Foundations of
Financial Risk

Foundations of Financial Risk

An Overview of Financial Risk and Risk-Based Regulation

Richard Apostolik
Christopher Donohue

*This book is dedicated to GARP's Board of Trustees,
without whose support and dedication
to developing the profession of risk management
this book would not have been necessary or possible,
and to the Association's volunteers, representing thousands
of organizations around the globe, who work on
committees and share practical experiences in numerous
global forums and in other ways, and whose goal is
to create a culture of risk awareness.*

Contents

CHAPTER 5

The New World of Banking

Banking after the Global Financial Crisis

T he global financial crisis of 2007–2009 will shape the ways **banks** are managed for many decades to come. It will also continue to affect the ways that politicians, regulators, analysts, and the general public think about banks and behave toward them.

Banking crises are not unusual. The Argentinian **currency** revaluation in 2001 led to a crisis for its banks, the Asian financial crisis of 1997 led to the **insolvency** of many of the region's banks, Sweden suffered a banking crisis in the early 1990s, and in the mid-1970s many second-tier British banks suffered huge losses as a result of a collapse in property prices.

Yet the 2007–2009 global financial crisis stands out from other banking crises due to its global extent, its impact on economic growth, and the far-reaching policy responses that have followed it. In all three respects, what happened in 2007–2009 resembles the financial crash and economic depression of the late 1920s and early 1930s more than it does any of the other banking system crises of more recent years.

The events of 2007–2009 challenged many of the widely held assumptions about how banks and banking systems worked. In simple terms, many things that would have been dismissed as unthinkable a few years before actually happened.

For example, it had always been assumed that banks and other commercial institutions would invariably make **liquidity** available to other financial institutions even if they charged very high rates for it. Yet during the days that followed the collapse of Lehman Brothers in September 2008, short-term financing markets dried up as banks refused to extend liquidity at any price. The level of uncertainty in financial markets was such that banks did not want to increase their exposure to anyone else, however strong they seemed to be.

Among the other ideas challenged by the crisis was the distinction between **off-balance-sheet** and on-balance-sheet items, the value of credit ratings, and the ability of many new capital instruments to absorb losses.

More generally, the long-term trend toward deregulation of financial markets that had begun in the 1970s and gathered pace during the 1990s fell out of favor. The belief that bankers themselves best understood the risks that they were taking was discredited. Politicians who had to explain to their voters why the failure of private sector banks had led to higher unemployment and public sector wage freezes wanted to exert control over the way banks operated in the future to try to ensure that a similar global crisis could not reoccur.

As a result, the level of regulation and public scrutiny of banks is far greater today than it has been for many decades, and this is unlikely to change in the near future.

Although the crisis was global in the sense that banks and economies throughout the world were affected, some were affected more than others. Emerging market banks that did not rely on global funding streams and had little exposure to **assets** and **financial instruments** originated in Western economies were barely affected. For example, in 2007–2009, the performance of Egyptian banks was driven more by the progress of their **central bank's** domestic financial reform program than by events in global financial markets.

Nevertheless, the fact that it was banks and economies in developed markets, particularly the United States and Europe, that were most affected has had far-reaching consequences for banks everywhere. Officials from North American and European countries and from the developed economies of Asia dominate bodies such as the **Basel Committee on Banking Supervision** that set standards for **international banks** and other financial institutions. It was banks from these countries that were most affected by the global financial crisis, so officials from these countries have been determined to put in place new standards—for example, on minimum capital levels and corporate governance—that they hope will reduce the possibility of another global financial crisis happening.

The standards that are set by bodies such as the Basel Committee are applicable to banks worldwide. So, for example, Egyptian banks may have been minimally affected during the financial crisis, but they are now judged against new international standards on bank capital and liquidity just like everyone else.

THE EUROPEAN FINANCIAL CRISIS OF 2009–2013

European banks and financial markets were badly affected by the global financial crisis, but from early 2010 European financial markets suffered additional problems specifically related to economic trends in Europe. These problems particularly affected the **Eurozone**—the group of 17 countries that had adopted the euro as their currency and whose monetary affairs were therefore governed primarily by the European Central Bank.

The difficulties experienced by European financial markets over this time were the result first and foremost of a sovereign debt crisis arising from unsustainable spending and borrowing by some governments. However, one of the features of the crisis was the close connection that emerged between the sustainability of government finances in a particular country and the health of that country's banking system.

The response to the crisis has had far-reaching consequences for the way in which banks are regulated and supervised in the European Union (EU)—for both Eurozone and non-Eurozone countries.

Ireland was the first EU country to need financial support from the European Union and the International Monetary Fund, although Ireland's problems arose from problems in its banking system that became apparent in 2007–2008, rather than from budgetary difficulties. As a result, the European crisis is deemed to have begun with Greece in 2009.

In late 2009, concerns began to grow that the Greek government would not be able to repay its debts, and in February 2010 the European Union announced a financial support package for Greece that was coupled with requirements that the Greek government drastically reduce public spending. Over the course of 2010, new figures revealed that the Greek government's financial situation was even worse than expected, and further support from international bodies was provided.

Although the Greek crisis originated with problems in the Greek government's finances, it quickly became clear that Greek banks would be affected. Most obviously, they held large amounts of their own government's bonds, and the government's ability to repay these bonds was now in doubt. Furthermore, as investors worried about the ability of the Greek government to repay its debts, they pushed up the cost of new borrowing to Greece and this in turn led to higher funding costs for Greek banks. More generally, the Greek government's budgetary crisis revealed broader mismanagement within the

Greek economy, including state-owned enterprises that were not servicing the loans that they had received from banks.

As the problems in Greece unfolded, analysts turned their attention to other Eurozone countries that had been running large budget deficits, such as Portugal, Spain, and Cyprus. Although the fundamental problems lay with government budgets, banks based in these countries also experienced difficulties either as a result of their direct exposure to their governments, because international investors were refusing to provide funds to any institutions in that particular country, or because the problems at the government level were symptomatic of broader economic mismanagement whose full extent only came to light as a result of the crisis.

The difficulties of resolving the European financial crisis were exacerbated by a lack of clarity over who was responsible for solving the problems. It was clearly in the interest of the Eurozone as a whole to prevent financial collapse in any member country, but some countries were reluctant to commit their own taxpayers' **money** to resolve problems in other countries that had been caused by years of overspending. These issues have now been largely resolved though the implementation of a "banking union" among Eurozone countries, with a central fund to support troubled banks and centralized supervision conducted by the European Central Bank.

The European financial crisis illustrated not only how budgetary problems at the government level lead to problems for individual banks, but also how lack of clarity over who is responsible for resolving banking crises can result in those crises deepening and becoming more widespread.

THE RISE OF SHADOW BANKING

Until recent times, the provision of credit and the collection of **deposits** were performed almost exclusively by banks that were regulated by a central bank or an equivalent institution, and these banks could expect to receive support from their central bank in the event that they ran short of liquidity. In the mid-1980s in the United States, and shortly after that in other developed financial markets, a variety of nonbank institutions and investment vehicles began to conduct many of these banking activities alongside the traditional banks. This network of nonbank institutions and vehicles is known as **shadow banking**.

Examples include finance companies that make loans for specific purposes, such as car purchases; money market mutual funds that offer deposit facilities similar to those offered by banks, but with the prospect of higher returns than banks can pay; financial vehicles that are created by banks to issue short-term commercial paper and invest in longer-dated assets while remaining off the balance sheets of the banks themselves; and special purpose vehicles created to securitize assets such as mortgages and sell them to institutional investors.

Shadow banks perform many of the functions of banks but exist outside the regulated banking industry. A report published by the Federal Reserve Bank of New York in 2010 estimated that in March 2008 the size of the shadow banking industry in the United States had reached USD 20 trillion, almost twice the size of the traditional banking industry.

It was often the case that activities were conducted through shadow banks in order to avoid the regulatory scrutiny accorded to banks and to take advantage of lower capital requirements than those imposed on banks.

One of the many causes of the global financial crisis of 2007–2009 was that regulators and bankers did not understand how important these shadow banking institutions had become to the everyday functioning of financial markets. Since the financial crisis, regulators have moved to impose rules and standards on shadow banking activity as well as reporting requirements that enable them to monitor the extent and influence of shadow banking on global financial markets.

The volume of shadow banking activity declined as a result of the global financial crisis. (The Federal Reserve Bank of New York report mentioned above estimated that the size of the market had fallen to about USD 16 trillion by the first quarter of 2010.) Factors contributing to this decline included reduced activity in securitization markets and the winding up of many structured investment vehicles.

Despite increased regulatory scrutiny, shadow banking is here to stay. As a result, those analyzing banks and financial markets must take account of competitive pressures on banks from nonbank financial institutions, and the effect that the behavior of large nonbank financial institutions could have on the health of a financial system as a whole.

EXAMPLE

On September 16, 2008, Reserve Primary Fund, a U.S. money market fund, announced that the net asset value of its shares had fallen below USD 1 per share and that it was therefore not able to repay investors in full if they asked for their money back. This was the first time since 1994 that a money market fund was not in a position to repay depositors in full.

Money market funds had grown rapidly in the United States as an alternative to bank deposits. Money market funds offered customers instant access to their money but paid higher interest than that offered by banks. On the eve of the global financial crisis, the amount of money invested in money market funds in the United States was more than the amount of money placed in **commercial bank** deposits. Reserve Primary's asset size of USD 125 billion at the end of June 2008 was equal to that of the biggest and best-known U.S. banks.

Coming just one day after Lehman Brothers had filed for bankruptcy, Reserve Primary's announcement that it had "broken the buck" (meaning that it was not able to repay customers a full dollar for every dollar invested) added to the panic that was engulfing U.S. and international financial markets. The effect was not confined to those investors who had placed their money in Reserve Primary and similar institutions. Money market funds had been major buyers of short-term bonds issued by banks and other financial institutions and as such had been important providers of liquidity to the financial system as a whole. As investors withdrew their money, the funds were no longer able to buy new financial instruments and as a result liquidity tightened across the financial system.

The difficulties of Reserve Primary also demonstrated the effect of **interconnectivity** and **contagion** in financial markets (see next section). Reserve Primary had bought large amounts of bonds issued by Lehman Brothers. When Lehman declared bankruptcy, signaling that it would not be able to repay its investors, Reserve Primary knew that it would not be able to fully repay its own investors.

INTERCONNECTIVITY AND CONTAGION

As international financial markets have become larger and more complex in recent decades, they have become interconnected, and the risk of contagion has increased (see Section 3.2.1). For example, a banking crisis in one country, or even problems within a single large institution, can lead to problems in other countries and other institutions. Although problems can arise as a result of direct financial relationships—for example, when the failure of Lehman Brothers led the Reserve Primary money market fund to announce that it would be unable to pay investors in full—they can also arise as a result of perceptions and fear rather than actual financial exposure and risk.

For example, when Thailand devalued its currency in mid-1997, banks and investors began withdrawing money not only from Thailand but also from other Southeast Asian countries. In the aftermath of the crisis questions were raised about the strength of these other Southeast Asian economies, but in most cases the withdrawal of investment funds from these countries and the currency crises that they suffered were triggered directly by investors' fear that what was happening in Thailand might also happen in neighboring countries. In effect, investors did not want to run the risk that other regional economies might be harboring the same problems that had appeared in Thailand, but when they took the initiative to reduce their exposure, they precipitated the very crisis that they were seeking to avoid.

As financial systems become more international (for example as a result of companies and banks in one region raising bonds and deposits from investors in other regions) and electronic payment systems become more sophisticated, the ability of banks and investors to move money quickly from one place to another is increasing. In turn, this increases the risk that problems in one region will spread quickly to others.

INTERNATIONAL BANK REGULATION

The global financial crisis discredited the approach, prevalent before the crisis, that banks and banking systems work best if regulation and supervision are kept to a minimum. (In the United Kingdom this approach was known as "light touch" regulation and supervision.) As a result, the years since the crisis have seen a large number of initiatives to extend the scope of financial regulation worldwide and to intensify the scrutiny imposed on banks. This new regulatory landscape will continue to govern how banks are run well after memories of the crisis have faded and the people who were running banks at the time have retired.

Efforts to reform the global financial system were initially led by the **G20** group of developed market economies. Finance ministers and central bankers from the G20 countries set the agenda, defined the priorities for financial market reforms, and delegated specific tasks to more specialized bodies, such as the Basel Committee on Banking Supervision (whose work has included new capital and liquidity standards for banks) and the **International Organization of Securities Commissions (IOSCO)** (whose work has included new rules on how to trade financial instruments). The **Financial Stability Board** has also undertaken work on issues such as **corporate governance** and best practices for bankers' pay. Standard setters, such as the Basel Committee, do not have the power to enforce their recommendations. Their recommendations carry a lot of weight, because they have been drawn up by representatives from many countries after a lot of consultation, but to take effect they need to be incorporated into the laws and regulations of individual countries.

In the United States, many of the new standards governing financial activity were defined in the Dodd-Frank Wall Street Reform and Consumer Protection Act (named after the two congressmen who sponsored the legislation), although the process of writing the detailed rules is delegated to specialized agencies such as the Federal Reserve Bank and the Securities and Exchange Commission. In Europe, new standards have been adopted by the European Union and then transmitted down to the Union's member states through directives and regulations.

Acknowledgments

GARP's *Foundations of Financial Risk* has been developed under the auspices of the Banking Risk Committee of the GARP Risk Academy, who guided and reviewed the work of the contributing authors.

The committee and the authors thank **Alastair Graham, Amanda Neff, Graeme Skelly, Christian Thornæs, Mark Dougherty,** and Editor, **Andrew Cunningham,** for their contributions to the 2015 revision. *Foundations of Financial Risk* builds upon a previously published book titled, *Foundations of Banking Risk*, co-authored by Richard Apostolik, Christopher Donohue and Peter Went. We would like to specifically acknowledge that Peter Went's work along with the *Foundations of Banking Risk* other co-authors provides a material basis for the *Foundations of Financial Risk*, and would like to thank Peter on his much appreciated contributions.

Introduction

This textbook, previously published in 2009 as the *Foundations of Banking Risk* has been revised, updated and expanded. GARP has renamed the book to reflect the additional content which includes a new chapter on insurance risk.

The role of **risk management** is becoming more important as banks, insurance firms, and supervisors around the world recognize that good risk management practices are vital, not only for the success of individual firms, but also for the safety and soundness of the financial system as a whole. As a result, the world's leading supervisors have developed regulations based on a number of "good practice" methodologies used in risk management. The banking regulations, outlined in the International Convergence of Capital Measurement and Capital Standards, known as the Basel Accord, and the insurance regulations, known as Solvency 2, codify such risk management practices.

The importance of these risk management methodologies as a basis for regulation is hard to overstate. The fact that they were developed with the support of the international financial community means that they have gained worldwide acceptance as the standards for risk management.

The implementation of risk-based regulation means that staff, as well as supervisors, will need to be educated and trained to recognize risks and how to implement risk management approaches. Consequently, GARP offers this program, the *Foundations of Financial Risk*, to provide staff with a basic understanding of banking, banking risks, insurance risks, **regulation** and supervision. This study text has been designed to assist students in preparing for the *Foundations of Financial Risk* assessment exam. It is presented in a user-friendly format to enable candidates to understand the key terms and concepts of the industries, and their risks and risk-based regulation.

This study text concentrates on the technical terms used in banking and risk management, while providing an insight to the similar risk in the insurance industry. These terms are defined either in the text or in the glossary. As the material is at the introductory level, candidates are not expected to have a detailed understanding of risk management or significant experience in banking. In this text, they will gain an understanding of the commonly used terms in the finance industry.

Each chapter contains a number of examples of actual financial events, as well as case study scenarios, diagrams, and tables aimed at explaining banking, banking risks, and risk-based regulations. This study text has adopted the standard codes used by banks throughout the world to identify currencies for the purposes of **trading**, settlement, and displaying of market prices. The codes, set by the International Organization for Standardization (ISO), avoid the confusion that could result as many currencies have similar names. For example, the text uses USD for the U.S. dollar, GBP for the British pound, EUR for the euro, and JPY for the Japanese yen.

Functions and Forms of Banking

Chapter 1 introduces **banks** and the banking system: their roles in facilitating economic activity, and their relevant risks banks face. The three core banking functions—collecting deposits, arranging payments, and making loans—and their attendant risks are described. As this chapter intends to provide a foundation for the more detailed discussions in subsequent chapters, most of the key topics are presented within a risk management framework. A glossary is provided at the end of the book.

Chapter Outline
  1.1   Banks and Banking
  1.2   Different Bank Types
  1.3   Banking Risks
  1.4   Forces Shaping the Banking Industry

Key Learning Points
  ▪ Banks provide three **core banking services**: deposit collection, payment arrangement, and loan **underwriting**. Banks may also offer financial services such as cash, **asset**, and risk management.
  ▪ Banks play a central role in facilitating economic activity through three interrelated processes: **financial intermediation, asset transformation,** and **money creation**.

- **Retail banks** primarily serve retail customers, and **wholesale banks** primarily serve corporate customers. A country's central bank sets monetary policy on behalf of the country's government, liaises with other central banks, and may act as the bank regulator. Sometimes a body other than the central bank is responsible for the regulation of individual banks.
- The main risks that banks face are credit, market, operational, and **liquidity risks**. Other types of risk include business, and **reputational risk**. As economies, banks, and societies as a whole develop and change, the risks faced by banks may also change, and new risks may emerge.
- Multiple forces shape the banking industry, including regulation, competition, product innovation, changing technology, and the uncertainty surrounding future interest and **inflation rates**.

FUNCTIONS AND FORMS OF BANKING

1.1   Banks and Banking

To understand banking risk and regulation, it is important to understand the range of services banks provide and the key role that banks play in a modern economy.

1.1.1   Core Bank Services

Banks offer many products and services. While there is variation among banks and across regions, the core services that banks traditionally provide are:

- **Deposit collection**—the process of accepting cash or money (deposits) from individuals and businesses (depositors) for safekeeping in a bank account, available for future use.
- **Payment services**—the process of accepting and making payments on behalf of the customers using their bank accounts.
- **Loan underwriting**—the process of evaluating and deciding whether a customer (**borrower**) is eligible to receive credit and then extending a loan or credit to the customer.

As banking has evolved, the complexity of the three core banking functions has increased. For instance, in early banking, depositors received a certificate stating the amount of money they had deposited with the bank.

Later, deposit certificates could be used to make payments. Initially a cumbersome process, the concept of using deposit certificates for payments further evolved into passbooks, checks, and other methods to conveniently withdraw deposits from the bank. Today, deposits, withdrawals, and payments are instantaneous: withdrawals and payments can now be made through debit cards, and payments are easily made via electronic fund transfers (EFTs). See Figure 1.1 for examples of bank products and the services each provides.

Underwriting has many different meanings in finance and banking. This book focuses on lending or credit. Banks underwrite loans in two steps. First, the bank analyzes the borrower's financial capacity, or the borrower's ability and willingness to repay. This process will be discussed in detail in Chapter 4. Then, the bank pays out, or funds, the loan (cash or other forms of payment) to the borrower.

Services	Examples of Bank Products
Collecting Deposits, or Deposit Collection	▪ Checking/current accounts ▪ Certificates of deposit ▪ Savings accounts
Arranging Payments, or Payment Services	▪ Debit cards ▪ Electronic banking ▪ Foreign exchange ▪ Checking accounts
Underwriting Loans	▪ Commercial and industrial loans ▪ Consumer loans ▪ Real estate/mortgage loans ▪ Credit cards

FIGURE 1.1 Examples of Bank Products and Core Bank Services

Providing all these core services is not enough for an institution to be called a bank in a modern economy, however. In order to provide these services, a modern bank must also hold a **banking license** and be subject to regulation and supervision by a banking regulator.

1.1.2　Banks in the Economy

Through the core bank services mentioned, banks are critical facilitators of economic activity.

- Banks channel savings from depositors to borrowers, an activity known as financial intermediation.
- Banks create loans from deposits through asset transformation.
- Banks, through financial intermediation and asset transformation, engage in money creation.

When a bank accepts deposits, the depositor in effect lends money to the bank. In exchange, the depositor receives interest payments on the deposits. The bank then uses the deposits to finance loans to borrowers and generates income by charging interest on the loans. The difference between the interest that the bank receives from the borrowers and the interest it pays to the depositors is the main source of revenue and profit to the bank.

When underwriting a loan, a bank evaluates the credit quality of the borrower—the likelihood that the borrower will repay the loan. However, depositors, who lend money to the bank in the form of deposits, typically do not evaluate the credit quality of the bank or the bank's ability to repay the deposits on demand. Depositors assume that their deposits with the bank are safe and will be returned in full by the bank "on demand." This puts depositors at risk because, as we will see in later sections, banks occasionally do fail and are not able to repay deposits in full (Section 3.1). To protect depositors against bank failures, governments have created safety nets such as **deposit insurance** (Section 3.4). These safety nets vary from country to country and generally do not provide unlimited protection, thus leaving a certain percentage of deposits exposed to the risk that a bank will **default** and the depositors will not be able to receive their deposits in full.

By collecting funds in the form of deposits and then loaning these funds out, banks engage in financial intermediation. Throughout the world, bank loans are the predominant source of financing for individuals and companies. Other financial intermediaries such as finance companies and the financial markets (such as stock or bond markets) also channel savings and investments. Unlike other financial intermediaries, though, banks alone channel deposits from depositors to borrowers. Hence, banks are also called depository financial intermediaries.

Financial intermediation emphasizes the qualitative differences between bank deposits and bank loans. Bank deposits (e.g., **savings accounts**, checking accounts) are typically relatively small, consisting of money entrusted to the bank by individuals, companies, and other organizations for safekeeping. Deposits are also comparatively safe and can typically be withdrawn at any time or have relatively short maturities. By contrast, bank loans (e.g., home mortgage loans, car loans, corporate loans) are generally larger and riskier than deposits and have repayment schedules typically extending over several years. The process of creating a new asset (loan) from **liabilities** (deposits) with different characteristics is called asset transformation (see Figure 1.2).

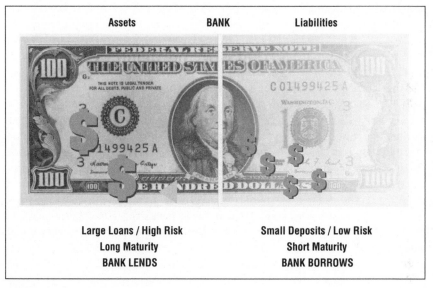

FIGURE 1.2 Asset Transformation

1.1.3   Money Creation

Banks earn revenues from the financial intermediation/asset transformation process by converting customer deposits into loans. To be profitable, however, the **interest rates** that the bank earns on its loans must be greater than the rate it pays on the deposits that finance them. Since the majority of deposits can be withdrawn at any time, banks must balance the goal of higher revenues (investing more of the deposits to finance loans) with the need to have cash on hand to meet the withdrawal requests of depositors. To do this, banks "reserve" a relatively small fraction of their deposit funds to meet depositor demand. Banking regulators determine the **reserve requirements**, the proportion of deposits a bank must keep as reserves in the vault of the bank. Keeping only a small fraction of the depositors' funds available for withdrawal is called **fractional reserve banking**. This system allows banks to create money.

Money creation is the process of generating additional money by repeatedly lending, through the fractional reserve banking system, an original deposit to a bank.

EXAMPLE

Suppose Bank A has collected deposits totaling USD 100 and retains 10% of those deposits as reserves to meet withdrawals. Bank A uses the remaining 90%, or USD 90, for lending purposes. Suppose the USD 90 is lent to one person, who then spends all the funds at one store. This USD 90 is effectively "new" money. The store then deposits the USD 90 in Bank B. At that point there are deposits in the two banks of USD 190 (the initial deposit of USD 100 plus the new deposit of USD 90). Bank B now sets aside 10% of the USD 90, or USD 9, in reserves, and loans the remaining USD 81, which is then deposited by the borrower in Bank C. There is now USD 100 + USD 90 + USD 81, or USD 271 of deposits in the three banks. As this process continues, more deposits are loaned out and spent and more money is deposited; at each turn, more and more money is made available through the lending process.

Figure 1.3 below shows the amount of money that an initial USD 100 deposit generates, assuming a 10% reserve requirement, transaction by transaction. (The dark shading is the reserve requirement held back from each loan (10%), and the lighter gray shading is each successive loan amount). Over the course of 21 separate transactions, USD 801 of deposits is generated, from an initial deposit of only USD 100. Allowed to continue indefinitely, this process would generate a total of USD 1,000 in deposits—the original USD 100 deposit plus USD 900 created through subsequent loans.

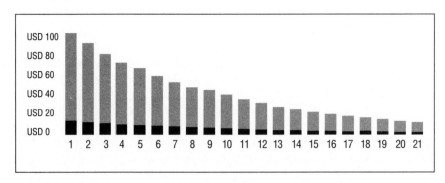

FIGURE 1.3 Money Creation (USD 801 in New Lending from Initial USD 100 Deposit)

In the example, the cycle started with an initial deposit of USD 100; no additional money was put into the system. Portions of the original USD 100 repeatedly flowed through the system, increasing both bank deposits and bank loans. The amount of money created at each deposit is 90% of the previous step (100% less the 10% held in reserve).

Reserve requirements limit how much money an initial deposit can create in the fractional reserve banking system. The **money multiplier,** the inverse of the reserve requirement, is a formula used to determine how much new money each unit of currency can create. As the following example shows, the higher the reserve requirement, the more the bank must keep as regulatory reserves in the vault of the bank and the less money the bank can create.

EXAMPLE

With a reserve requirement of 10%, the money multiplier is 10 (1/10% = 10). Thus, the amount of money that can be created on a USD 100 deposit is USD 1,000. Out of USD 1,000, USD 900 (or 90%) is new money and USD 100 (or 10%) is the original deposit.

With a reserve requirement of 20%, the money multiplier falls to 5 (1/20% = 5). Thus, the amount of money that can be created on a USD 100 deposit would be USD 500. Out of this USD 500, USD 400 (or 80%) is new money and USD 100 (or 20%) is the original deposit.

Globally, banks represent the largest source of financing for businesses and are therefore critical to economic development. Banks provide financing directly, by extending loans and buying **bonds,** and they also help companies secure financing by arranging for others to lend them money or invest in their bonds. Banks can also help companies secure financing by arranging share issues for them or even taking direct ownership stakes in them. Debt and equity are the two types of financing and two sources of capital.

Banks also provide financing for consumers, who use bank loans to purchase and finance assets they might not otherwise be able to afford, such as a car or a house. Credit cards, another type of bank loan, provide consumers with convenient access to credit that enables them to make purchases and can also stimulate economic growth. Chapter 4 will discuss in greater detail the various loan products and how they are used. Through their core functions—financial intermediation, asset transformation, and money creation—banks play a central role in advanced economies.

EXAMPLE

The global financial crisis of 2007–2009 vividly showed the interrelationship between bank functions and economic activity. Because banks were unable to collect on loans that were made to low credit quality borrowers called subprime borrowers, banks became unable to recirculate deposits and lend to other parties. This in turn meant there was less credit available for the use of companies and individuals who depend on bank loans to finance their purchases. Consequently, the companies and individuals made fewer deposits, creating less money. The effects were widely felt around the world and led to a substantial reduction in credit, which first led to a reduction in the demand for goods and services and further reduced the amount of money being deposited at banks. This caused an even further tightening of credit availability, which was one of a number of different causes and consequences related to the financial crisis.

1.1.4   Payment Services

Depositors can use their deposit accounts at banks to make and receive payments between depositors and between banks. Payments refer to the settlement of financial transactions between parties and usually involve the transfer of funds between the parties. There are various **payment systems** that facilitate transfer of funds for transactions, including checks, payment orders, bill payment, and electronic payments in the form of wire services and other electronic settlement systems. Payment systems can also help large corporations and government organizations handle their payments for goods and services.

Apart from settlement for payments, banks can also offer payment services by providing their customers with foreign currencies to make international payments. In arranging international payments, banks facilitate international transactions by, on one hand, offering facilities that enable the creation of payment documents that foreign banks accept and, on the other hand, by accepting payment documents that foreign banks have issued. By using international payment networks between banks, banks can also send payments according to their customers' requests.

1.1.5   Other Banking Services

Apart from its core services, a bank usually offers other financial services, sometimes in competition with nonbank financial service providers that typically include finance companies, brokerage firms, risk management consultants, and insurance companies. Banks and the companies offering these services typically receive fees, or "fee income," for providing these services.

Fee income is the second main source of revenue to banks after the interest the bank receives from its borrowers. Other banking services may include:

- *Cash management.* As a part of their core deposit collection and arranging payments function, banks provide cash or treasury management services to large corporations. In general, this service means the bank agrees to handle cash collection and payments for a company and invest any temporary cash surplus.
- *Investment- and securities-related activities.* Many bank customers demand investment products—such as mutual funds, unit trusts, and annuities—that offer higher returns, with higher associated risks, than bank deposits. Historically, customers have turned to nonbanks for these investment products. Today, however, most banks offer them in an effort to maintain customer relationships.

   Banks also offer other securities-related activities, including brokerage and investment banking services. **Brokerage services** involve the buying and selling of securities (e.g., stocks and bonds) on behalf of customers. **Investment banking** services include advising commercial customers on mergers and acquisitions, as well as offering a broad range of financing options, including direct investment in the companies themselves.
- *Derivatives trading.* **Derivatives** such as **swaps,** options, forwards, and futures are financial instruments whose value is "derived" from the intrinsic value and/or change in value of another financial or physical asset, such as bonds, stocks, or commodities such as gold or oil. Derivative transactions help institutions manage various types of risks, such as foreign exchange, interest rate, commodity price, equity price, and credit **default risks.** Derivatives and their use are discussed in Chapter 6.
- *Loan commitments.* Banks receive a flat fee for extending a loan commitment of a certain amount of funds for a period of time, regardless of whether the full amount is drawn down by the borrower. When the borrower uses the loan commitment, either in full or in part, the used portion of the commitment is recorded on the bank's balance sheet. The unused portion remains off its balance sheet.
- *Letters of credit.* When a bank provides a **letter of credit,** it guarantees a payment (up to the amount specified in the letter of credit) on behalf of its customer and receives a fee for providing this guarantee.
- *Insurance services.* Many banks, particularly those outside the United States, offer insurance products to broaden their customer base. Insurance services are a logical progression for banks since insurance products have financial intermediation and asset transformation features similar to traditional bank products. Life insurance policies, for instance, are

often similar to many of the long-term deposit products that banks offer: all are savings tools, but they deliver their savings benefits differently.

■ *Trust services.* Some bank customers, particularly wealthy individuals, corporate pension plans, and estates, prefer to have professionals manage their assets. Therefore, many banks offer trust services that professionally manage a customer's assets for a fee. These assets under management do not show up on the balance sheet of the bank.

■ *Risk management services.* As banks have expanded into more complex businesses, they have had to confront more complicated and composite risks such as interest rate, **exchange rate**, and price risks. Banks have developed sophisticated skills and complicated tools to manage these complex risks. For a fee, banks now offer the same risk management skills and tools to their customers.

1.2   Different Bank Types

This section illustrates different types of banks by focusing on the types of customers served and the range of services offered. Variations of the types of banks described here exist in different parts of the world.

1.2.1   Retail Banks

Retail banks' primary customers are individuals, or "consumers." Many retail banks also offer services to **small and medium enterprises (SMEs)**. Retail banks may have different specializations:

■ *Retail and consumer banks, savings and loans companies (thrifts, building societies), cooperatives, and credit unions.* These offer loans primarily to individuals to finance house, car, or other purchases (e.g., Woodlands Bank in the United States, TSB Bank in the United Kingdom, or OTP Bank in Hungary). The particular features of cooperatives and credit unions are addressed below.

■ *Private banking firms.* These provide wealth management services, including tax and investment advice, typically to rich individuals (e.g., Coutts & Co. in the United Kingdom and Bank Julius Baer in Switzerland).

■ *Postal banks.* These offer banking services to customers in post offices. This structure, where the postal service owns or collaborates with a bank, is widely used throughout the world (e.g., Postbank A.G. in Germany, Japan Post Bank in Japan).

Although retail banks can come in many forms, most have a network of local branches that enable them to focus on retail consumers in one specific geographic area such as a city or a region of a country. However, there are a number of very large retail banks that have extensive branch networks that cover entire countries or portions of countries (e.g., HSBC and Industrial and Commercial Bank of China) and link to retail branches in networks owned through their affiliated entities in other parts of the world (e.g., Citigroup and Santander).

1.2.2   Wholesale Banks

Wholesale banks' customers are primarily corporate and noncorporate businesses. Although the range of business customers varies, it usually includes larger domestic and international companies. Wholesale banks also offer advisory services tailored to the specific needs of large businesses. Types of wholesale banks include:

- *Commercial banks.* These offer a wide range of highly specialized loans to large businesses, act as intermediaries in raising funds, and provide specialized financial services, such as payment and risk management services.
- *Correspondent banks.* These offer banking services to other banks, often in another country, including loans and various investment alternatives.
- *Investment (sometimes called "merchant banks").* These offer professional advice to corporations and governments about raising funds in the capital markets such as the stock, bond, or credit markets. In the case of companies, they also provide advice on buying or selling companies as a whole or in part. In the case of governments, they will advise on privatizing public assets. They may also serve as underwriters and investors in these activities.

BANKING IN FOCUS

The number of investment or merchant banks has diminished since 2008 due to the effects of the global financial crisis that started in 2007.

In 2008, in the wake of the collapse of the subprime mortgage market, investment banks Bear Stearns and Lehman Brothers went out of business. Bear Stearns was sold to JPMorgan Chase, and

Lehman Brothers declared bankruptcy. Merrill Lynch, the third largest investment bank in the United States, merged with Bank of America. Two of the remaining major U.S. investment banks, Goldman Sachs and Morgan Stanley, legally converted their operations to those of bank holding companies. This move allowed them to accept deposits and thereby raise funds through customer deposits to support their ongoing operations. It also gave them access to emergency funding from their central bank, which was perhaps more important than their new ability to collect deposits.

This was a monumental change to banking because the investment banking model—which relies on accessing the credit markets daily for financing while being exposed to financial market risks—has been called into question.

In Europe, some large banks, such as Barclays, reduced their investment banking activity, although because they had significant businesses in other areas (such as retail banking) they were better able to survive than those banks that were wholly reliant on investment banking business.

Although the large investment banks in the United States have either converted to banks or collapsed, there are still investment banks remaining in the United States. Many of them are smaller, highly specialized investment banks. They are not as reliant on wholesale funding, and typically focus on providing advice to corporate customers about raising money in the financial markets (e.g., Keefe, Bruyette & Woods).

Many wholesale banks finance international trade and often operate in several countries through representative offices or smaller branches. These banks are known as international, multinational, or global banks. Banks that offer financial services, including insurance, along with the core banking functions are called **universal banks**. Citibank, Deutsche Bank, HSBC, and BNP Paribas are examples of large universal banks.

1.2.3   Bank Holding Companies

Bank holding companies are companies that own one or more banks but do not conduct banking business themselves. Bank holding companies are primarily a feature of the U.S. banking system where regulators were concerned to limit the ability of banks to engage in nonbanking activity. Bank holding companies could own subsidiaries that, between them, covered the full range of financial service activities, but each individual operating institution engaged in only a limited sector of the financial markets.

When analyzing U.S. banks, it is important to differentiate between the holding company or the operating company. For example, Wells Fargo & Company is a holding company that owns Wells Fargo Bank. It is Wells Fargo Bank that conducts banking business.

There are some large non-U.S. banking groups that operate through a holding company structure, such as HSBC Holdings and Royal Bank of Scotland.

Bank holding companies often raise funding on behalf of their group and then "downstream" it to their operating companies. They are able to service interest on the debt from **dividends** that are "upstreamed" from the operating companies.

1.2.4　Cooperative Banks

Cooperative banks are owned by their customers and usually have a large branch network that covers small towns and villages as well as larger cities. Their core strength is often lending to and taking deposits from individuals and small businesses.

For most banks, there is a distinction between **shareholders**, who invest in the bank and who therefore own it, and customers, who do business with the bank but have no ownership rights. In contrast, someone who deposits money with a cooperative bank automatically becomes a shareholder in that cooperative bank. In some cooperative banks, customers who receive loans also become shareholders. Such customers are, in principle, entitled to vote and to control how the local cooperative bank is run. Cooperative banks are structured like a pyramid, with individual customers controlling local cooperatives, these local cooperatives in turn controlling regional organizations, and these regional organizations controlling a national organization that oversees the network as a whole.

Examples of such cooperative banks include Rabobank in the Netherlands, the Nationwide Building Society in the United Kingdom, and the Shinkin cooperative bank network in Japan.

Although cooperative banks usually have strong ties to local communities, many have become very large and in some ways behave just like other banks. Rabobank, in the Netherlands, is one of the biggest banks in the world. The BPCE Group in France works with large companies and offers sophisticated financial products.

Many of the larger cooperative banks have a central entity—still ultimately owned by the members—that manages liquidity and risk for the
group as a whole.

1.2.5   Credit Unions

Credit unions are similar to cooperative banks in that they are owned by
their customers. However, in practice, credit unions tend to be small, closely
connected to their local community, and focused on meeting the needs of
low-income groups. Frequently, customers may borrow from a credit union
only if they also have a savings account there. Although credit unions are
seen all over the world and are an important feature of the financial landscape, there are no credit unions that have the size of, say, Rabobank or that
compete in international markets.

An example of a credit union is the Croydon, Merton, and South Sutton
Credit Union that operates in an area of southwest London in the United
Kingdom.

1.2.6   Micro-finance Institutions

Micro-finance institutions (MFIs) exist to extend small amounts of money
to low-income customers, usually in developing countries. The amounts lent
can be as little as USD 20, though they can sometimes reach a few thousand
dollars. The purpose of these loans is to enable customers to rise out of
poverty and become more economically self-reliant, for example by buying
materials with which to manufacture simple goods that can then be sold in
a local marketplace. MFIs often try to replace unscrupulous lenders that
exploit customers and charge exorbitant rates of interest. Much MFI activity
is directed to women.

The most famous example of an MFI is Grameen Bank, which was set
up in Bangladesh in the 1970s to lend money to poor people in small villages.
Grameen has since become a large institution, though it retains its strategy
of making small loans to underprivileged, largely rural borrowers.

Micro-finance lending now occupies a central position in economic
development programs worldwide, with significant networks in South America, Asia, and sub-Saharan Africa. Some large commercial banks provide
funding to MFIs as part of their corporate responsibility programs or even
as part of their regular lending programs.

1.2.7 Central Banks

Central banks are the principal monetary authority of a country (or, occasionally, a group of countries) and are crucial to the functioning of all banks, financial markets, and the economy. Central banks manage the amount of money and credit in an economy—usually in an effort to contain inflation rates and/or to foster economic growth. They typically accomplish this through their daily activities of buying and selling government debt, determining and maintaining core interest rates, setting reserve requirement levels, and issuing currency. Some central banks are also charged with maintaining certain foreign exchange rate levels for the home currency. Central banks also arrange payments between banks.

Historically, central banks have usually combined this role as the principal monetary authority with two other roles: oversight of the banking system as a whole (**macroprudential supervision**) and the regulation and supervision of individual banks (**microprudential supervision**). Even before the global financial crisis, there were moves to separate these functions (for example, the British government took banking supervision away from the Bank of England in 1997 and gave it to the newly created Financial Services Authority), and in the aftermath of the crisis there has been intense discussion among politicians and bank regulators about how these roles should be assigned. Views differ on how to divide the responsibilities, and no clear consensus has formed on the right way to do it.

The body that is given responsibility for microprudential supervision usually has responsibility not only for **bank regulation** but also for **bank supervision**. Regulation refers to the process of writing rules that govern how banks operate and behave (for example, setting minimum levels of capital, or requiring banks to set aside a proportion of their deposits as a reserve) whereas supervision refers to the enforcement of those rules (for example, by examining a bank's financial statements or sending inspectors to speak to a bank's management).

Examples of central banks include the Central Bank of Bahrain, the Bank of Japan, the People's Bank of China, and the Federal Reserve System.

INTEREST RATES AND INFLATION RATES

An interest rate is the price of credit, or the rate a lender charges a borrower for using borrowed funds. The inflation rate is the change in the purchasing value of money.

> Bank B lends EUR 1,000,000 to Compagnie Petit, a French corporation, for one year. In exchange for the corporation using these funds, the bank charges 6% interest rate per year. At the end of the year, Compagnie Petit must pay EUR 60,000 in interest to the bank as well as repay the original EUR 1,000,000.
>
> At the beginning of the year, Jean Molineaux paid EUR 100 for various groceries at the store. At the end of the year, the same groceries at the same store cost EUR 105. Since the price of the same groceries increased by 5% during the year, the purchasing power of the money declined by approximately 5%. This decline in purchasing power is the inflation rate.

1.3 Banking Risks

There are multiple definitions of risk. Everyone has a definition of what risk is, and everyone recognizes a wide range of risks. Some of the more widely discussed definitions of risk include the following:

- The likelihood an undesirable event will occur
- The magnitude of loss from an unexpected event
- The probability that "things won't go well"
- The effects of an adverse outcome

Banks face several types of risk. All the following are examples of the various risks banks encounter:

- Borrowers may submit loan repayments late or fail to make repayments.
- Depositors may demand the return of their money at a faster rate than the bank has reserved for.
- Market interest rates may change and hurt the value of a bank's loans.
- Investments made by the bank in securities or private companies may lose value.
- A bank may discover that it has acted in a way that is contrary to a law or regulation and be fined by its regulator or by a court of law.
- Human input errors or fraud in computer systems can lead to losses.

To monitor, manage, and measure these risks, banks are actively engaged in risk management. In a bank, the risk management function contributes to the management of the risks a bank faces by continuously measuring the risk of its current **portfolio** of assets and other exposures; by communicating the risk profile of the bank to others within the bank, to the bank's regulators, and to other relevant parties; and by taking steps either directly or in collaboration with other bank functions to reduce the possibility of loss or to mitigate the size of the potential loss.

From a regulatory perspective, the size and risk of a bank's assets are the most important determinants of how much **regulatory reserve capital** the bank is required to hold. A bank with high-risk assets faces the possibility that those assets could quickly lose value. If the market—depositors—perceives that the bank is unstable and deposits are in peril, then nervous depositors may withdraw their funds from the bank. If too many depositors want to withdraw their funds at the same time, then fear that the bank will run out of money could break out (Section 3.1 discusses how **bank runs** occur). And when there is a widespread withdrawal of money from a bank, the bank may be forced to sell its assets under pressure. To avoid this, regulators want a bank with high-risk assets to have more reserves available. Therefore, understanding banking regulation requires understanding financial risk management.

This section introduces the various types of risk a bank may face and provides examples that demonstrate each risk. Later chapters explore these risks and their regulatory implications in more detail. The key risks discussed below are those identified by the **Basel Accords**, the cornerstone of international risk-based banking regulation. The Basel Accords, described in greater detail in Section 3.3 and throughout the book, are the result of a collaborative attempt by banking regulators from major developed countries to create a globally valid and widely applicable framework for banks and bank risk management.

The Basel III Accord, the most recent of these accords, focuses primarily on four types of risk (see Figure 1.4):

1. Credit risk
2. Market risk
3. Operational risk
4. Liquidity risk

The Basel Accords also recognize that there are other types of risk that may include these different core risk types.

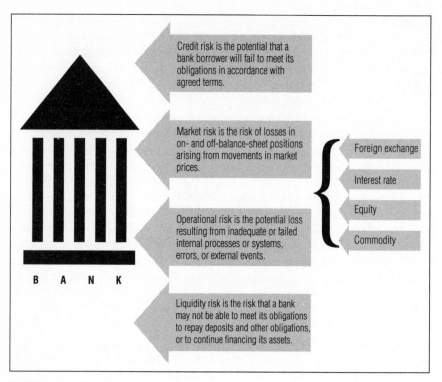

FIGURE 1.4 Bank Risks

1.3.1   Credit Risk

Credit risk is the risk that a bank borrower, also known as a counterparty, may fail to meet its obligations—pay interest on the loan and repay the amount borrowed—in accordance with agreed terms. Credit risk is the largest risk most banks face and arises from the possibility that loans or bonds held by a bank will not be repaid either partially or fully. Credit risk is often synonymous with default risk.

EXAMPLE

In December 2007, the large Swiss bank UBS announced a loss of USD 10 billion due to the significant loss in value of loans made to high-risk borrowers (subprime mortgage borrowers). Many high-risk borrowers could not repay their loans, and the complex models used by UBS to predict the likelihood of credit losses turned out to be incorrect. Other major banks all over the world suffered similar losses due to incorrectly assessing the likelihood of default on mortgage payments. The inability to assess or respond correctly to this risk resulted in many billions of U.S. dollars in losses to companies and individuals around the world.

Credit risk affects depositors as well. From the depositors' perspective, credit risk is the risk that the bank will not be able to repay funds when they ask for them.

The underwriting process aims to assess the credit risk associated with lending to a particular potential borrower. Chapter 4 contains a detailed description of the underwriting process. Once a loan is underwritten and the loan is received by the customer, the loan becomes a part of the bank's **banking book**. The banking book is the portfolio of assets (primarily loans) the bank holds, does not actively trade, and expects to hold until maturity when the loan is repaid fully. Section 2.2 discusses the banking book further. Nearly all of a bank's credit risk is contained in the credit risk of the assets in its banking book, although some elements of credit risk can also exist in the **trading book**.

1.3.2   Market Risk

Market risk is the risk of losses to the bank arising from movements in market prices as a result of changes in interest rates, foreign exchange rates, and equity and commodity prices. The various components of market risk, and the forces that give rise to them, are covered more extensively in Chapter 6. The components of market risk are as follows:

- **Interest rate risk** is the potential loss due to movements in interest rates. This risk arises because bank assets (loans and bonds) usually have a significantly longer maturity than bank liabilities (deposits). This risk can be conceptualized in two ways. First, if interest rates rise, the value of the longer-term assets will tend to fall more than the value of the shorter-term liabilities, reducing the bank's equity. Section 2.2 discusses bank assets, liabilities, and equity further. Second, if interest rates rise, the bank will be forced to pay higher interest rates on its deposits well before its longer-term loans mature and it is able to replace those loans with loans that earn higher interest rates.

EXAMPLE

American **savings and loans** (S&Ls), also called thrifts, are essentially mortgage lenders. They collect deposits and underwrite mortgages. During the 1980s and early 1990s, the U.S. S&L system underwent a major crisis in which several thousand thrifts failed as a result of interest rate risk exposure.

Many failed thrifts had underwritten longer-term (up to 30-year) fixed-rate mortgages that were funded by variable-rate deposits. These deposits paid interest rates that would reset, higher or lower, based on the market level of interest rates. As market interest rates increased, the deposit rates reset higher, and the interest payments the thrifts had to make began to exceed the interest payments they were receiving on their portfolios of fixed-rate mortgages. This led to increasingly large losses and eventually wiped out the equity of thousands of S&Ls and led to their failures. As shown in Figure 1.5, as interest rates rose, the payments the S&Ls had to make on variable rate deposits became larger than the payments received from the fixed-rate mortgage loans, leading to larger and larger losses.

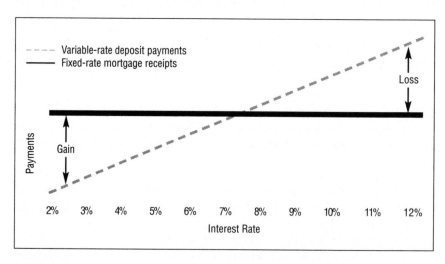

FIGURE 1.5 Gains vs. Losses for American S&Ls as Interest Rates Rise

■ **Equity risk** is the potential loss due to an adverse change in the price of stock. Stock, also referred to as shares or equity, represents an ownership interest in a company. Banks can purchase ownership stakes in other companies, exposing them to the risk of the changing value of these shares.

EXAMPLE

In the early part of this century, the functionality and use of technology for social media grew rapidly. The Facebook networking site transformed the way in which hundreds of millions of people communicated. It also transformed the way companies advertised to existing and potential customers. When Facebook went "public" on May 17, 2013, investor excitement pushed the launch price higher based on expectations and forecasts of advertising revenue. The opening share price was USD 38, but the price soon fell, dropping to USD 20 shortly afterward due to questions being asked about the effectiveness of Facebook advertising and the company's growth potential. The share price later rebounded, but its initial opening volatility was reminiscent of the dot-com bubble of 1997–2001; when it burst, the share prices of many technology companies fell, causing losses (due to equity risk) of 50% or more.

■ **Foreign exchange risk** is the risk that the value of the bank's assets or liabilities changes due to currency exchange rate fluctuations. Banks buy and sell foreign exchange on behalf of their customers (who need foreign currency to pay for their international transactions or receive foreign currency and want to exchange it to their own currency), and they also hold assets and liabilities in different currencies on their own balance sheets.

EXAMPLE

The Crimean Crisis that started in February 2014 put Russia and the United States, along with the European Union on a collision course. While military conflict, although unfortunate, was largely contained, by late 2014 the crisis continued and its main theatre of operation moved to the international financial markets and banking and payment systems. A number of sanctions were imposed by countries around the globe on Russian individuals, businesses, and on the Russian State herself.

The sanctions ranged from travel bans, money transfer bans, bans on access to foreign bank accounts, reduced or denied access to raising capital in international financial markets, bans on correspondent bank activity in favor of identified individuals and companies, bans of imports from and exports to Russia of certain defined goods, including energy-related goods.

The net effect of these sanctions was a slowdown of Russian business activity, reduction of personal freedoms, unavailability of international consumer products in Russia—and a collapse in the international value of the Russian ruble.

The ruble was valued at 32.6587 against the USD on January 1, 2014—a value level it had held since the onset of the Financial Crisis in 2008—and was still valued at 33.8434 on July 1, 2014—a modest decline of 3.6%. However, towards the end of October and early November, the ruble fell dramatically. On November 1, 2014 its value was 39.3519, and on November 7, 2014, it was valued at 45.1854, or a 38% decline since the beginning of the year. These prices for USD/RUB were official Russian Central Bank prices, suggesting that the effective foreign exchange rate for Russian customers and companies were many times higher for real transactions. The effect on Russian businesses was an increase by at least 38% in the price of foreign goods and/or a 38% decline in earnings from exports to other countries.

Although designed to be a measure against Russia as a whole, and her leadership in particular, the measures were expected to impact small and medium-sized Russian companies much more than large corporations. So, although the currency movements were dramatic, at the end of 2014, it remained to be seen if any lasting impact on economic and commercial life in Russia would take place.

■ **Commodity risk** is the potential loss due to an adverse change in commodity prices. There are different types of commodities, including agricultural commodities (e.g., wheat, corn, soybeans), industrial commodities (e.g., metals), and energy commodities (e.g., natural gas, crude oil). The value of commodities fluctuates a great deal due to changes in demand and supply.

EXAMPLE

During the 1970s, two American businessmen, the Hunt brothers, accumulated 280 million ounces of silver, a substantial position in the commodity. As they were accumulating this large position—approximately one-third of the world's supply—the price of silver rose. For a short period of time at the end of 1979, the Hunt brothers had cornered the silver market and effectively controlled its price. Between September 1979 and January 1980, the price of silver increased from USD 11 to USD 50 per ounce, during which time the two brothers earned an estimated USD 2 to 4 billion as a result of their silver speculation. At its peak, the position held by the brothers was worth USD 14 billion. Two months later, however, the price of silver collapsed back to USD 11 per ounce, and the brothers were forced to sell their substantial silver holdings at a loss.

Market risk tends to focus on a bank's **trading book**. The trading book is the portfolio of **financial assets** such as bonds, equity, foreign exchange, and derivatives held by a bank either to facilitate trading for its customers or for its own account or to hedge against various types of risk. Assets in the trading book are generally made available for sale, as the bank does not intend to keep those assets until they mature. Assets in the bank's banking book (held until maturity) and trading book (not held until maturity) collectively contain all the various investments in loans, securities, and other financial assets the bank has made using its deposits, loans, and shareholder equity.

Distinguishing between the trading and banking books is essential to understand how banks operate and how they manage their risks. The value of assets and liabilities in the trading book can change quickly, and the bank has to recognize those changes immediately. In contrast, changes to the value of the banking book generally take longer to happen.

The Basel Accord does not provide a definition for the term banking book; this is an important and easily forgotten point. In effect, what is included in the banking book is what is not included in the bank's trading book, which *is* defined by the Basel II and Basel III Accords. The trading and banking books will be discussed in later chapters (see Section 2.2).

1.3.3 Operational Risk

Operational risk is the risk of loss resulting from inadequate or failed internal processes, people, and systems or from external events. This definition includes **legal risk**, but excludes strategic and reputational risk.

EXAMPLE

In 1995, Baring Brothers and Co. Ltd. (Barings) collapsed after incurring losses of GBP 827 million following the failure of its internal control processes and procedures. One of its traders in Singapore hid trading losses for more than two years. Because of insufficient internal control measures, the trader was able to authorize his own trades and book them into the bank's systems without any supervision. The trader's supervisors were alerted after the trades started to lose significant amounts of money and it was no longer possible for the trader to keep the trades and the losses secret.

Compared to credit, market, and liquidity risk, operational risk is the least understood and most challenging risk to measure, manage, and monitor.

A wide range of loss events can be categorized as operational risk events. Chapter 7 discusses how banks measure and manage the different types of operational risks they are exposed to as part of the banking business.

1.3.4 Liquidity Risk

Liquidity risk is the risk that a bank may not be able to meet its obligations to repay deposits and other funding, or to continue financing its assets. There has been far greater focus on banks' liquidity risk following the global financial crisis of 2007–2009 when several banks needed to be supported by their governments because they were unable to meet their obligations to repay depositors and bondholders. The most recent Basel Accord includes new standards on banks' liquidity to complement its standards on banks' capital levels: Basel I and Basel II had provided standards only for capital levels. Liquidity risk will be discussed in greater detail in Chapters 3 and 6.

EXAMPLE

In August 2007, Northern Rock, a bank focused on financing real estate in the United Kingdom, received emergency funding from the Bank of England. The bank was relatively small and did not have a sufficient depositor base to fund new loans from deposits. It financed new mortgages by selling the mortgages it had already originated to other banks and investors, and by taking out short-term loans. This strategy made it increasingly vulnerable to changes in financial markets. How much financing Northern Rock could raise depended on two factors. The first was the demand for mortgages it had originated to sell to other banks. The second was the availability of credit in the credit market to finance these mortgages. Both of these depended on how the overall banking marketplace, particularly the availability of funding to finance lending, was performing. When the credit markets came under pressure in 2007, the bank found it increasingly difficult to sell the mortgages it had originated. At the same time, the bank could not secure the short-term financing it required. Simply put, Northern Rock could not finance its assets, was unable to raise new funds, ran out of money, and, notwithstanding the emergency financing from the Bank of England, was ultimately taken over by the government.

1.3.5 Systemic Risk

Systemic risk refers to the possibility that an entire banking system may face losses or even collapse, with all banks operating in that system being affected.

Systemic risk can arise due to macroeconomic or monetary events, such as a currency devaluation, or it can result from the failure of a single "systemically important" financial institution, whose problems cause difficulties for all other banks in the system.

EXAMPLE

In 1991, Argentina pegged its currency to the U.S. dollar, but over time people came to believe that this relationship was not sustainable and that the Argentine government would be forced to devalue the peso. In November 2001, interest rates rose dramatically in response to expectations of a devaluation, and depositors began to withdraw funds from their banks. The following day, the minister of the economy announced restrictions on banks' ability to pay clients and on customers' ability to withdraw deposits. All banks in the system were affected by these restrictions. Even banks that had been financially strong and conservatively managed were not able to meet their obligations.

1.3.6   Other Risks That Banks Face

Beyond the types of risk mentioned previously, there are other risks banks face and must manage appropriately. Here is a listing of some of them:

- **Business risk** is the potential loss due to a decrease in the competitive position of the bank and the prospect of the bank prospering in changing markets.

EXAMPLE

In 2003 HSBC bought the U.S. consumer, credit card, and mortgage lender Household International (later named HSBC Finance Corporation) to gain a slice of the booming U.S. property market. Expansion into this new market was seen as the answer to improving profitability and return on capital, although it was a departure from HSBC's traditional conservative banking culture.

Household International was a poor fit with HSBC operations, as much of its business was in second-line mortgages (equity loans or lines of credit which use the home as collateral) known in the United States as piggyback loans, marketed to low-income homeowners who used the loans to make a down payment on their home to avoid mortgage insurance, or purchase cars and other consumables. These loans were ultimately considered of dubious quality and a result of poor underwriting standards coupled with high-pressure selling.

When house prices fell in the United States, the equity supporting these loans was reduced to the point that in many cases the total loans outstanding were greater than the value of the property, resulting in negative equity.

Household International, which was bought for USD 15.3 billion, by 2006 had lost USD 30 billion for HSBC. The chairman said that, in retrospect, HSBC should not have acquired Household International.

In 2009 HSBC Finance Corporation announced the discontinuation of loan origination of all products by its consumer lending business, but continued to service, assist, and collect the existing receivable portfolio as it closed down its business.

- ■ **Reputational risk** is the potential loss resulting from a decrease in a bank's standing in public opinion. Recovering from a reputation problem, real or perceived, is not easy. Organizations have lost considerable business for no other reason than loss of customer confidence over a public relations problem, even with relatively solid systems, processes, and finances in place.

EXAMPLE

In 2012, Standard Chartered reached an anti-money-laundering settlement with the New York Department of Financial Services (NY DFS) for failures in its transaction surveillance systems. The bank had to suspend dollar-clearing activity for high-risk business clients, mostly small and medium enterprises (SMEs) in Hong Kong and the United Arab Emirates (UAE). It was also barred from accepting new clients without prior approval from NY DFS. The regulator believed that the bank allowed millions of suspicious payments to go unreported for several years.

The bank also agreed to pay a fine of USD 340 million to the regulator as part of an overall USD 667 million settlement in 2012. In addition to the financial losses, the bank closed much of its SME business in the Middle East and received wide negative publicity.

EXAMPLE

Wonga, a so-called payday consumer lender in the United Kingdom, also suffered significant losses in 2014 when, under pressure from the Financial Conduct Authority, it had to write off more than GBP 220 million of nonperforming loans (333,000 customers), as Wonga had not followed underwriting due diligence with individual borrowers to ensure they were in a position to repay the loans and pass an affordability test.

The firm suffered serious financial and reputational damage and had to rethink its business model.

■ **Compliance risk** is the risk that a bank may suffer losses as a result of its failure to comply with laws and regulations or with internal policies and procedures that govern the way it operates. This risk has been increasing in recent years, and oversight and scrutiny of banks have intensified following the global financial crisis of 2007–2009. The result is that the number of laws and regulations that a bank has to comply with has greatly increased, and so has the risk of non-compliance. Furthermore, regulations on money laundering and financial crime (including tax evasion) have become stricter in recent years, and governments and regulators are far less tolerant of any breaches than they were in the past.

1.4   Forces Shaping the Banking Industry

There are numerous other aspects of banking that have not been covered in this chapter but will be briefly touched upon in later parts of the book—either directly or as part of a discussion about other topics.

■ *Regulation, deregulation, and globalization.* In the 1990s and the early years of the 21st century, deregulation led to a relaxing of restrictive banking regulations in many countries around the globe. This allowed many banks to compete against each other and other financial services providers with less direct government oversight. The theory behind less oversight was that increased competition among banks would increase their efficiency. Deregulation puts market pressures on banks from organizations that offer similar banking services.

Additionally, it was felt that banks would, in their own self-interest, effectively regulate themselves with little need for heavy-handed oversight from government regulators. The idea was that it is in a bank's self-interest to ensure that it functions properly to compete in an increasingly competitive world. However, as became apparent during the global financial crisis of 2007–2009, banks were unable to police themselves effectively. Their lack of discipline resulted in a virtual collapse of the global financial system. It has also become clear that many banks are now considered **"too big to fail"** due to their global connectivity and importance to the worldwide financial system. Since then, governments have introduced numerous banking regulation reforms and have, for the first time, been considering adopting some type of cooperative system to allow for the rapid sharing of information among world financial regulators with the intent of more proactively addressing future financial services–related risks and issues.

The trend toward deregulation of financial markets that was seen in the years that preceded the global financial crisis has now been put into reverse. Not only are banks more heavily regulated than before, but there is general agreement among policy makers and regulators that this heavier regulation is justified. There has also been much more attention given to how banks conduct themselves and whether they are treating customers fairly, regardless of whether they are operating in a financially prudent manner.

- *Competition.* Banks are facing increasing competition from specialized financial services providers. Examples of such non-depository financial intermediaries that now compete with banks include:

  - Retirement systems—pension plans and retirement funds
  - Collective investment pools—mutual funds, unit trusts, and hedge funds
  - Finance companies—leasing and equipment finance
  - Payment services
  - Insurance companies
  - Hedge funds
  - Private equity companies

- *Securitization.* Bundling together various debt capital assets, such as mortgages, credit cards, and loans, and selling securities representing various types of ownership in the resulting portfolio, is a relatively new financial product. The securitization process is explained in greater detail in Section 5.2.3. Securitization is a threat to banks since it enables non-banks to offer loans and financing at a lower cost than what banks historically charge. Securitization, however, can also benefit banks by offering them a way to sell some of the higher-risk assets they would prefer not to hold on their books.

- *Technological advances.* Improvements in computing power, telecommunications, and information technology have allowed banks to offer new ventures such as Internet-based banking. Technological advances continue to reduce the cost of routine banking services, such as payments and withdrawals.

■ *Inflation and interest rate uncertainty.* Both bank balance sheets and profits are highly sensitive to changes in interest rates. When inflation increases, interest rates tend to increase, and many banks—as we will see in later sections—suffer. When interest rates change considerably and frequently, banks must focus on managing these risks.

In this chapter, the foundations were laid for understanding banks, the banking industry, and the risks they face. Later chapters discuss in greater detail the relationship between bank risks and regulation.

Managing Banks

Chapter 2 builds on the first chapter and introduces bank management topics that are particularly relevant to risk management and regulation. This chapter examines bank corporate governance, the financial statements banks use to communicate their activities, the function of **asset and liability management** in banking, and how banks manage loan losses.

Chapter Outline
- 2.1 Balance Sheet and Income Statement
- 2.2 Loan Losses
- 2.3 Asset and Liability Management
- 2.4 Corporate Governance

Key Learning Points
- Banks report their assets, liabilities, and the effects of their various business transactions in financial statements. Financial statements provide a comprehensive view of performance for shareholders, depositors, **stakeholders**, and regulators.
- Banks treat performing and **nonperforming loans** differently; banks build up reserves in their financial statements to reduce the potential negative effects of nonperforming loans.

- Banks manage their assets and liabilities with the overall objective of reducing risks while maximizing returns to shareholders.
- Bank corporate governance refers to the framework banks use to manage their operations and deal with the often conflicting interests of bank stakeholders.

MANAGING BANKS

2.1   Balance Sheet and Income Statement

One responsibility that a bank's board and senior management team must fulfill is to record correctly and account for all the bank's transactions. Transactions include the bank's loans, investments, and other assets as well as deposits. These records form the underlying basis for the bank's financial statements: its balance sheet, **income statement**, statement of cash flows, and the notes to these statements. Through financial statements, a bank is able to communicate its financial position to its stakeholders and regulators. This section focuses on the balance sheet and the income statement.

- The balance sheet shows all the assets, liabilities, and equity the bank has at one particular point in time, such as at the end of a year. It is a snapshot of what the bank owns (assets) and owes (liabilities), and the difference between them, the bank's equity.
- The income statement records all the revenues (income) and costs (expenses) that the bank has encountered over a specific time period, such as one month, one quarter, or one year.

2.1.1   Bank Assets

A bank typically has cash, investments in securities and loans, real estate holdings, and other assets on its balance sheet. The majority of a bank's assets are held in either the bank's banking book or its trading book. A small proportion of the bank's assets are held in cash, either in the vault of the bank to meet immediate needs for payments and withdrawals, as reserves at the central bank, or deposited with other banks to fulfill its regulatory reserve requirements (see Chapter 1).

Figure 2.1 shows a simple balance sheet for a hypothetical bank, Bank A, a typical medium-sized bank that provides credit for commercial and industrial purposes. The bank finances its assets—the bonds it owns and the loans it underwrites—using a combination of deposits and borrowings. We will use this hypothetical balance sheet as our example throughout the remainder of this chapter.

Assets in million USD	Amount	Liabilities in million USD	Amount
Cash	10	Short-term deposits	300
Government bonds	100	Long-term deposits	250
		Subtotal deposits	*550*
Loans to local government, net	190	Short-term financing	200
Loans to SMEs, net	200	Long-term bonds	150
Loans to large corporations, net	500	*Subtotal other liabilities*	*350*
Total loans	*890*	Total liabilities	900
		Equity	100
Total	**1,000**	**Total**	**1,000**

FIGURE 2.1 Bank A's Balance Sheet

From a management perspective, the bank's assets are divided in two "books":

- The **trading book** includes the investments the bank has made in securities such as bonds, equities, and commodities. The trading book is chiefly exposed to market risk. Chapter 6 will discuss in further detail the risks of the various financial assets usually found in the trading book.
- The **banking book** refers to the loans the bank has made. The primary risk in the banking book is credit risk. Interest rate risk is also a major consideration when managing the bank's banking book (see Section 2.3.1). Chapters 4 and 5 will discuss in detail the risks of the various loan types that banks routinely underwrite.

Figure 2.2 below depicts the difference between the trading book and the banking book for our hypothetical bank, Bank A.

Assets in million USD	Amount	Book
Cash	10	
Government bonds	100	Trading
Loans to local government	190	
Loans to SMEs	200	Banking
Loans to large corporations	500	
Total	**1,000**	

FIGURE 2.2 Trading and Banking Books

Bank A's trading book consists of the government bonds the bank owns, and the banking book consists of three distinct portfolios: local government loans, small and medium enterprise (SME) loans, and large corporate loans. The value of the banking book equals the value of the bank's loans.

In addition, banks will usually own real estate (buildings and other premises) and machinery and equipment (computer and other technology networks) used to support operations.

2.1.2   Bank Liabilities

A bank's liabilities consist of its deposits and its borrowings. Most of a commercial bank's liabilities are the deposits made by its customers (depositors). These deposits are generally placed in either **transaction accounts** or savings accounts. Figure 2.3 shows the balance sheet with the various liabilities the bank holds.

- Transaction accounts are accounts where the depositor can withdraw the deposits on demand using checks, debit cards, or similar payment instructions. Transaction accounts usually allow a large number of withdrawals with minimal time restrictions. In exchange for the convenience of immediate access to deposits, banks pay no, or low, interest to the depositors. Checking or debit accounts are examples of transaction accounts.
- Savings accounts may limit the number of withdrawals a depositor can make over a specified period of time, and offer higher interest rates to depositors. Because access to funds in a savings account is limited and withdrawal in certain cases may be restricted by time, savings accounts are important to a bank's asset and liability management function (see Section 2.3 for more details). Examples of savings accounts are time deposits, passbook savings, and certificates of deposit.

A bank may also borrow money from other banks overnight or from its central bank for various time periods. Additionally, banks may issue bonds and other debt instruments that are publicly traded. Figure 2.3 shows Bank A's debt financing.

Liabilities in million USD	Amount		Liability type
Short-term deposits	300		Transaction deposit
Long-term deposits	250		Savings deposit
Total deposits		*550*	
Short-term financing	200		Other bank liability
Long-term bonds	150		Other bank liability
Other debt financing		*350*	
Total liabilities		**900**	

FIGURE 2.3 The Bank's Debt Financing

2.1.3   Equity

The difference between the bank's assets and liabilities equals its equity.

$$\text{Assets} - \text{Liabilities} = \text{Equity}$$

EXAMPLE

Bank A has USD 1,000 million in assets with USD 900 million in liabilities; the difference of USD 100 million is the bank's equity.

Equity represents the ownership stake of the bank's shareholders and consists of two parts:

1. **Paid-in capital,** the capital that the owners have provided to the bank
2. **Retained earnings,** all the earnings the bank has generated since its inception, less any income it returned to the owners as dividends

A bank can raise equity in two ways. First, it can sell new stock (equity) to its existing shareholders or the public. When the bank turns to the public to sell new equity in the form of shares, the process is called a **public offering.**

An alternative approach to raising equity is a **private offering**, when the bank turns to a selected group of qualified investors to raise the equity capital. The bank can also generate **net income** that is added to its existing equity capital as retained earnings. Dividends are discretionary payments from the bank to its shareholders. The bank returns part of its income to its owners through dividends. The **board of directors** usually decides whether to pay dividends.

Typically, equity consists of preferred and common stock. One of the fundamental differences between preferred and common stock is that common stock allows its owners to make decisions that affect the bank by voting, including voting for the board of directors. Owners of preferred stock generally do not have this right, which they give up in exchange for set dividend payments and priority over the common shareholders in the event the bank is liquidated. Preferred stock is considered a **hybrid security,** as it has both debt- and equity-like features. The debt-like features are the set return and the fact that preferred shareholders, in case the bank is liquidated, receive payments before the common shareholders. The equity-like features include that preferred shareholders may receive dividends that may be structured to reflect corporate profits, and the fact that if the bank is liquidated, they receive payment after the bondholders but before the common shareholders.

2.1.4   Income Statement

The income statement records the effects of the financial transactions the bank carried out over a specified time period, usually quarterly or annually. The income statement specifically shows the effect of costs on revenues. The difference between the revenues earned and the costs incurred over a set time period is called profit (or loss). In sum, profit (or loss) is the difference between the bank's income and its expenses.

The bank's greatest source of income is the difference between the interest rate the bank earns on the loans it makes and the interest rate it pays to the depositors for their deposits. This difference is called the **interest rate margin.** Banks profit only when their interest income (paid by the borrowers to the bank) is greater than interest expenses (paid by the bank to the depositors). Managing the bank's **net interest income,** the difference between interest income and interest expense, is an important function of bank management.

EXAMPLE

Using the balance sheet presented in Figure 2.1 and the bank's stated rates of return, we can calculate its net interest income. Looking at the assets (left) side of the balance sheet, we see that the USD 10 million in cash Bank A holds on hand currently earns nothing. The interest income the bank derives from the next four items and their total is shown in Figure 2.4.

Assets in million USD	Amount	Annual return	Annual interest income
Cash	10	0%	10 * 0% = 0
Government bonds	100	2%	100 * 2% = 2
Loans to local government, net[1]	190	3%	190 * 3% = 6
Loans to SMEs, net	200	5%	200 * 5% = 10
Loans to large corporations, net	500	7%	500 * 7% = 35
Total			**53**

FIGURE 2.4 The Bank's Interest Income[1]

Looking at the liabilities (right) side of the same balance sheet, the bank's interest expense comes from the first four items, and is shown in Figure 2.5.

Liabilities in million USD	Amount	Annual cost	Annual interest expense
Short-term deposits	300	1%	300 * 1% = 3
Long-term deposits	250	2%	250 * 2% = 5
Short-term financing	200	3%	200 * 3% = 6
Long-term bonds	150	4%	150 * 4% = 6
Total			**20**

Interest income	USD 53 million
– Interest expense	USD 20 million
= Net interest income	USD 33 million

FIGURE 2.5 The Bank's Interest Expense

---

1. For reasons of presentation simplicity, the number relating to loans to local government, net, is rounded from USD 5.7 million to USD 6.0 million.

A second major source of revenues generated by the bank comes from the various fees banks charge their customers for services provided. For example, fees are charged for opening an account, applying for a loan, arranging a payment, or receiving advice for complex financial services. Fee income is a substantial source of income. Many banks try to maintain some type of balance between the revenues they earn from interest income and fee income.

The most significant cost the bank has apart from its interest expenses is for personnel (employees). Other important costs are the cost for the premises where it operates and the physical infrastructure (computer and other networks) the bank owns.

After all costs have been deducted from the bank's revenue, the bank's earnings before taxes are calculated. Banks, like almost all other companies, pay tax on their earnings to local, state, and national governments. After the bank pays any taxes due, the remainder is the bank's net income. If the net income is negative, it is called a loss.

EXAMPLE

In building on the example above, assume Bank A generates USD 15 million in fee income but has USD 23 million in personnel and other expenses. Thus, its earnings before taxes may be calculated as:

Net interest income	USD 33 million
+ Fee income	USD 15 million
− Personnel and other expenses	USD 23 million
= Earnings before taxes	USD 25 million

These examples present a very simplified approach to calculating profits and losses. In reality, there are numerous, and often complex, tax, legal, regulatory, and other considerations that a bank, and any company, must take into account before it can calculate profit(s) or loss(es).

Banks can use their positive net income in any number of ways. As mentioned earlier, the net income can be added to the bank's already existing equity capital as retained earnings, thereby increasing the amount of the bank's equity capital, or the bank can return part of this income to its shareholders as dividends or through the repurchase of existing stock.

2.1.5   The Role of Bank's Equity

Equity plays an important role in the management of the bank. If the bank makes a loan to a borrower who defaults on the obligation, the bank will lose some of its assets, affecting the bank's equity and reducing the shareholders' stake in the bank. The depositors, who have entrusted their money for safekeeping at the bank, expect to be protected from any losses the bank suffers on its loans.

As noted in Chapter 1, the processes of financial intermediation and asset transformation are key to bank operations and are also at the core of bank risks. Underwriting, the process of evaluating a borrower's ability to repay funds to the bank, places the bank in a unique position. The bank must determine how much credit can be extended (if any) and the conditions (or terms) it must impose on the loan to decrease the possibility of loss. In addition, the bank must consider the total amount of credit risk it is willing to take across all its borrowers (see Section 2.4 on corporate governance). In fact, how well a bank succeeds in its underwriting process affects the bank's profits, financial health, and survival.

EXAMPLE

Bank A has extended many loans to SMEs, including a USD 4 million loan to XYZ Construction Inc. The bank's balance sheet, just after it makes the loan to XYZ Construction, is shown in Figure 2.6.

Assets in million USD	Amount	Liabilities in million USD	Amount
Cash	10	Short-term deposits	300
Government bonds	100	Long-term deposits	250
		Subtotal deposits	*550*
Loans to local government, net	190	Short-term financing	200
Loans to SMEs, net	200	Long-term bonds	150
Loans to large corporations, net	500	*Subtotal other liabilities*	*350*
Total loans	*890*	Total liabilities	900
		Equity	100
Total	**1,000**	**Total**	**1,000**

FIGURE 2.6 Bank A's Balance Sheet

Now, suppose that XYZ Construction is unable to repay the loan and defaults. This loan default impacts the bank in several ways:

- The bank will not receive any additional interest income from the loan. Assuming the interest rates on loans to SMEs are 5%, the bank would lose USD 200,000 in annual interest income. In the meantime, Bank A still has to pay interest to its depositors. This will reduce the net interest income of the bank.
- If Bank A cannot recover the loan it has provided to XYZ Construction, the bank loses USD 4 million, which it charges off, or removes, from its balance sheet. (Section 2.2 will discuss in greater detail how banks manage nonperforming loans.) The charge-off affects the bank's balance sheet by reducing two items:

1. Assets by the loss of USD 4 million
2. Equity by the loss of USD 4 million

Losses to the bank reduce first its equity. Deposits are usually insulated from these losses, as equity and other sources of capital—such as the bank's own borrowings—bear the primary impact of losses. Banks create various reserves to counterbalance some of the effects of loan losses; how these reserves work will be discussed in Section 2.2. Some countries provide deposit insurance as an additional guarantee for bank depositors, further reducing the potential risk to depositors (see Section 3.4 for more on deposit insurance).

After the USD 4 million loss, the bank's balance sheet looks like Figure 2.7, showing total assets and liabilities (plus equity) of the USD 996 million.

Assets (in USD millions)	Amount	Liabilities	Amount
Cash	10	Short-term deposits	300
Government bonds	100	Long-term deposits	250
Loans to local government, net	190	Short-term financing	200
❶ Loans to SMEs, net	196	Long-term bonds	150
Loans to large corporations, net	500	❷ Equity	96
Total	996	Total	996

FIGURE 2.7 Bank A's Balance Sheet after the Loss

The two effects of the loss on the balance sheet of the bank are the following:

1. The value of loans is reduced by the amount of the loss. The USD 4 million loan loss reduces the "Loans to SMEs" from USD 200 million to USD 196 million.
2. The value of equity is reduced by the amount of the loss. The USD 4 million loan loss reduces equity from USD 100 million to USD 96 million.

As in Figure 2.7, the USD 4 million loss is small in relation to all of the bank's assets, just 0.4% of assets of USD 1,000 million. It is, however, a considerable loss in relation to the bank's equity of USD 100 million. It is 4% of the capital. The bank's equity absorbs the losses the bank suffers when loans or other investments go sour. That is why banks carefully evaluate their borrowers. Should losses accumulate, the bank's equity would be in peril. Losses tend to accumulate during bad economic times, when banks are most vulnerable.

If the losses are large enough, the entire capital of the bank disappears. In practice, in this particular case, the bank can only withstand an additional USD 96 million in losses before its equity becomes zero. With USD 996 million in loans outstanding, if a little less than 1/10 of the total amount the bank lent to the customers is lost, the equity of the bank becomes zero. In practice, in most countries, a bank would be closed by the regulators before it lost all of its equity. A bank with a larger equity base is better able to absorb potential losses from nonperforming and defaulted loans and is considered more stable. In the example, 90% of the assets are financed through debt. Leverage (or gearing) is the ratio of debt to equity.

During the global financial crisis of 2007–2009, some banks suffered large losses on their loan portfolios and had to reduce the value of their capital by significant amounts. In several cases, the losses were so large that governments had to step in to support the banks.

EXAMPLE

Initially, Bank A's USD 1,000 million in assets were financed through USD 900 million in debt and USD 100 million equity. The **leverage** was 9-to-1 (9:1); each dollar of equity supported USD 10 in assets. In relation to many other businesses, banks are highly leveraged.

When compared to other businesses, banks are inherently highly leveraged. Let's revisit Bank A's balance sheet with the previous loan loss example to see how quickly bank equity can disappear when a bank has higher leverage and suffers losses. (See Figure 2.8.)

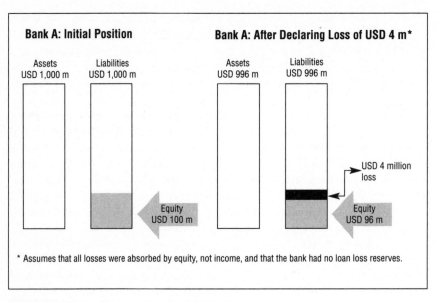

FIGURE 2.8 Effect of Losses on a Bank's Equity

EXAMPLE

Looking at the same loss of USD 4 million discussed earlier, the impact on Bank A will be far greater when leverage increases. Let us assume that instead of 9-to-1 leverage (9:1), Bank A's initial leverage was 19-to-1 (19:1). In this scenario, the bank's assets of USD 1,000 million would be financed with USD 950 million in debt and only USD 50 million in equity. Here, each dollar of equity supports USD 19 in debt (USD 950/USD 50 = USD 19). Figure 2.9 shows the combined effects of losses and smaller equity base.

Assets (in USD millions)	Amount	Liabilities	Amount
Cash	10	Short-term deposits	300
Government bonds, net	100	Long-term deposits	250
Loans to local government, net	190	Short-term financing	250
❶ *Loans to SMEs, net*	*196*	Long-term bonds	150
Loans to large corporations, net	500	❷ *Equity*	*46*
Total	**996**	**Total**	**996**

FIGURE 2.9 Simplified Balance Sheet—Smaller Equity Base or Higher Leverage

1. The value of loans is reduced by the amount of the loss. The USD 4 million loan loss reduces the "Loans to SME" from USD 200 million to USD 196 million.
2. The value of equity is reduced by the amount of the loss. The USD 4 million loan loss reduces equity from USD 50 million to USD 46 million.

Losing USD 4 million, or 0.4% of its assets in this case, reduces equity from USD 50 million to USD 46 million, but this erosion will reduce equity by 8% (USD 4/USD 50 = 8%). The bank now can only withstand an additional USD 46 million in losses before its equity becomes zero. With USD 996 million in loans outstanding, if a little less than 5% of the total amount the bank lent to the customers is lost, the equity of the bank becomes zero.

The higher the leverage, the faster the equity disappears when the bank has to take losses on loans that default. The impact that losses have on equity is why bank regulations and regulators have historically focused on the bank's equity. Regulators consider the bank's equity the core tool to motivate bank managers and owners to reduce risks and to provide a sufficient cushion against losses.

More equity and lower leverage represents the following:

- Bigger commitment by the owners, on the aggregate, to the future of the bank, as they have more of their wealth tied to the fortunes of the bank and potentially more to lose.
- Greater cushion for the bank to absorb and withstand potential losses.

In fact, over the years, both regulators and economists have found that prudently managed banks have higher capital-to-total-assets ratios and suffer losses less frequently. They have found that the amount of capital a bank must have to support its operations reduces the risks it will take and increases the likelihood that the equity of the bank is sufficient to withstand loan losses as well as liquidity pressures. In fact, contemporary banking regulation, such as the Basel Accords (described in Section 3.3), is risk based and links the riskiness of the bank's assets to its equity.

2.2 Loan Losses

Banks recognize that some of the loans they underwrite may default, and they anticipate the impact this could have on both the bank's earnings and its profits. As will be seen in later chapters, banks have developed sophisticated and highly structured approaches to predict, manage, and reduce potential loan losses. Since loan losses diminish the equity capital and consequently may affect the long-term survival of the bank, banks must incorporate into their planning and budgeting processes a reasonable level of loan losses as a "cost of doing business," similar to expenses they budget for employees, office space, and equipment. For good corporate governance, a bank's board of directors should set and approve the bank's loan loss policies. That is why each year banks set aside part of their income to offset the potential impact of loan losses in a way similar to budgeting for salaries and other common expenses.

Complex rules govern the way banks are required to publicly report the assets they have in their trading and banking books. Regulators, shareholders, and other stakeholders have an interest in having high-quality, reliable, and up-to-date information on the financial position of the bank. One core concern is how well the recorded value of loans and other assets reflects their true value. This issue of asset valuation is one of the underlying reasons for the credit crisis that began in 2007.

This section discusses how banks record and value assets in their trading and banking books, and, in general, what rules they are required to follow to properly treat and value loans that do not perform. The section also describes methods to manage loan losses and the reserves that are held by the bank to deal with them.

2.2.1   Valuing Assets in the Trading Book

Assets in the trading book are usually held for sale, and their value on the balance sheet of the bank should reflect what these assets would fetch in the financial markets (Chapter 6). Thus, the value of these assets has to be **marked-to-market**; that is, their value on the balance sheet must reflect the fair market value. The **fair market value** is the price the asset would bring if sold immediately on the market to a willing buyer.

EXAMPLE

Bank A, our hypothetical bank, has purchased a **bond** for USD 1 million. As a result of severe financial turmoil, the bond dropped in value by 10%, and it can only be sold for USD 900,000. The bank's financial records must record the fair market value of the bond at USD 900,000 and not the purchase price of USD 1 million. The difference of USD 100,000 is an unrealized loss (a book loss that has not been actually incurred, as the bond has not yet been sold in the market). The unrealized loss will reduce the bank's assets and equity at the time it is recorded. The effects of this loss are similar to the loss the bank suffers if one of its loans defaults and the ensuing loss reduces the bank's earnings.

Several months later, the financial turmoil subsided, and the price of the bond increased to USD 1,010,000. As a result of the price of the bond increasing in the market, the previous loss of USD 100,000 is erased, and both the bank's assets and equity increase in value. Although the bond can be sold for USD 1,010,000 in the market, at a gain of USD 10,000, this gain is considered an unrealized gain until the bond is sold. Most accounting rules are generally more restrictive in treating unrealized gains than unrealized losses. The bank must initially record the bond on its books at the purchase price of USD 1,000,000. The unrealized gain of USD 10,000 will have to wait for a period of time or until the bond is actually sold for that gain to be recognized in the financial statements.

2.2.2 Value of Assets in the Banking Book, Performing Loans

Assets held in the banking book, mostly loans, are usually not made available for sale. As such, they are different from assets held in the trading book that, as already noted, are usually held for sale.

Loans whose borrowers make payments as agreed are considered **performing loans**. Loans whose borrowers fail to make payments, or make delayed payments, may be considered nonperforming loans (NPLs).

In the banking book, if the loans held by the bank are not sold off to third parties, then for accounting purposes they are considered to be held until they are repaid or held to maturity. Since these assets are held long-term, changes in their value do not necessarily have to reflect their fair market value. Their value, however, does have to reflect what the bank reasonably can expect to receive from the borrower. If the bank expects the loan to be repaid in full, no adjustments are necessary.

EXAMPLE

Bank A has extended a USD 5 million, five-year loan to XYZ Construction Inc. and records the loan on its balance sheet as USD 5 million since it expects to hold the loan until the loan is fully repaid. Regardless of how well XYZ Construction performs over the next five years (absent bankruptcy or other materially adverse problems), Bank A can carry the loan on its books at that face value.

2.2.3   Value of Assets in the Banking Book, Non-performing Loans

If a bank does not expect full or partial repayment of a loan on time, it must then be classified as a nonperforming loan, and adjustments must be made to the recorded value of the loan in the bank's financial statements. The bank has to adjust the recorded value of nonperforming loans on its balance sheet so that shareholders, management, regulators, and other stakeholders can correctly assess the strength of the bank. The loan's newly recorded value must be changed to reflect the expected amount the bank can reasonably recover from the borrower. As a consequence of a borrower not repaying the loan in full, the bank must categorize the nonperforming loan as past due, written down, or charged off.

- A loan is past-due when the repayment of principal and interest is in doubt because the borrower has missed several payments to the bank or the bank has a clear indication that the borrower may not repay the loan; that is, there is doubt about the borrower's ability or willingness to pay. A **past-due loan** may eventually be fully repaid by the borrower.
- A loan is **written-down** if it is past due, and the bank has made a determination that it will not be able to recover fully the amount it has lent to the borrower. Therefore, the bank has to adjust the value of the loan in its financial statements to the value that the bank expects to recover from the borrower. The amount by which the bank reduces the value of the loan is also called the write-down.
- A loan is **charged-off** if it has been removed from the bank's financial statements because the bank believes that it will collect nothing of the loan from the borrower. A charged-off loan will reduce the bank's equity. Even though a loan may be completely charged off, the bank may continue to try to collect on it.

EXAMPLE

Due to unforeseen circumstances, XYZ Construction Inc., the borrower from the previous example, became unable to make principal and interest payments in a timely manner. XYZ Construction, a home builder, has been materially impacted by the softening real estate market and is largely incapable of selling its already-built property inventory. As a result, it has not been able to raise sufficient funds to make loan payments as scheduled.

When Bank A first received an indication that XYZ Construction would not be able to continue making its loan principal and/or interest payments on time, it flagged the loan as nonperforming or doubtful. As is true with any bank, nonperforming loans receive additional attention from Bank A's management, as well as its regulators. Initially, the bank exercises forbearance by working with XYZ Construction and providing additional time to make the payments or, alternatively, to reduce (at least temporarily) the interest rate on the loan. Under this situation, Bank A may not have to make any adjustments to the value of the loan. If XYZ Construction Inc. is able to catch up with its payments, the loan will no longer be classified as nonperforming. However, if the forbearance does not help XYZ Construction and it is not able to catch up with the payments, Bank A will then typically decide that it is unlikely that the borrower will make all the payments it owes the bank. In that case, the bank must adjust the value of the loan recorded on its balance sheet. This can be achieved by either a write-down or through a specific provision (more about provisions in the next section).

When a loan is written down, the value of the loan is reduced to a value the bank expects to recover. For example, if Bank A believes that it can recover only 80% of the outstanding loan, it would reduce the value of the loan by 20%, or USD 1 million. The loan will then be recorded at its net value or USD 4 million, with the USD 1 million that was written down reducing the bank's assets and consequently its equity.

If the situation worsens further and it becomes more likely that XYZ Construction Inc. will be unable to repay even 80% of the USD 5 million loan, the bank will have to write down the loan even further to a value that it deems to be reasonable. If Bank A does not expect the loan to be repaid at all—due to significantly worsening economic conditions or other factors—the bank faces no other option but to charge off and remove the entire remaining loan of USD 4 million as it is recorded on the bank's balance sheet.

In this scenario, the bank charged off the loan in two steps. First, it wrote down the loan. Next, because XYZ Construction was unable to make any payments, the bank had to remove the entire loan from its balance sheet.

How a bank deals with nonperforming loans depends on the regulatory rules it operates under, how conservative the bank's risk management policies are, and the degree of prudence the bank's management exercises in its overall bank management.

Prudent management is a function of the bank's corporate governance and reflects the risk management culture promoted by the bank's board of directors and the operational structure of the bank. Very conservatively, or prudently, managed banks may aggressively charge off the entire loan as soon as the loan becomes nonperforming. Other banks may exercise a less conservative approach and delay writing down or even charging off loans for as long as they can. Although regulators provide guidance on how to treat nonperforming loans on the bank's books, some banks, particularly those that have limited financial strength, may tend to be less conservative when it comes to writing down or charging off assets and may keep them on their books at face value much longer.

Because there is discretion afforded to a bank in dealing with nonperforming assets, regulators pay a great deal of attention to how banks deal with nonperforming loans, often demanding that banks make additional write-downs. Delaying write-downs or charge-offs can easily lead to an incorrect valuation of the bank's financial condition, because the value of its loans will be overstated. Overstating the value of loans negatively affects the bank's earnings capacity and the size of its equity capital. This could hinder its ability to support operations and absorb future losses, and would be misleading to the shareholders.

2.2.4   Provision for Loan Losses and Loan Loss Reserves

As will be seen in later chapters, particularly in Chapter 5, the bank's entire underwriting process focuses on making a prediction about the borrower's likelihood of defaulting. Even though the bank thoroughly analyzes all the loans it underwrites, circumstances can change so that what was initially considered to be a good, high-quality loan becomes a nonperforming loan. Banks know this and expect a reasonable level of losses on the loans they make. To compensate for the expected loan losses, banks price their loans accordingly: the interest rate and other fees the borrower pays for the loan are calculated to compensate for the risk the lender undertakes, including the potential loan losses the bank would suffer if the borrower defaults. That is why higher-risk borrowers pay a higher interest rate to the bank.

Another approach a bank can use to manage the effect of loan losses is to create a **loan loss reserve** in its balance sheet. Through provisions in their income statements, banks set aside part of their earnings to cover the losses they expect to suffer from bad loans. The **provision for loan losses** reduces the bank's income as recorded in the income statement and creates a loan loss reserve on the balance sheet that reduces the value of the loans recorded on the bank's balance sheet. The loan loss reserve is also referred to as an "allowance for loan losses" or a "credit loss reserve."

EXAMPLE

Using the income statement example in Section 2.1.4, earnings before taxes were USD 25 million. When the bank makes a provision for loan losses, its earnings are directly reduced. If the bank decides to make a USD 2 million provision for loan losses, it reduces its earnings by the amount of the provision.

Earnings before provision for loan losses	USD 25 million
– Provision for loan losses	USD 2 million
= Earnings after provision for loan losses and before taxes	USD 23 million

Banks pay taxes on earnings after the provision for loan losses is calculated.

There is an important difference between the provision for loan losses and the loan loss reserve. *The provision for loan losses is recorded in the income statement of the bank and affects the earnings of the bank. The loan loss reserve is recorded on the balance sheet of the bank and affects the value of the bank's assets.*

During good times, banks generally perform well, experience infrequent defaults, and generate high earnings. Stability coupled with high earnings allows banks to make loan loss provisions as a part of their normal business operations to ultimately bolster the bank's loan loss reserve in anticipation of an economic downturn. Banks budget for losses on loans each year based on historical experience and business judgment. When actual loan losses start accumulating, usually during weaker economic times or recessionary environments, the loan loss reserves can be used to absorb some, if not all, of the losses the bank will suffer. Since the bank made provisions for potential losses in previous years, the loan losses will reduce the loan loss reserves first, not the earnings of the bank. Because of this, losses are not recognized in that year's income statement unless the accumulated loan loss reserves are depleted that year and additional provisions have to be made. In effect, by maintaining an appropriate loan loss reserve, the bank is able to smooth its earnings.

Regulators pay close attention to the size of the loan loss reserve, as inadequate provisions for loan losses can hurt the bank's equity capital during economic contraction, when banks need the most protection to withstand potentially sizable losses.

2.2.5 Loan Loss Reserves and Loan Losses

The loan loss reserves that a bank builds up over the years should be sufficient to offset future charge-offs the bank expects to make, but if loan loss reserves are not sufficient, then the bank needs to use its earnings to add to its reserves. If neither existing reserves nor the bank's earnings are sufficient to cover loan losses, then the bank will have to reduce the value of its equity.

EXAMPLE

1. Bank's A's balance sheet totaled USD 1,000. Its assets comprised a mixture of loans, some government bonds, and some cash. Its liabilities comprised deposits and equity.

Assets in million USD	Amount	Liabilities in million USD	Amount
Cash	10	Short-term deposits	300
Government bonds	100	Long-term deposits	250
		Subtotal deposits	*550*
Loans to local government	190	Short-term financing	200
Loans to SMEs	200	Long-term bonds	150
Loans to large corporations	500	*Subtotal other liabilities*	*350*
Total loans	*890*	Equity	100
Total	**1,000**	**Total**	**1,000**

FIGURE 2.10 Typical Bank Balance Sheet

2. One of the bank's loans to large corporations is a loan of USD 5 million to XYZ Corporation. At the end of the year, the bank judges that XYZ Corporation is unlikely to be able to repay the full USD 5 million that it owes. It thinks that USD 4 million is a more realistic estimate of what it will receive. Bank A therefore decides to create a loan loss reserve of USD 1 million against the XYZ Corporation loan.

    During the year, Bank A made a profit before provisions of USD 1 million. All of this is used to create the loan loss provision against the XYZ Corporation loan. As a result, the bank declares net profits of zero.

    After Bank A has created the USD 1 million loan loss reserve, net loans to large corporations are USD 499 million—that is, the amount that the bank expects to collect. Gross loans are still USD 500 million. The amount of total assets on the bank's balance sheet remains the same, but assets other than loans increase by USD 1 million. In our example, this USD 1 million is added to cash, increasing cash on the balance sheet to USD 11 million from USD 10 million.

    Assuming no other changes, its balance sheet now appears as follows:

Assets in million USD	Amount	Liabilities in million USD	Amount
Cash	11	Short-term deposits	300
Government bonds	100	Long-term deposits	250
		Subtotal deposits	*550*
Loans to local government	190		
Loans to SMEs	200	Short-term financing	200
Loans to large corporations	*500*	Long-term bonds	150
Loan loss reserve	*(1)*		
Net loans to large corporations	499		
Total loans (net)	*889*	*Subtotal other liabilities*	*350*
		Equity	100
Total	**1,000**	**Total**	**1,000**

FIGURE 2.11 Creating a Loan Loss Reserve

If the bank had not been able to use the USD 1 million in pre-provision profits to create the loan loss reserve, it would have had to reduce the value of its equity to USD 999 million: Cash would have remained at USD 10 million and net loans would have been USD 889 million, with the result that total assets would have become USD 999 million.

3. At the end of the following year, Bank A judges that XYZ Corporation's financial position has deteriorated further and that it is now realistic to expect only USD 3 million of the original USD 5 million loan to be repaid. The bank therefore decides to add another USD 1 million to its existing loan loss reserve against the XYZ Corporation loan. During this year, Bank A made pre-provision profits of USD 2 million. After deducting the USD 1 million loan loss provision, it declares a net profit of USD 1 million.

After adding the additional USD 1 million to the loan loss reserve, net loans to large corporations are USD 498 million, which is the amount that the bank now expects to collect, and gross loans are still USD 500 million.

Net assets other than loans are increased by the amount of the net profit before loan loss provisions. This increase is reflected in an increase in cash of USD 2 million. Looked at another way, retained earnings (which are part of equity) have increased by USD 1 million, reflecting the bank's net profit of USD 1 million, so liabilities and equity now equal USD 1,001 million. Assets must equal liabilities, so with net loans now at USD 498 million, cash increases to USD 13 million.[2]

2. The bank does not have to allocate its profits to cash. It could use that money to extend more loans or to buy more bonds, but in order to keep this example simple, we assume that the bank always allocates this money to cash and keeps it in cash.

Assets in million USD	Amount	Liabilities in million USD	Amount
Cash	13	Short-term deposits	300
Government bonds	100	Long-term deposits	250
		Subtotal deposits	*550*
Loans to local government	190		
Loans to SMEs	200	Short-term financing	200
Loans to large corporations	*500*	Long-term bonds	150
Loan loss reserve	*(2)*		
Net loans to large corporations	498		
Total loans (net)	*888*	*Subtotal other liabilities*	*350*
		Equity	101
Total	**1,001**	**Total**	**1,001**

FIGURE 2.12 Profits Reduced by Additional Provision

4. At the end of the next year, XYZ Corporation's financial position has deteriorated even further, and Bank A decides that it is unlikely to repay any of the USD 5 million loan. Bank A therefore decides to write off the entire loan. It already has USD 2 million in loan loss reserves, leaving USD 3 million to write off. During this year, the bank made profits before provisions of USD 2 million.

Since the bank has only USD 2 million in pre-provision profits but is making a loan loss provision of USD 3 million, it declares a net loss of USD 1 million.

Net loans to corporations are now USD 495 million, reflecting the full write-down of the USD 5 million loan. The bank has no loan loss reserves; they have all been used to write down the value of the XYZ Corporation loan. As a result, net loans are now the same as gross loans.

Cash on the balance sheet increases by USD 2 million; the bank has allocated USD 3 million from its income statement as loan loss provisions, but this has resulted in a net loss of USD 1 million. The net loss must be accounted for on the balance sheet. As a result, while net loans are reduced by USD 3 million, the net increase in assets other than loans is USD 2 million.

Assets in million USD	Amount		Liabilities in million USD	Amount
Cash		15	Short-term deposits	300
Government bonds		100	Long-term deposits	250
			Subtotal deposits	*550*
Loans to local government	190			
Loans to SMEs	200		Short-term financing	200
Loans to large corporations	*495*		Long-term bonds	150
Total loans (net)		*885*	*Subtotal other liabilities*	*350*
			Equity	100
Total		**1,000**	**Total**	**1,000**

FIGURE 2.13 Additional Loan Loss Provision Creates Net Loss

5. The following year, it turns out that XYZ's financial condition improves and it is able to repay USD 2 million to Bank A. During the year, the bank made pre-provision profits of USD 1 million (before taking account of the debt recovery from XYZ Corporation). As a result of the recovery of USD 2 million from XYZ Corporation, it declares net profits of USD 3 million. This is shown as an increase in the bank's cash of USD 3 million. Total assets therefore increase by a total of USD 3 million to USD 1,003 million. Loans to corporations remain the same at USD 495 million; the money received from XYZ Corporation does not affect the amount of loans.

    Because assets now total USD 1,003 million, liabilities and equity must also total USD 1,003 million, so the bank's equity increases by USD 3 million to USD 102 million. Assets must equal liabilities, and this is reflected in an increase in cash to USD 18 million.

Assets in million USD	Amount		Liabilities in million USD	Amount
Cash		18	Short-term deposits	300
Government bonds		100	Long-term deposits	250
			Subtotal deposits	*550*
Loans to local government	190			
Loans to SMEs	200		Short-term financing	200
Loans to large corporations	*495*		Long-term bonds	150
Total loans (net)		*885*	*Subtotal other liabilities*	*350*
			Equity	103
Total		**1,003**	**Total**	**1,003**

FIGURE 2.14 Writing Back Loan Losses Increases Cash

2.3 Asset and Liability Management

Banks face two additional key risks that have not yet been discussed: **interest rate risk** and **liquidity risk**.

- *Interest rate risk refers to the potential loss in value of an asset due to changes in interest rates.* For example, a bank pays one interest rate to its depositors and receives another from its debtors. If interest rates change, the profitability of the bank changes as well. Interest rate risk affects both the banking book and the trading book.
- *Liquidity risk refers to the potential inability of a bank to meet its payment obligations when they are due.* In particular, a bank must manage its ability to pay its depositors interest and to repay depositors seeking to withdraw any part of their money. Liquidity risk is also called **funding liquidity risk**.

The liquidity discussed in this section is different from another type of liquidity, the ability to trade in markets without significant price concessions, which will be discussed in Chapter 6.

The bank's asset and liability management (ALM) function manages both the interest rate risk in the bank's banking book and liquidity risk. In particular, the ALM function in a bank focuses on:

- Maintaining liquidity for the bank
- Analyzing the shape and structure of the bank's balance sheet
- Maintaining a stable net interest margin

2.3.1 Interest Rate Risk

Interest rate risk in the banking book refers to a possible monetary loss caused by adverse changes in interest rates affecting the underlying structure of the bank's business: its lending and deposit-taking activities. The dangers of not managing interest rate risk in the banking book were highlighted by the savings and loan crisis that affected the United States during 1980s and 1990s.

EXAMPLE

In the United States, savings and loan associations (S&Ls), also known as thrifts, are banks that are predominantly mortgage lenders. During the 1980s and early 1990s, many S&Ls

collapsed due largely to a mismanagement of interest rate risk that allowed a severe mismatch of assets and liabilities.

During the 1980s, S&Ls underwrote fixed-rate, 30-year mortgages at around 6% and financed these loans from short-term deposits at interest rates around 2%. The mortgages were relatively profitable until U.S. interest rates rose and the S&Ls had to pay 9% to 10% on their deposits, the same deposits that financed the funds that were loaned out for 30 years at only 6%. In the end, several hundred S&Ls collapsed.

Ultimately, the U.S. government financed the collapsed S&Ls. Some reports put the bailout figure around USD 150 billion. There are, however, estimates that reach up to USD 500 billion. (See Section 1.3.2 about the S&L crisis.)

In managing the bank's assets and liabilities, the ALM function has to consider and balance several factors simultaneously:

- *The bank's balance sheet is a dynamic portfolio of loans and deposits.* As new loans are extended, as existing loans mature, and as new deposits arrive, existing deposits may be withdrawn.
- *The interest rate on liabilities and assets.* Some will be fixed, but the interest rate on other liabilities and assets will change periodically according to market rates, resulting in fluctuations in the value of floating-rate liabilities and assets.
- *Timing differences between changes in market rates and in the interest rates on retail products such as bank loans to customers.*
- *The bank's current liquidity needs.* The current market interest rates for all maturities and competition among banks determine the interest rates offered on deposit products.
- *Commercial (e.g., corporate loans) and retail (e.g., home mortgage loans) products.* Both allow for the early termination of the loans, but the terms and conditions can be widely different among individual commercial or retail loans, as well as between commercial and retail loans in general.

To manage interest rate risk in the banking book, banks consider the impact of interest rate changes on both their assets and liabilities, and the particular features of their assets and liabilities, including, among other things, terms and timing. How well the bank manages its assets and liabilities, the revenues from its assets, and the costs of its liabilities has a direct impact on the net interest margin of the bank.

2.3.2   Liquidity Risk

Liquidity is defined by the Basel Committee as the ability of a bank to fund increases in assets and meet obligations as they come due, without incurring unacceptable losses. Liquidity risk has been given much greater attention by standard setters and regulators, and by banks themselves, since the global financial crisis of 2007–2009, when many banks faced severe liquidity difficulties. At that time banks were facing both asset liquidity risk (inability to liquidate large holdings of collateralized debt obligations) and funding liquidity risk (inability to obtain funds from the interbank, or indeed any other, market).

From both a bank's and its regulator's point of view, the structure of the bank's assets and its related liquidity needs may highlight potential weaknesses over time. Liquidity corresponds to the bank's ability to make payments to its customers punctually. Ultimately, its ability, or inability, to make these payments in a timely manner will directly affect the banking institution's **solvency**, or its ability to pay its debts with available cash.

Solvency is different from a bank's ability to make a profit. A bank can be solvent (have more assets than liabilities) and not make a profit if its expenses are greater than its revenues. A solvent bank may be able to generate cash to make payments by selling off assets, but if these transactions are at a loss, then the sale of its assets could erode the bank's solvency, leading to insolvency. A bank can be profitable without being solvent if its revenues are greater than its expenses but its assets are worth less than its liabilities.

Banks actively manage their liquidity risks to ensure that they have sufficient funding to pay their obligations when they become due. Liquidity obligations run to both a bank's depositors and its loan customers. Depositors demand liquidity; they expect to be able to withdraw their deposits at any time without delay. Since fractional reserve banking means that banks can keep only a fraction of their deposits available for immediate withdrawal, improperly managing the bank's liquidity risk could lead to serious consequences (see Section 3.1 on liquidity and bank runs). Customers who borrow money from the bank require that the bank provide them with access to the funds they have borrowed without delay when the funds are needed. If a highly leveraged bank needs to secure liquidity quickly to fulfill its obligations, but can do so only by selling its assets hastily and at low prices, then it can easily become insolvent.

As with interest rate risk, banks model how their liquidity requirements may change over time in a wide array of circumstances. Banks have several tools at their disposal to assess their liquidity. Among these tools, scenario analysis and stress testing play a chief role in enabling a bank to examine its liquidity in a variety of adverse situations. **Scenario analysis**, or what-if analysis, analyzes the potential outcome of various scenarios by setting up several possible situations and analyzing the potential outcomes of each situation. Scenario analysis often includes multiple steps and complex programming. **Stress testing** analyzes the potential outcome of a specific change to a risk model parameter (e.g., asset correlations and volatility) or to the business and operating environment that is fundamental, material, and adverse.

EXAMPLE

Bank A considers a scenario in which it loses its main depositor, a large car manufacturer. When the ALM department conducts a scenario analysis, it models how the bank would meet its liquidity needs without the car manufacturer's funds. The ALM department also conducts a stress test whereby it analyzes the potential impacts on its liquidity should a large number of its loans default and a substantial number of smaller depositors withdraw their deposits at once, while the bank cannot secure funding elsewhere. This type of analysis allows the bank, and its supervisory agency, to gain a clearer picture of the risks the bank is facing and to proactively determine how to deal with those risks.

A particular concern of liquidity monitoring relates to the potential for a run on a bank. Banks need to have sufficient and readily available funds to meet regular withdrawals of deposits and to fulfill their loan obligations (see Chapter 1). If a bank is rumored to be in financial difficulty, depositors may rush to withdraw their funds. Unanticipated demand could reduce the bank's cash on hand, very likely causing the bank to become illiquid and, ultimately, insolvent.

EXAMPLE

In September 2007, Northern Rock, a British bank, found itself in a **liquidity crisis**. In prior years, mortgage lending in the United States to subprime borrowers (that is, less qualified borrowers who may make either little or no down payment on their home loans) had grown considerably. As the U.S. housing market slowed in early 2007, the rate of subprime mortgage defaults increased sharply, leading to considerable losses to the banks and financial institutions that owned these loans. Because of the U.S. subprime crisis, financial institutions globally became nervous about lending to mortgage banks.

As a large mortgage lender, in mid-2007 Northern Rock suddenly found it very difficult to obtain the short-term loans from other banks or other funding sources it needed to repay its depositors. After the news was released publicly in mid-September 2007 that the bank had a liquidity problem and needed immediate assistance from the Bank of England, depositors rushed to withdraw their funds, further exacerbating its predicament. At the time, the UK government's deposit protection scheme covered only up to GBP 31,700 (100% of the first GBP 2,000 in deposits and 90% of the next GBP 33,000 in deposits), possibly contributing to depositor anxiety. Subsequent to these events, in October 2008, UK deposit insurance was temporarily increased to GBP 50,000. By January 2008, Northern Rock had borrowed in excess of GBP 25 billion from the Bank of England. In February 2008, it was announced that the British government would nationalize the bank, taking it over to protect the depositors and assure that it would be able to fulfill its obligations.

Banks, including central banks, often provide support to each other to meet short-term liquidity needs through **repurchase agreements**. A repurchase agreement (also known as a repo) allows one party to sell an asset for cash with the understanding, supported by a legal repurchase agreement, that it will be repurchased at a later date at an agreed-on price (usually higher than the sales price).

EXAMPLE

Atlas Bank needs USD 10 million for five days. It enters into a repurchase agreement with Capital Bank, whereby it sells to Capital Bank a USD 10 million bond for USD 10 million and agrees to repurchase it for USD 10,005,000. At the end of the five days, Atlas Bank pays Capital Bank USD 10,005,000 and receives the bond back. Atlas Bank has increased its liquidity for five days at a cost of USD 1,000 for each day. Figure 2.15 shows the flow of money between the two banks involved in this repurchase agreement transaction.

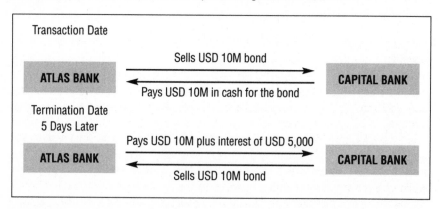

FIGURE 2.15 Repurchase Agreement

In a repo transaction, the actual ownership of the **security** passes to the buyer from the seller. The repo markets are a major source of funding for the liquidity needs of banks around the globe.

In addition to the liquidity needs described above, bank supervisors often require banks to maintain a minimum holding of either cash or assets that can be readily turned into cash in case the bank encounters an unexpected cash demand. Highly liquid assets generally include the bank's deposits held at the central bank and domestic government debt held by the bank.

Finally, since the collapse of Herstatt Bank (see Section 3.3.1 for further details), bank supervisors have also been concerned with banks' ability to meet their obligations to each other. A particular concern for regulators are the ripple effects of a bank owing money to other banks as a result of its position in a payments system (e.g., a check clearing system or a government bond payment and delivery system). If a bank's customers who use these payment systems default, the bank may not have sufficient cash to be able to pay its banking counterparties on behalf of their customers (the other banks). To counter this risk, banks often rely on collateral, usually high-quality government bonds and other securities.

Collateral is an asset(s) pledged by a borrower to secure a loan or other credit and to act as a guarantee to the lender in the event of a default. If the borrower is unable or unwilling to repay the debt, the lender has the option to accept the collateral as full or partial payment of the loan's principal, accrued interest, fees, and expenses. (The role of collateral will be explained further in Section 4.4.5.)

EXAMPLE

Bank Little, a small bank, and Bank Large, a large international bank, engage in various transactions with each other. In most of these transactions, Bank Little buys securities, mostly government bonds, from Bank Large. The terms of payment for these transactions are three days. For example, for a transaction entered on Monday, payment is expected on Thursday. During this three-day period, Bank Large effectively extends credit to Bank Little and assumes the risk that Bank Little may not be able to pay for the transaction at the end of the three days.

Since Bank Little is smaller than Bank Large, there is a concern that Bank Little may be exposed to significant liquidity risks and may not be able to pay for its government bond transactions as contracted. To reduce the risk of this happening and to further support the transactions between the two banks, Bank Little posts collateral with Bank Large equal to a certain percentage of the value of the transaction. Bank Large will usually specify the amount and type of collateral it will accept from Bank Little. If Bank Little is unable to pay for its transactions with Bank Large, the collateral Bank Little posted to Bank Large can be used by Bank Large to pay for the purchase of the government bonds. This reduces the risk to Bank Large. Figure 2.16 shows this.

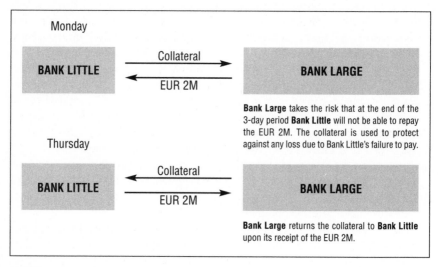

FIGURE 2.16 The Use of Collateral

2.3.3   Liquidity Standards in Basel III

Typically, bank failures are due to the combination of substantial credit losses and limited or disappearing liquidity to adequately fund assets during times of stress. Consequently, regulators have considered access to adequate funding and liquidity levels crucial for the long-term stability of each bank. Prior to the Basel III Accord, international banking regulations did not have global liquidity standards, or consistent regulatory monitoring in cross-border supervisory oversight. (The Basel III Accord will be explained further in Section 3.3.9.)

Under the new regulatory framework, the new short-term **liquidity coverage ratio,** to be implemented starting in 2015, focuses on the ability to maintain adequate liquidity coverage for extreme stress conditions of up to 30 days. This will be complemented by a longer-term structural **net stable funding ratio,** to be implemented by 2018, that relates the long-term and stable sources of funding to the liquidity characteristics of on- and off-balance-sheet items.

2.4   Corporate Governance

A bank is required to consider the often conflicting requirements of its individual customers, borrowers, depositors, investors, employees, shareholders, regulators, and the public, collectively called stakeholders. All stakeholders have an interest in the future success of the bank. For instance, if the bank is successful, customers benefit from continued business relationships, depositors have continued access to their money, and employees have jobs and receive salaries. Banks attempt to balance the conflicting interests of all its stakeholders, yet recognize that ultimately all decisions should increase the value of the bank and wealth of the owners of the bank, the **shareholders**.

Shareholders elect the board of directors that supervises management that controls the day-to-day operations of the bank. **Corporate governance**, the set of relationships between the board of directors, shareholders, and other stakeholders of a company, is a framework banks use to enhance their success. Corporate governance creates a relationship structure that helps management to:

- Set corporate and strategic business objectives and run daily operations
- Consider the interests of all its stakeholder groups, separately as well as jointly
- Manage the bank in a safe and sound manner
- Comply with relevant laws and regulations
- Protect the interests of its depositors

2.4.1   Corporate Governance Structures

The structure of a bank's corporate governance depends on its host country's legal system, business customs, and the historical development of the bank. Although there is no single structure that can be prescribed as ideal, there are generally accepted governance concepts and ideas that have been shown to support an adequately functioning governance system. Good corporate governance seeks to establish rules that help corporations, such as banks, create internal processes that benefit both the bank and its stakeholders.

Several national and international organizations, agencies, corporations, and institutions have attempted to define what creates good corporate governance. Some of the elements identified are described in this section.

The board of directors has the ultimate responsibility for the management and performance of a company and is responsible for its governance. The board of directors should do the following:

- Set the overall strategic direction of the bank, including the establishment of the bank's risk tolerance levels
- Advise on recruitment and human resources (HR); oversee, guide, and review the performance of senior management; and set senior management compensation
- Monitor the performance of the bank, and review regular financial and risk reports
- Be qualified, both personally and professionally, to act as directors with integrity and in the interest of shareholders
- Meet regularly with senior management and internal auditors to establish and approve policies
- Review reporting lines, authority, and responsibilities of the bank's senior management

In particular, outside directors should be independent of internal and external influences and provide sound advice without participating in the daily management of the bank.

Specialized committees support the overall work of the board and allow board members to oversee specific areas. These committees will cover areas such as risk management, audit, compensation, and board nominations. Particularly in smaller banks, a board-level committee can be tasked to review major loan decisions.

When the board of directors establishes the bank's strategy and risk tolerance levels, it effectively decides what types of assets the bank should primarily underwrite. Essentially, any bank can choose between pursuing a low-risk strategy and a high-risk strategy.

- A low-risk strategy entails underwriting high-quality bonds (in particular, government bonds) and loans with stringent underwriting standards (Chapter 4), including collateral demands. These assets are considered conservative, with little risk of default. Chapter 6 will discuss bonds.
- A high-risk strategy entails underwriting lower-quality bonds (in particular, lower-rated corporate bonds) and loans with less stringent underwriting standards. All these assets are considered risky, having a greater risk of default.

Whether a bank pursues a low-risk strategy or a high-risk strategy, the board of directors has to determine how prudently, or conservatively, the bank should be managed. A prudent bank closely monitors the loans it underwrites, has more than adequate liquidity, and generally has stringent internal controls on all aspects of its operations. From a regulatory perspective, a prudently managed bank that pursues a low-risk strategy is optimal. A bank that is not prudently managed and pursues a high-risk strategy usually causes considerable concern to regulators.

A bank's organizational structure is determined by the board and directed by the CEO. The board has oversight responsibilities, with day-to-day decision-making lying in the hands of the CEO and senior management. At the head of the organization is the board of directors. Immediately below the board of directors is the company's CEO or president, who oversees the senior management. The senior managers, in turn, oversee the activities of business units, junior managers, and employees. This hierarchical structure ensures that corporate activities are coordinated across the various businesses. An example of this structure is depicted in Figure 2.17.

FIGURE 2.17 Typical Organizational Structure with Board of Directors

In many countries, the corporate governance structure includes a supervisory board. As the name suggests, this board supervises the state of play, course of business, and managing board, led by the interests of both the company and its stakeholders. The supervisory board also gives support and advice to the managing board. An example of this structure is depicted in Figure 2.18.

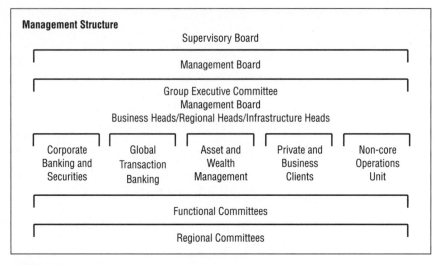

FIGURE 2.18 Typical Organizational Structure with Supervisory Board

2.4.2   Corporate Governance Techniques

The structure of corporate governance in banks varies depending on local customs, legal restraints, and the historical development of each bank. Figure 2.19 lists techniques typically adopted by a bank to implement good corporate governance.

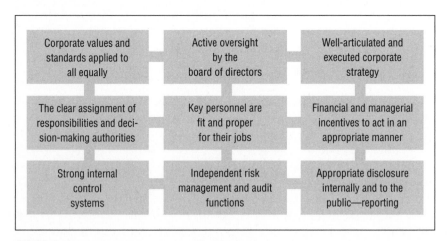

FIGURE 2.19 Corporate Governance Techniques

Although there is no single structure or set of techniques that can be prescribed as ideal, there are important governance issues that must be addressed in order to ensure adequate checks and balances are built in. These are:

- Oversight by the board of commissioners, board of directors, or supervisory board.
- Oversight by individuals not involved in the day-to-day running of the various business areas.
- Direct line supervision of different business areas.
- Independent risk management and audit functions.
- Key personnel who are fit and proper for their jobs.
- Regular reporting.

2.4.3 Senior Management and Corporate Strategies

Senior management has comprehensive oversight of managers (managers are held directly responsible for the development of a specific line of business or operational function). An important task for senior managers is to communicate the responsibilities and ensure the performance of each staff member. Senior management also has a key role in the setting and implementation of a bank's strategic objectives. A bank that does not have strategic objectives will find it difficult to manage its activities, as there will be a lack of focus in the use of its resources.

2.4.4 Values and Culture

It is important for a bank to have a strong corporate culture. By establishing a corporate culture, a bank will be able to conduct its business according to clearly defined values. Equally important is the communication of such policies to all areas of the bank.

The company's set of values should be applied to all areas of the bank, including the board of directors. They should encourage the reporting of problems in a timely fashion and prohibit corruption and bribery both internally and externally. These values should be supported by policies to prevent situations that can challenge the operation of good corporate governance. An example would be a clear policy setting out a procedure for employees to follow if their work creates a conflict of interest with their outside interests. A clear policy reinforces a bank's values in dealing with such situations.

2.4.5   Financial Incentives

It is important that the board of directors develops a compensation policy that reflects the bank's culture, objectives, strategy, and control environment. The board should set the compensation for senior management and other key personnel. Any such compensation scheme should ensure that it does not create an imbalance between risks and rewards, as it is important to align pay and bonus structures with long-term risk management.

Compensation schemes should encourage individuals to consider long-term issues over short-term revenue generation, while attracting and retaining talent. The compensation scheme should be designed to motivate senior management to act in the best interests of the bank. It should discourage short-term performance measures that may leave the bank exposed to long-term risks. Salary scales should be set so that personnel are not overly dependent on short-term performance in relation to their total remuneration package.

2.4.6   Internal and External Auditors

Internal and external auditors validate the information provided by senior management to the board of directors, regulators, and the public. Both internal and external auditors play a central role in corporate governance. The board of directors supports and protects the auditors' interaction in the following ways:

- The board supports auditor independence by engaging auditors to prepare an unbiased assessment of the company's financial position based on accepted standards and to report the findings directly to the board.
- Boards engage external auditors to judge the effectiveness of the company's internal controls.
- Boards should review, in a timely and effective manner, the auditors' findings and recommendations and require prompt correction by senior management of problems identified by auditors.

2.4.7   Transparency

Transparency helps stakeholders, investors, the public, and regulators to evaluate the performance of the bank and how effectively senior management and the board fulfill their responsibilities. The degree of transparency relates to the degree of **disclosure**. At a minimum, public disclosure should include:

- The size and qualifications of the board of directors and its subcommittees.
- The structure, qualifications, and responsibilities of the company's senior management.
- Information about the bank's basic organizational structure, including its legal structure.
- Information regarding senior employee incentive structure and compensation policy (typically restricted to a few senior and well-compensated employees).
- The nature and extent of transactions with affiliates and related parties.

CHAPTER 3

Banking Regulation

C hapter 3 introduces bank regulation and outlines the impact regulations have on bank operations. This chapter discusses why banks need to be regulated, what regulatory processes are in effect, how international cooperation helps shape bank regulation, and what role deposit insurance plays in banking stability. Chapters 1, 2, and 3 together provide a comprehensive foundation for the remaining chapters.

Chapter Outline
 3.1 The Evolution of Risk Regulation in Banking
 3.2 Foundations of Bank Regulation
 3.3 International Regulation of Bank Risks
 3.4 Deposit Insurance

Key Learning Points
 ■ When a bank lacks the funds to repay its depositors on demand, the bank is in a liquidity crisis. The mere rumor of a liquidity crisis could lead to a bank run—when a large number of depositors demand a return of their deposits from one bank simultaneously. If a bank run spreads to other banks, there is a contagion that has the potential to spread further panic and runs on other banks.

- Bank regulation seeks to ensure that banks are operated prudently, that **nonsystemic risk** is reduced, and that there are systemwide support mechanisms to assist banks and provide stability before they reach a crisis. Bank regulation achieves these objectives using two main tools: **licensing**, the granting of the right to operate a bank; and supervision, regulatory and recurring monitoring of the bank's operations and activities.
- The Basel Accords are the international regulatory frameworks that govern the activities of banks. The three Basel Accords acknowledge that the risk of the bank's assets and operations is related to, and can be minimized by, a minimum regulatory capital standard. In the **Basel II Accord**, this minimum regulatory capital covers credit, market, and operational risks. The third Basel Accord also recognizes the importance of liquidity risk.
- Deposit insurance provides protection for depositors in case a bank suffers a liquidity crisis, and is intended to reduce both bank runs and panics by reducing the incentives for depositors to withdraw funds from a bank.

BANKING REGULATION

3.1   The Evolution of Risk Regulation in Banking

The banking industry is different from other industries in that the failure of a bank, either partial or total, will have an impact on the entire economy; hence bank failure carries systemic risk. This chapter broadens the discussion. It first reviews the reasons for banking regulation and then explains the progression of the Basel Accords.

Successive Basel Accords provide regulators, supervisors, and banks with a structured approach to identify risks and link capital to these identified risks. Initially, the Basel Accords focused on assessing the **credit risk capital** requirements for internationally active banks, an approach that subsequently was deemed inadequate by both the banks and regulators. The approach of Basel I was to impose very generic and schematic **regulatory capital requirements** for credit risk; these methodological computations were very simplistic and exhibited limited risk sensitivity. Given the reactive nature of regulation, the first Basel Accord has been replaced by a series of more complex agreements.

The Basel II Accord, which provides the regulatory framework for most banking and financial regulators, expanded on Basel I by incorporating specific methodologies to measure market risk and operational risk and to directly link capital requirements to these risks. In addition to credit, market, and operational risk, the Basel II Accord also outlined other general principles to link capital to some hard-to-measure risks. The Basel III Accord that emerged after the global financial crisis of 2007–2009 incorporates lessons from that crisis. Since the crisis was partially caused by **illiquidity** in the markets and inadequate capital levels to withstand substantial losses in the market, the new internationally agreed framework imposes not only quantitative and qualitative measurements, but also quantitative liquidity requirements.

3.1.1 Why Banks Are Special and Need to Be Regulated

Banks play a crucial role in the economy by offering payment services and providing credit. Because any disruption to the banking system could have widespread effects on businesses and people, all governments regulate banking. It was not always so, however. In fact, up until the early 20th century, there were still parts of the world where banking was unregulated. Anyone able and willing to open a bank could do so without any qualifications, hindrance, or permission. However, such an uninhibited banking environment was unstable—bank failures were common—so, over time, governments began to regulate banks actively.

3.1.2 Liquidity Crises and Bank Runs

As noted in Chapter 1, when a bank makes a large number of loans that borrowers cannot repay, the bank's liabilities (deposits and borrowings) could exceed the bank's assets, rendering the bank insolvent. As it relates to a bank's (or a company's) balance sheet, insolvency means that its liabilities exceed its assets—it has zero or negative equity. While this implies an inability to repay creditor claims when they become due, it does not mean that an insolvent bank may be unable to raise cash to meet depositor withdrawal needs. However, because the fractional reserve banking system allows banks to retain only a fraction of their deposits on hand as cash, insolvency problems can be magnified. This problem can be particularly acute if the bank experiences severe defaults.

Without adequate liquidity, a bank may have insufficient cash readily available to pay its depositors' claims when they come due. While a bank may have assets that could be sold or leveraged to raise cash, it may not always be possible to do so in a timely fashion. This inability to make payments when they are due is termed illiquidity, and can lead to a liquidity crisis. A liquidity crisis, in turn, can lead to a bank run, as described in the following example.

EXAMPLE

An increasing number of Bank A's borrowers have failed to repay their loans at all or in a timely manner. This has placed a severe strain on the bank's liquidity position. For the last two months, Bank A has depleted its cash reserves to make payments to its depositors and bondholders because the cash received from its borrowers has fallen short of what is required to pay out in new loans and deposit withdrawals. Suddenly, Bank A has found itself in the position that its available cash reserves are insufficient to pay its creditors' interest payments when due. Moreover, Bank A has found that the credit markets it has occasionally tapped for funds are no longer willing to loan it money. Since the bank does not have the funds available to make its payments and cannot borrow the funds, the bank finds itself in a liquidity crisis. As a result, its depositors and creditors are at risk of not receiving their funds when due.

The only option Bank A has to raise cash and to pay its depositors is to sell off its assets—loans and bonds—to other banks. However, because of its urgency, poor market conditions or both, such a sale would likely be at prices below the value at which the loans were recorded. Selling the loans to another bank at a loss would exacerbate the bank's worsening financial position—further eroding its equity position (see Section 2.1.5)—and increase the likelihood of balance sheet insolvency. This puts Bank A in a no-win situation because if information about its position becomes public it would add to concerns about the bank's stability, potentially causing even more depositors to attempt to withdraw their funds. The unexpected and excessive demand for withdrawals would position Bank A for possible failure since it has no viable, timely alternatives other than to appeal to its customers for patience while it attempts to arrange for some immediate cash or capital infusion from other institutions or investors, unfortunately making the problem public, something it did not want to do in the first place, thereby worsening an already tenuous situation. Alternatively, the bank could look to merge its business with a another organization, or seek a capital infusion from a private third party source. Unfortunately, all these alternatives take time, which works to Bank A's disadvantage.

If no solution is found and the bank fails to raise sufficient funds to continue its operations, the bank may collapse, potentially wiping out the depositors' funds in the bank. Such a collapse could have widespread ramifications for other banks, the availability of credit, other businesses, and the economy, termed a "contagion" effect (Section 3.1.3).

When a solvency or liquidity crisis is limited to one bank, then that crisis is generally considered to represent **nonsystemic risk.** In a nonsystemic crisis, one bank's unique circumstances precipitate the crisis, in that its conditions and circumstances do not apply to other banks, and are not expected to have widespread effect. The issues resulting from the crisis will generally be limited to that bank's customers or its local economy.

However, systemic crises can also result from a run on the deposits of one bank, requiring extraordinary government efforts to keep it what was a more localized crisis from spreading beyond the one bank. Probably one of the most famous and early examples of this happening on more modern times is the bailout of Continental Illinois National Bank.

EXAMPLE

In May 1984, Continental Illinois National Bank in the United States suffered a run on its deposits, which, in turn, prompted the largest bank bailout in U.S. history up to that time. The run was started by rumors that the bank was heading for bankruptcy over poor credit risks, particularly from loans assumed from Penn Square Bank, which had collapsed in 1982. Nonperforming loans at Continental had risen to USD 3.3 billion by April 1984.

Continental Illinois was particularly vulnerable because it relied heavily on short-term financing. Short-term financing is very sensitive to both market interest rates and the short-term investors' perception of the bank's financial safety. It is an elusive financing source. As long as the investors were satisfied that the bank would repay these short-term loans, they were willing to lend to Continental Illinois. Suddenly the bank found that investors did not renew their short-term loans at maturity and that overseas depositors, concerned about the rumors, had begun to shift their deposits away from Continental. Following failed attempts by the bank to arrange a rescue package with a consortium of 16 other banks, Continental's domestic depositors also began to withdraw their funds.

The global nature of the Continental Illinois funding base and the bank's size (at the time it was the seventh largest bank in the United States) made it imperative for U.S. regulators to step in to stop the run and prevent it from spreading to other U.S. banks. The cost of this rescue: U.S. regulatory agencies, with a consortium of banks, assumed the liability and risks for USD 3.5 billion in Continental Illinois debt. In the case of Continental Illinois, therefore, regulators acted to prevent a nonsystemic crisis from spreading to other banks and becoming a systemic crisis.

3.1.3   Bank Panics

Even the rumor of a liquidity problem at one bank can spread quickly and cause depositors at other banks to rush to withdraw their funds. Thus, a problem that exists at one bank can spread to multiple banks. If unchecked, this process can grow into a **bank panic**, when depositors from multiple banks simultaneously seek to withdraw their deposits.

This type of situation can put an entire banking system at risk. Effectively, a multiple and concurrent run on banks, or a bank panic, is an example of a systemic risk. Systemic risk is the risk of the collapse of the entire banking system or financial market. A systemic crisis would have very wide-ranging effects. It is very probable that the effects of a severe bank panic and the accompanying instability in a regional financial system would cross country borders and adversely affect the banking systems of other countries.

Also, the failure of a major globally active bank, the negative effects of a material decrease in asset prices (such as home values), or a bank panic in one country can create shocks that can spill over into other countries. Even upon hearing about a crisis, there is potential that depositors in other countries could become nervous about their deposits. The term for this transference of concern or **spillover effect** between countries (or even markets) is **contagion**. Extreme financial events or economic stress, whether a contagion or a bank panic, raises systemic risks for the banking system. Systemic risks can impart significant negative effects across many industries and countries and are likely to have widespread negative consequences for bank employees, customers, shareholders, and, ultimately, the economy. For small and developing countries, foreign deposits are often a critical source of capital, and their withdrawal—as a response to contagion or rumors of contagion—can have devastating effects on these economies.

EXAMPLE

The near collapse of the Icelandic banking system is a recent example of a bank run leading to a potential bank panic. The three major Icelandic banks—Kaupthing, Glitnir, and Landsbanki—grew very aggressively after the deregulation of the Icelandic financial sector in 2001. As Iceland is a small and geographically isolated country with roughly 320,000 inhabitants, the bank's desire for aggressive growth could not be supported by the domestic market. Consequently, these banks rushed to establish branch networks around Europe. As the banks established operations outside of Iceland, they became heavily reliant on the interbank market, where banks borrowed funds from other banks for short periods of time to fund their daily banking activities rather than rely on customer deposits as their primary funding source. At the end of July 2008, it was estimated that these three banks had foreign debt in excess of EUR 42 billion compared to Iceland's gross domestic product (GDP) of EUR 8.5 billion.

In early September 2008, after the collapse of Lehman Brothers, a U.S. investment bank, the interbank market for short-term loans between banks froze. This change in the funding markets adversely affected the Icelandic banks' ability to secure the necessary funding to keep their widespread international banking networks adequately funded, thereby experiencing increased liquidity and funding concerns.

Then on September 29, 2008, the Icelandic authorities announced that the smallest of the three largest banks, Glitnir, would be partially nationalized. Glitnir was about to face repayment of EUR 600 million in short-term debt, funds that Glitnir did not have and was unable to raise.

The decision to partially nationalize Glitnir had effects on both Kaupthing and Landsbanki. Nervous depositors, both in Iceland and in other European countries where the Icelandic banks had a presence, started withdrawing funds. The coverage in the media was also particularly negative. The fact that the Icelandic banks owed more than the Icelandic gross domestic product was widely emphasized, particularly in light of potentially substantial bailout costs. In the ensuing days, as the word spread about the banks' problems, the Icelandic economy was shaken, the value of its currency tumbled, and interest rates increased. This had a ripple effect on all the foreign operating subsidiaries of the Icelandic banks, causing them to experience significant and unprecedented withdrawal requests. The fear arose that the widespread collapse of Icelandic banking so soon after the collapse of Lehman Brothers could lead to a global financial meltdown. Moreover, due to the size of a potential government bailout of the Icelandic banks, rumors circulated that the country itself would face bankruptcy.

Early on October 7, only about a week after Glitnir was nationalized, Landsbanki was nationalized to protect its depositors. The same day, Icesave, an online bank operated by Landsbanki in both the United Kingdom and the Netherlands, suspended withdrawals. On October 9, the day after British and other European banking regulators closed down the local branches of some Icelandic banks, the Icelandic government started to shut down and nationalize Iceland's major banks. After the shutdown, the Icelandic banks continued their operations but under government ownership. The bailout costs were substantial—the equity alone of the newly nationalized banks equaled approximately 30% of Iceland's gross domestic product. The Icelandic government sought and received emergency funding from other governments. The aid package is estimated to have been around EUR 9 billion from the International Monetary Fund, European Union, Nordic countries, and elsewhere.

Here, we introduced four concepts that are key drivers for banking risks and regulation. A bank run on a single, non-systemically important bank is a nonsystemic risk. If an individual run is neither avoided nor managed properly, its effects could become systemic and lead to a panic among other banks. Bank panics, as the Icelandic example shows, can lead to contagion. The relationship between these concepts is illustrated in Figure 3.1.

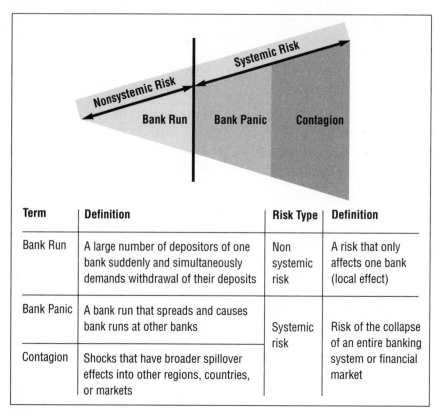

FIGURE 3.1 From Bank Run through Bank Panic and Contagion

3.2   Foundations of Bank Regulation

Avoiding a run on a bank is a chief concern not only of a bank's stakeholders, including management, shareholders, customers, and employees, but also of bank regulators and various agencies and authorities in charge of managing the economy. Effective bank regulation reduces systemic risk by addressing individual underlying risks that could rise to the level, either along or in concert with other risks, of systemic-related issues. The objective of regulation is to identify where oversight is needed and to then implement the appropriate supervision of individual banks to reduce the chance that runs on individual banks will happen, or if they do to prevent them from escalating to systemwide bank panics, contagion, and economic crises.

3.2.1 Regulatory Objectives

To avoid the devastating economic effects of bank failures and to ensure a stable banking industry in well-functioning financial markets, banking and financial regulators actively aim to meet the following objectives:

- *Ensure that banks are operated prudently.* Regulators set rules that give banks incentives to follow strict operational standards and to avoid risky loans. Regulators also impose capital requirements on banks—requirements that take into account the risk inherent in banks' activities.
- *Reduce systemic risk.* Regulators and bank supervisors, through examinations, inspections, and regulatory audits, monitor banks on an individual basis. In these examinations, the bank supervisors focus on identifying nonsystemic sources of risks that can increase the possibility of a bank run. Usually banks with low equity and regulatory capital levels, risky loans, internal managerial problems, weak earnings, and limited funding sources receive additional regulatory monitoring.
- *Implement system-wide support mechanisms.* These mechanisms reduce the impact of a possible bank run by offering deposit insurance that insures each depositor's money (see Section 3.4 for a detailed discussion on deposit insurance). Other approaches include reserve requirements and access to various liquidity support systems in the banking system. Ultimately, the country's central bank or monetary authority can act as the **lender of last resort** and may step in to offer temporary emergency liquidity support to weak but otherwise viable banks (see Section 3.2.3 for a detailed discussion on the lender of last resort).

3.2.2 The Regulatory Process

Bank regulation is a complex process and generally consists of licensing and supervision. The first component, licensing, sets certain requirements on those who want to start a new bank. The second component, supervision, provides for the monitoring of banks to ensure that they are in compliance with regulations. In other words, regulation is the drafting of suitable rules and practices, and supervision is the enforcement of regulation.

Licensing
Licensing provides license holders the right to operate a bank. The licensing process is specific to the regulatory landscape of the country and/or state where the bank is located and operates. Licensing involves an evaluation of an entity's intent and ability to observe the regulatory guidelines that will

govern the bank's operations, financial soundness, and managerial actions. The process is ordinarily somewhat cumbersome and expensive, which, although not intentional, tends to weed out entities that might not be as dedicated to making the longer-term commitment required to obtain the license and operate a bank. When regulators are satisfied that the owners and managers of a newly established bank have fulfilled all their requirements, the regulators will grant the bank a license to operate.

Regulatory Supervision

The second part of regulation is an extension of the license-granting process and consists of the supervision of the bank's activities by a government regulator. **Regulatory supervision** ensures that the operations and functioning of the bank comply with the regulatory guidelines that banks are obliged to follow when they receive their license. Supervision also monitors and attempts to resolve deviations from regulatory standards.

Regulatory supervision varies, depending on the type of institution, and is at the discretion of regulatory authorities. Bank supervisors subject riskier banks to more invasive supervision. Some regulatory agencies or regulatory supervisors require a physical inspection of the records, operations, and processes of regulated banks, while other regulators simply evaluate reports submitted by the banks. Complying with regulatory requirements is often resource consuming and expensive to banks, but it is, quite simply, a cost of doing business.

Examples of banking regulators and supervisors include the Federal Reserve System in the United States, the Prudential Regulatory Authority (PRA) in the United Kingdom, the Single Supervisory Mechanism of the European Union as noted below, and BaFin or Bundesanstalt für Finanzdienstleistungsaufsicht in Germany, among others. Since 2014, many European banks have been supervised through the European Union's Single Supervisory Mechanism (SSM), which oversees about 6,000 banks in the European Community. States in the Eurozone are obliged to participate in the SSM. Member states of the European Union outside of the Eurozone can voluntarily participate through a "close cooperation agreement" with the European Central Bank (ECB) if they so choose. The ECB has no jurisdiction over non-Eurozone states, so it can enforce the SSM only on Eurozone members.

3.2.3   Stabilization: The Lender of Last Resort

Liquidity and solvency are as relevant today as they were in the 19th century when the current banking system in industrialized countries took form. Early regulators sought solutions to solvency crises at individual banks before these crises transformed into widespread bank panics, and determined that the regulators had to play a role as the lender of last resort. The central bank, as the lender of last resort, helps maintain the stability of the financial system by providing emergency funds to banks undergoing solvency or liquidity problems.

EXAMPLE

At the time the Icelandic banking sector collapsed in October 2008, the Icelandic banks had widespread branch networks in the United Kingdom, the Netherlands, Luxembourg, Switzerland, and Scandinavia. The collapse of the three major Icelandic banks also severely affected their European branch banks. For instance, Kaupthing, the largest Icelandic bank, had operations in Sweden—Kaupthing Bank Sverige AB. The day before the Icelandic authorities closed down Kaupthing, the Swedish central bank—as the lender of last resort—extended emergency funding to the Swedish subsidiary of Kaupthing. According to the Swedish authorities, although the Swedish subsidiary of Kaupthing was still solvent, the funding—EUR 520 million—was extended simply to allow an orderly shutdown of that bank.

Governments hope to ensure the efficiency and resiliency of the financial system. **Financial stability** is the extent to which financial institutions and markets are able to mobilize savings to provide liquidity. In the first example of the Icelandic banking crisis in Section 3.1.3, the actions of the Icelandic government (providing capital support through nationalization of Glitnir in September 2008) were designed to maintain financial stability in both Iceland and countries where its banks operated. This support, while substantial, was limited given the considerable disparity between the asset size of the Icelandic banks and the Icelandic economy. Ultimately, the bailout of the Icelandic banks depended on the coordinated action of regulators from different countries as illustrated by the previous example.

Monetary stability is the extent to which the value of money is maintained (i.e., low and stable inflation). One of the many roles that central banks play is to maintain stable prices by reducing inflation to an acceptable range, usually considered to be in the range of 2% to 3% per year. Central banks achieve this by setting interest rates and controlling the amount of credit and money available in the economy. Discussion of the specific mechanisms by which central banks achieve monetary stability is beyond the coverage of the material here. Monetary stability should not be confused with financial stability; although they can often exist together, they are not necessarily fellow travelers. For instance, very high inflation in a country—a sign of monetary instability—tends to disrupt the financial stability of that country. Starting in 2007 (and continuing in 2009), developed countries suffered from a financial crisis, which caused shorter, yet very significant, periods of financial instability. Well-functioning markets suddenly froze and established banks failed. Notwithstanding this unprecedented financial instability, monetary stability—a stable inflation rate—was maintained in these countries, and in several of them, inflation rates actually declined.

3.3   International Regulation of Bank Risks

For a long time, banking regulation was national. That is, governments and their regulatory agencies developed rules and banking supervisory guidelines specific to the country's needs. Regulatory rules differed significantly between countries. Not until 1988, when the Basel I Accord was released, did international banking regulations take shape. The Basel Accords outline regulatory guidelines for international banks' operations and risk management.

3.3.1   Bank for International Settlements

The **Bank for International Settlements** (BIS), established in Basel, Switzerland, in 1930, is the principal center of international central bank cooperation. The BIS acts as:

- A forum to promote discussion and policy analysis among central banks and within the international financial community
- A center for economic and monetary research
- A prime counterparty for central banks in their financial transactions
- An agent or trustee in connection with international financial operations[1]

After the end of the Second World War, the BIS focused on cooperation among banks, first by implementing and defending the international exchange rate system and then by managing it. The BIS has always performed traditional banking functions—gold and foreign exchange transactions—for the central bank community, as well as trustee and agency functions. The BIS has also provided or arranged emergency financing to support the international monetary system when needed.

---

1. The BIS Profile, July 2008.

BANKING IN FOCUS

The collapse of Herstatt Bank (in German, Bankhaus Herstatt) and its effects on the international financial markets—particularly on the foreign exchange market—highlighted the close interdependence among international banks around the world. Herstatt Bank was a midsized West German bank active in the foreign exchange market. For a long time, the foreign exchange market was a relatively small and stable market, but it changed dramatically after 1973.

In 1974, Herstatt Bank collapsed after German supervisors withdrew its banking license. Unfortunately, the supervisors did not wait for the close of business to shut down the bank, but acted at lunchtime in Germany. Their timing had international ramifications. Herstatt was engaged in foreign exchange trading, where it was buying and selling foreign currency, mainly German marks. In accordance with custom, Herstatt Bank's counterparties had paid the bank in the morning local time, roughly six hours ahead of New York, for the foreign exchange transactions that Herstatt was engaged in. When the regulators closed the bank in Germany at lunchtime, or noon in Germany, New York banks were not yet open. The counterparties, who made the payments to Herstatt Bank in Frankfurt during the morning, expected that they would receive funds in exchange for their foreign currency in their New York accounts in the afternoon. Herstatt Bank was closed at lunchtime Frankfurt time, and Herstatt's U.S. bank, aware that Herstatt had been shut down, subsequently suspended all dollar payments on the parent bank's behalf. When the New York markets opened later in the day, Herstatt's clients were unable to access their exchanged funds. There followed a chain reaction that severely impacted the global payments and settlements system. In the three days following Herstatt's closure, the gross amount of funds transferred among banks for the purpose of payments and settlements fell by approximately 60%. Since then, **settlement risk** has commonly been called "Herstatt risk."

In the aftermath of the failure of Herstatt Bank, the central bank governors of developed BIS-member countries established the Basel Committee on Banking Supervision, also referred to as the **Basel Committee**. The committee's goal was to foster cooperation in regulating the activities of international banks. As noted, the failure of Herstatt Bank produced major problems for banks making international payments, particularly foreign exchange transactions. To reduce the chance of such an event happening again, the Basel Committee set out to improve international banking supervision.

The BIS provides the facilities for the Secretariat of the Basel Committee in Basel. The secretariat has a small staff of experienced banking supervisors from member institutions. The Secretariat provides administrative help for the committee and its subcommittees and is available to provide guidance to supervisory authorities in all countries.

3.3.2   The Basel Committee

The Basel Committee on Banking Supervision, commonly shortened to the Basel Committee, is a forum for regulatory cooperation between its member countries on banking supervision–related matters. Representatives of the central banks and banking supervisors are the committee members. It is not a global supervisory authority. Both the reports and recommendations issued by the committee lack legal force. Instead, the committee formulates broad banking supervisory standards (such as the Basel Accords), develops guidelines for both banks and regulators, and recommends statements of best practice.

The committee encourages the development of common banking regulatory and supervisory approaches for internationally active banks. It seeks to instill guiding regulatory principles without attempting to micromanage member countries' supervisory approaches. An overall objective of the committee's work has been to close gaps in international supervisory coverage in pursuit of two basic principles:

1.   Every international bank should be subject to supervision.
2.   The supervision should be substantial enough to ensure compliance.

To achieve this objective, the committee has issued several comprehensive documents since 1975 that seek to improve both regulatory understanding and the quality of banking supervision for international banks. The Basel Committee originally consisted of representatives from the members of the Group of 10 (known as the G10) countries, Spain, and Luxembourg. In 2009 the committee was expanded to include representatives from a total of 27 countries.

More recently, it has acted as a source of domestic legislation or banking supervision in the European Union (EU). In the EU, the Basel II Accord (explained in further detail below) was adopted, largely unchanged, as the basis for domestic banking and financial services supervisory legislation. This has led more and more countries outside the G10[2] and EU countries to either adopt or consider adopting Basel II as a basis for their respective banking legislation and regulations for domestic and international banks.

The Basel Committee has advanced several accords and one amendment. The timeline of these accords is set out in Figure 3.2. These documents are directly relevant for regulating the capital needed to balance the risks of internationally active banks. The accords are closely related to one another and reflect the development and increased sophistication of current-day finance and banking. The committee has also undertaken consultative activities.

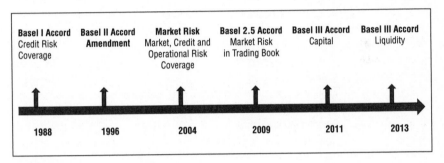

FIGURE 3.2 BIS—Banking Risk and Regulation

3.3.3 The Basel I Accord

The Basel Committee recognized an overriding need to strengthen the international banking system's ability to withstand shocks. The committee also sought to level the competitive playing field by standardizing national capital requirements. Lower capital requirements, or higher leverage, mean that a bank can use more debt to finance the loans it makes, which reduces the cost of funds and increases profitability. For example, prior to Basel I, international banks domiciled in Japan were allowed by their home regulator to maintain less capital than banks domiciled in other countries, giving the Japanese banks a competitive edge. In December 1987, the committee published a consultative study supporting a proposed system for the measurement of capital. The document is commonly referred to as the Basel I Accord.

---

2. There are 11 G10 countries: Belgium, Canada, France, Germany, Italy, Japan, the Netherlands, Sweden, Switzerland, the United Kingdom, and the United States.

It was approved by the governors of the central banks of the G10 countries, Spain, and Luxembourg and was released to banks in July 1988.

The capital measurement system provided for the implementation of a common framework for capital assessment as a function of the riskiness of assets.

The Basel I Accord introduced a system to help banks better assess their level of risk across all assets. The system established risk weightings based on the perceived relative credit risk associated with each asset class. The idea was to generate a risk identification system to make it possible to compare different types of banks and the different types of assets they held. To derive a balance sheet weighted by risk factors, each instrument, loan, or debt is grouped into four broad categories depending on its perceived credit risk. Figure 3.3 lists these risk weights.

Category	Examples	Risk Weight
1	Cash, loans to governments in OECD[3] countries	0%
2	Loans to banks in OECD countries	20%
3	Residential mortgages	50%
4	Corporate loans, consumer loans	100%

FIGURE 3.3 Risk Weights Associated with Certain Credits

In practice, banks had a multitude of different assets with different characteristics, and the actual risk weights used could vary according to the principles of the Accord and the discretion allowed in calculating the risk weight by the banking supervisor. This system allowed banks to consider all their assets, categorize each, and then calculate their total **risk-weighted assets (RWA)** as the sum of the absolute value of each asset multiplied by its risk weight. Risk-weighted assets include the bank's loans and securities recorded on the bank's **balance sheet** and also some commitments not recorded on the bank's balance sheet. For example, **off-balance-sheet** items would include financial derivatives, standby letters of credit, and other contingent liabilities that, if ever triggered, could expose the bank to financial risk.

---

3. The Organization for Economic Cooperation and Development (OECD) is a group of 30 developed countries with a democratic government and a market economy.

In addition, the Accord created a framework for the structure of bank capital, often called eligible capital. The Basel Committee considers equity capital as the preferred element of eligible capital for a bank. However, for **regulatory capital** purposes, most banks could hold capital in two tiers:

- *Tier 1*, core capital, is primarily the bank's equity.
- *Tier 2*, supplementary capital, mainly includes reserves and provisions as well as hybrid capital instruments and subordinated debt. **Tier 2 capital** was restricted to be at most 50% of total regulatory capital.

Finally, the Accord also set a minimum capital requirement of 8% for the ratio of risk-weighted assets to regulatory capital. The ratio of the risk-weighted assets (RWA) to the regulatory capital of the bank is called the **capital ratio** or capital standard. **Tier 1 capital** is usually the equity of the bank; combined Tier 1 and Tier 2 capital, with some adjustments, usually equals the regulatory capital. The minimum capital standard of 8% was to be implemented by the end of 1993. **Capital adequacy** is achieved when an institution's capital ratio meets or exceeds the minimum capital standard. The Accord's common framework for capital was progressively introduced in virtually all countries with active international banks.

EXAMPLE

Suppose Bank B currently holds the following assets:
1. EUR 1,000 million loan to UK government (OECD)
2. EUR 300 million loan to international bank in Germany (OECD)
3. EUR 700 million mortgage portfolio
4. EUR 800 million corporate loan portfolio

Figure 3.4 shows the calculation of the risk-weighted assets for Bank B.

Description	Size (EUR million)	Risk-Weighted Asset (EUR million)
Loan to UK government	1,000	0% 0
Loan to international bank in Germany	300	20% 60
Mortgages	700	50% 350
Corporate loans	800	100% 800
Total RWA		**EUR 1,210**

FIGURE 3.4 Calculation of Risk-Weighted Assets for Bank B

Thus, assuming the country in which Bank B operates uses the Accord's 8% minimum capital requirement, Bank B's minimum capital required is EUR 96.8 million (= EUR 1,210 million * 8%). Therefore, to meet the Basel I capital requirement, Bank B must have at least EUR 96.8 million in Tier 1 and Tier 2 capital. To meet the regulatory requirements, at least EUR 48.4 million has to be Tier 1 capital.

The Basel I Accord was the first international regulatory attempt to link a bank's risks to the bank's equity. Over the years, both regulators and economists have found that prudently operated banks are characterized by higher capital ratios, take fewer risks, and suffer losses less frequently. The more equity the bank has, the greater the cushion the bank has to absorb potential losses (see Section 2.1.5 on the role of the bank's equity).

3.3.4 The Market Risk Amendment

Banking changed dramatically after the original Accord was introduced. Due largely to other regulatory changes (deregulation) that allowed banks to have greater self-determination in how they conducted their activities, banks became broad-based providers of financial services. Because trading activities in banks began playing a more significant role, the Basel Committee in 1996 issued the **Market Risk Amendment,** formally titled Amendment to the Capital Accord to Incorporate Market Risks. The Amendment focused on the effect of a bank's positions in various market-traded financial assets—foreign exchange, debt securities, equities, commodities, and derivatives.

The risks arising from trading positions in bonds, equities, foreign exchange, and commodities were separated from credit risk calculations and assigned to a new risk category—market risk. The Amendment allowed banks to use their own systems for measuring market risk, subject to banking supervisory approval, and the capital required to cover that risk was based in part on how effective their models had been at measuring the bank's market risk. In particular, the Amendment allowed banks to use value-at-risk (VaR) models to measure **market risk capital** requirements. VaR then was a new methodology for measuring risk and has since evolved to become a cornerstone of financial risk management. Chapter 6 will further delve into the VaR methodology. It should be noted that VaR is now, in some circles, being replaced by, or is used in conjunction with a concept called "expected shortfall," which is a more conservative approach to assessing possible losses. Expected shortfall provides an estimate the of the expected loss in excess of the loss determined by the VaR calculation. Subsequently, the Market Risk Amendment was incorporated into the Basel II Accord. Further details will be discussed in Chapter 6.

3.3.5 Weaknesses of Bank Capital Requirements in Basel I Accord

The 1988 Accord was intended to evolve over time. In 1991, it was amended to provide a more precise definition of general provisions against bad debts that are included in general loan loss reserves. Since 1991, general loan loss reserves have been included as capital for purposes of calculating capital adequacy.

However, as implementation and use of the Accord progressed, it became evident that Basel I was too simplistic to address the activities of complex banks. For instance, according to Basel I, banks that lent to companies with a very good credit standing were obliged to hold exactly the same amount of regulatory capital as banks lending to companies with poor credit standing. But banks could charge higher interest on loans to companies with poor credit standing. Thus, the Basel I Accord provided banks—inadvertently—with the incentive to underwrite loans to companies with lower credit ratings. These credit ratings are provided by credit rating agencies that routinely evaluate the creditworthiness of a wide range of borrowers. (Section 5.5 discusses credit rating agencies.) A higher credit rating, such as an AAA rating, indicates a lower risk of default than a CCC rating. Since AAA-rated borrowers offer lower interest rates than CCC-rated borrowers, this structure provided banks fewer incentives to underwrite loans to companies with good credit ratings. (Figure 5.2 summarizes the various credit ratings and their interpretations.) While the purpose of the Accord was to reduce the overall risk of internationally active banks, these incentives actually encouraged banks to underwrite riskier loans.

Another concern with Basel I was that it did not recognize the benefits of **credit mitigation techniques**. Credit mitigation techniques help banks reduce the credit risk associated with loans through the use of collateral and loan guarantees. Although certainly not the intent, the Accord did not provide banks with the appropriate incentives to use credit mitigation techniques. Under the Accord, banks could employ these techniques but not receive any capital relief.

EXAMPLE

Bank C is evaluating a EUR 100,000,000 loan request from Bear Inc.; the company has fallen on hard times and has a CCC credit rating. The company has some undeveloped—and otherwise unencumbered—land worth EUR 125,000,000 that it can use as collateral for the loan. As the value of the collateral (see Section 4.4.5 for additional details on collateral) exceeds the value of the loan, Bank C is confident that even if the loan becomes nonperforming, Bear Inc. can sell the land and repay the loan. Because there is collateral and the value of the collateral exceeds the value of the loan, this loan is relatively safe. Yet, Bank C will be charged a risk weight of 100% toward the 8% regulatory minimum capital, notwithstanding the existence of collateral.

The Accord also did not recognize the benefits of diversification for credit risk reduction. A bank that lends to the same type of customer in the same region faces greater credit risk than a bank that lends to a diverse group of customers in the same or different regions of the world.

The committee initiated the Basel II Accord in an attempt to correct the drawbacks and inadvertent consequences of the Basel I Accord.

3.3.6   The Basel II Accord

In 1999, the committee issued a proposal for a new capital framework to replace the 1988 Accord. The new Accord proposed to connect capital requirements more closely to the actual risks incurred by a bank. It also aimed to broaden the risks banks considered when calculating their minimum capital requirements. The new Accord proposed approaches that would accommodate banks' differing complexities in their operations and businesses. Most importantly, it sought to provide incentives for banks to develop more sophisticated internal risk management systems that reduce nonsystemic risk in the banking system. From a regulatory perspective, the new Accord would provide banking supervisors with enhanced powers to redress weaknesses in individual banks.

In 2004, after lengthy consultations, a new capital framework, Basel II, was introduced. It consists of three pillars, shown in Figure 3.5.

- *Pillar 1.* Sets minimum capital requirements designed to improve upon the standardized rules set forth in the 1988 Accord. These minimum regulatory capital requirements should reflect the three major types of risk that a bank faces: credit risk, market risk, and operational risk. The approach in Basel II cures some of the arbitrariness or coarseness in Basel I. Under Pillar 1, banks can choose from different alternatives of varying complexity to calculate their minimum regulatory capital requirements. Basel II also represents the first attempt to assign a regulatory capital charge to the management of operational risk.

■ *Pillar 2.* Complements and strengthens Pillar 1 by establishing a prudential supervision process. It covers all the risks in Pillar 1 and adds some other considerations:

- The calculation by the bank of the amount of **economic capital,** the amount of capital a firm will require to survive during times of distress to cover Pillar 1 risks. Economic capital is discussed extensively in Chapter 8.
- The creation of a governance structure within the bank to ensure internal supervision and oversight from the board of directors and senior management.
- The evaluation by the banking supervisor of the bank's own risk profile level and the processes the bank used to determine that level.

■ *Pillar 3.* Outlines the effective use of market discipline as a lever to strengthen disclosure and encourage sound banking practices. **Market discipline** is public disclosure of a bank's financial condition to depositors and other interested parties, allowing these to assess the condition of the bank. It relates to transparency of the bank and its activities. Disclosure, or transparency, is the degree to which a bank or any company reveals its assets, liabilities, and/or inner workings. Disclosure affords the market—other banks, depositors, and borrowers—a better picture of the bank's overall risk position and allows the bank's counterparties to price, and deal appropriately.

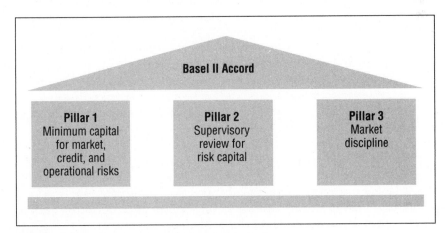

FIGURE 3.5 The Three Pillars of the Basel II Accord

The three pillars are intended to reinforce each other in an approach designed to strengthen the safety and soundness of the global financial system. The complex regulatory framework has two overarching objectives:

1. Improve how regulatory capital requirements reflect underlying risks
2. Address the effects of financial innovation that has occurred

3.3.7   Adopting Basel II

When a country incorporates the Basel Accord into its banking regulatory and supervisory framework, it must do so by adjusting it to its own laws and regulations. Most members of the Group of 20 (G20) have adopted the Accord by incorporating the requirements into their respective national laws and/or regulations with some amendments and adjustments. The Basel II Capital Accord has become the basis for the EU regulatory framework and has been implemented across EU countries through the European Union's Capital Requirements Directive (CRD) and other directives. The European Union adopted the CRD through an EU-wide legislative process. The Committee of European Banking Supervisors (CEBS) was created to ensure that Basel II is applied, interpreted, and implemented uniformly across all member states. In 2010 the European Banking Authority (EBA) replaced the CEBS, taking over all of its responsibilities.

A study by the Financial Stability Institute (FSI) reported that the vast majority of countries planned to implement, or have implemented, parts of Basel II. Of course, different countries will have different approaches to implementing these Accords. The decision to implement the Basel II Accord in a country is motivated by several factors.

- The relative success being enjoyed by banks that use risk-based capital
- The desire of many bank supervisors across the world to move toward risk-based regulation
- The desire of many countries to enhance the reputation of their banking system

Different countries have different banking industry structures and specific rules and regulations that govern their business activities. The Basel II Accord takes these country-specific differences into consideration by allowing the national bank regulators and supervisors in countries that adopt the Accord to customize certain Basel definitions, approaches, or thresholds that they plan to adopt when implementing the proposals. Implementation of rules and regulations are to be based on domestic market practice and experience and be consistent with the objectives of the Basel II Accord and its principles.

EXAMPLE

In determining the risk weights of loans secured against commercial real estate, national regulators have discretion to allow a 50% risk weight for certain loans that meet particular requirements, although the Basel II Accord sets out that loans secured against commercial real estate have a 100% risk weight.

3.3.8   Limitations of Basel II

The severity and complexity of the global financial crisis of 2007–2009 high-lighted the need to improve regulation and supervision of large, complex, and internationally active financial institutions. Basel II, although still relatively new, was found to be insufficient to deal with the modern and fast changing characteristics of the global banking industry and unable to keep the industry away from crisis. Basel II focuses on individual banks, assuming that by ensuring the stability of each bank the entire banking system would be stable. When the crisis occurred, it became clear that this was not the case. Basel II was found to have weaknesses. Below is a list of some of the more important ones:

- The Accord's provisions did not adequately assess risk capital.
- Assets could belong to either the banking book or the trading book.
- Its treatment of market risk failed to capture the effects of excess concentrations of credit exposure in the trading book.
- It failed to fully recognize the effect of liquidity on bank securitization practices.
- Liquidity management requirements were limited; there were no standards.
- Some risk weights and risk assessments were inadequately calibrated.
- A lack of understanding of correlation between risks.

After a series of discussions, the Basel Committee, subsequently, redesigned the Basel framework by considering the various experiences learned from the crisis. These changes have been incorporated in the Basel III Accord.

3.3.9   The Basel III Accord

In December 2010 the Basel Committee released the Basel III Accord that was approved by the G20 leaders. Learning from the incremental and fragmented implementation of Basel II, the Basel Committee emphasized the need for a consistent rigorous implementation approach across different countries with attention to internationally active banks. The Basel III framework overlays the currently existing Basel II Accord and is to be implemented in stages, to be completed in 2019. It attempts to address the evolution of modern banking and the complex relationships within the financial system. Unlike the two previous Basel Accords, Basel III includes **macroprudential** issues. While maintaining the **microprudential** (national or local) regulatory tool kit from Basel II that ensures the safe, sound, and prudent operations of banks, Basel III considers the effects of systemic risks that globally interconnected financial institutions may present, and seeks to address these risks.

To increase the resilience of individual banks, Basel III implements new bank capital requirements that address both the quality and the quantity of eligible capital. Additionally, Basel III introduces a concept called capital buffers above the minimum levels to capture procyclical and systemic risk.

An example of the pro-cyclicality effect is the prevalence of lending into so-called asset bubbles. Excessive lending during a booming market leads to unrealistic expectations of returns and unrealistic valuations of assets, as has occurred in commercial and residential real estate and equities markets at various times throughout history.

Additionally, Basel III requires systemically important institutions to raise extra capital. The framework recognizes that the failure of these globally important institutions can have a greater impact on the stability of the financial system. Basel III includes enhanced standards for both global and domestic systemically important banks. Indicators of global systemic importance are: size, interconnectedness, lack of substitutability, global activity, and complexity. The Basel III bank leverage ratio is defined in the Bank for International Settlements', Basel III leverage ration framework and disclosure requirements paper, January 2014, as follows:

$$\text{Leverage ratio} = \frac{\text{Capital measure}}{\text{Exposure measure}}$$

Capital measure is a bank's Tier 1 capital calculation as determined according to the Basel risk-based capital framework. The Exposure measure is generally defined as a bank's total exposures including on-balance sheet exposures, derivative exposures, securities financing transaction exposures and off-balance sheet items. In simple terms, a leverage ratio is the amount of capital a bank has in relation to its assets. A leverage ratio has the advantage of being a simple measure but the disadvantage of treating all assets the same, regardless of how risky they are. This could incentivize banks to hold riskier assets.

Strengthening the resilience of the financial system and ensuring sufficient levels of high-quality capital are not, in and of themselves, sufficient to ensure systemic financial stability. As noted above, poor liquidity management, among other things, can bring markets to a standstill or result in bank failures. Even though the Basel Committee emphasized the importance of sound liquidity management prior to the 2007–2009 crisis, these were not quantitative standards, but rather qualitative principles. The proposed liquidity framework in Basel III includes quantitative liquidity standards, addressing that earlier omission.

3.4   Deposit Insurance

One of the tools that ensures the safety and soundness of the financial system is deposit insurance. Deposit insurance is a promise by a government or an insurance system that, in the event of a bank failure, bank depositors will receive back all or some of the deposits they made with that bank.

Deposit protection is generally limited to a certain amount of the deposits held at each bank. Each country sets its own limit. The following table gives a sample of the levels at which deposit insurance protection is currently provided around the world:

Country	Deposit Insurance Limit
Australia	AUD 250,000
Canada	CAD 100,000
Eurozone countries (other than Ireland)	EUR 100,000
Hong Kong	HKD 500,000
Ireland	Unlimited
Kenya	KES 100,000
Japan	YEN 10,000,000
United Kingdom	GBP 85,000
United States	USD 250,000

The motivation for deposit insurance is to help prevent the risk that a bank run will grow into a broader bank panic. Knowing that their deposits would be repaid fully or in most part, even if the bank were to fail, means depositors have fewer incentives to withdraw their funds from an institution even when there is news that the institution is about to fail. As noted above, deposit insurance reduces bank runs, bank panic, and contagion.

3.4.1   Deposit Insurance Coverage

Historically, deposit insurance was voluntary and was offered by insurance companies, banks, and governments. Banks that wanted to participate in these deposit insurance systems were able to market this added protection against the failure of the institution to existing and potential depositors. Consequently, these banks were able to secure financing at lower costs than banks that did not offer deposit insurance coverage. Despite the advantage of lower financing costs to banks, few deposit insurance systems were popular, and many were severely underfunded, meaning the deposit insurance provider did not have sufficient funds available to repay the depositors in case of widespread bank failures. Many of the voluntary deposit insurance systems exhausted their assets during poor economic times when multiple banks failed. This original combination of voluntary participation and poor funding reduced the effectiveness of deposit insurance.

During the Great Depression in the United States starting in 1929, bank runs grew into a bank panic and led to widespread bank failures. As a result of sweeping legislation, in 1933 the United States created the world's first comprehensive, compulsory, and explicit deposit insurance system. Under this system, which continues to exist today, the Federal Deposit Insurance Corporation (FDIC), an independent agency, provides protection for deposits in U.S. banks.[4] Protection is subject to certain limits, constraints, and caps, but in effect a large proportion of deposits in the United States are protected against a bank's failing. This approach has been espoused by deposit insurance systems around the world. The FDIC regularly examines the safety and soundness of the banks it insures to determine their capitalization and overall financial health. The decisions the agency makes based on the bank examinations, in a sense, are the same as an underwriting activity for a bank, and lead to a determination of the premium the bank will pay to the FDIC for deposit insurance. The FDIC has become one of the principal bank supervisors in the United States. At the end of 2008, well-capitalized U.S.

---

4. The United States has several government agencies that provide deposit insurance to different types of banks. The chief deposit insurance agency is the FDIC.

banks that belonged to the lowest supervisory risk rating (the lowest overall risk of operations, loans, and investments) paid between 5 and 7 **basis points** (bp) of deposits for insurance coverage per year. A basis point is one-hundredth of 1%, or 0.0001. A bank paying 7 bp of deposits in deposit insurance premium would pay USD 7 for each USD 10,000 in deposits.

Undercapitalized banks that belong to the highest supervisory risk rating group (the highest overall risk of operations, loans, and investments) pay 43 bp of deposits for insurance coverage. Other factors may adjust these deposit insurance assessment levels, but at the core the difference in deposit insurance premiums between risky and prudent institutions can be substantial.

EXAMPLE

Both Bank D and Bank E have USD 1,000 million in deposits. While Bank D is well-capitalized and holds the lowest supervisory risk rating, Bank E is both undercapitalized and holds the highest supervisory risk rating. Bank D pays 5 bp in insurance, or USD 500,000, while Bank E pays 43 bp, or USD 4.3 million. The difference in premium, USD 3.8 million, reflects the higher risk of Bank E.

3.4.2 Deposit Insurance Around the World

In July 2013, there were 112 countries with deposit insurance systems in operation, and 19 countries with deposit insurance systems that are pending, planned, or under development.[5] Several countries have multiple deposit insurance systems. For instance, Austria has five different deposit insurance providers. There are also deposit insurance systems that cover multiple countries/territories: the Marshall Islands and Micronesia, and Puerto Rico are insured by the U.S. Federal Deposit Insurance Corporation (FDIC).

Many countries have adopted the FDIC's approach to deposit insurance, making participation in deposit insurance programs compulsory for all banks and financial institutions that accept deposits from the public. Insurance can be provided either by a government agency or through private insurance companies. These approaches are different, but ultimately all seek to protect depositors in case of bank failure. Deposit insurance coverage varies across countries. In most countries, retail customers' deposits are protected at the expense of commercial customers. The reason for this two-tiered approach is that commercial customers are generally believed to be more sophisticated than retail customers and maintain multiple banking relationships that reduce

---

5. International Association of Deposit Insurers, Country System List, updated June 30, 2013.

their overall risks if one bank should fail. Also, regulators consider commercial depositors to have the capability to assess the possible risk of a bank failing.

EXAMPLE

In 2003, the deposit insurance system of Serbia and Montenegro covered deposits of banks up to RSD 5,000 (Serbian dinars), the equivalent of USD 87 at the then prevailing international exchange rate between the RSD and the USD. This was the lowest deposit insurance coverage in the world at that time. At the same time, the Dominican Republic, Thailand, Turkey, and Turkmenistan all provide unlimited coverage for deposits. In 2011, Serbia increased the coverage to EUR 50,000, with Montenegro covering the same amount from 2013. As of October 2013, the countries within the Eurozone have coverage of at least EUR 100,000.[6]

While there are 100 countries that have explicit deposit insurance systems in operation, there are several countries that provide implicit deposit insurance coverage. An **explicit deposit insurance system** is where the government, through an agency, has created a deposit insurance system to guarantee deposits. Such a system relies on regulation through the government or a dedicated agency, banking and other legislation, and active involvement of regulators as well as a law that explicitly states the coverage limits of deposit insurance, the assessment of deposit insurance premia, and regulatory rules. An **implicit deposit insurance system** is a system where the government has not created a specific agency providing deposit insurance, but has stated its willingness to guarantee deposits when so needed.

EXAMPLE

In the early 1990s, Sweden suffered a major banking crisis. At that time Sweden had neither an explicit nor an implicit deposit insurance system. In the early days of the crisis, it became clear that due to the substantial losses many banks were suffering from speculative real estate lending, which was the cause of the crisis, most banks would not be able to withstand a run and the system would soon be engulfed in a bank panic. As the signs of a bank panic became more evident, the Swedish government sought to avoid it by stating its readiness to guarantee all bank deposits. This implicit guarantee reduced the incentives for bank runs and was successful in averting widespread bank panic and bank failures. Later, the government created an explicit deposit insurance system.

---

6. Article 7(1a) of Directive 94/19/EC (European Forum of Deposit Insurers).

Credit Risk

T his and the following chapter provide a comprehensive introduction to credit risk: Chapter 4 focuses on the analysis of credit risk, and Chapter 5 explains the management of credit risks. This chapter addresses credit risk by focusing on three related topic areas. The first section introduces credit risk by defining and explaining the source of credit risk. The following sections provide a detailed overview of lenders and borrowers, characteristics of credit products, and features of specific credit products used for retail and commercial lending. The final two sections describe the credit process and specifically **credit analysis**—how banks evaluate credit risk.

Chapter Outline
  4.1 Introduction to Credit Risk
  4.2 Lenders
  4.3 Borrowers
  4.4 Characteristics of Credit Products
  4.5 Types of Credit Products
  4.6 The Credit Process
  4.7 The Credit Analysis Process
  4.8 Information Services

Key Learning Points

- One of a bank's core risks is the possibility that borrowers will not repay their loans on time, or at all.
- Lenders distinguish between retail and commercial borrowers and tailor products to meet each group's unique financial needs.
- Loan products can be characterized by **maturity**, repayment method, loan use, the different types of security the borrower needs to provide the lender (collateral), or the restrictions the borrower must agree to in order to obtain the loan (**covenants**).
- There is a wide variety of credit products, and similar products can be used to meet both retail and commercial borrowing needs.
- The credit process contains several sequential steps, including identifying the credit opportunity, evaluating credits, and monitoring credits on an ongoing basis.
- To analyze the borrower's ability to repay, banks engage in a complex credit analysis process that critically assesses the financial position of the borrower using several different methods and sources of information.
- The five C's of credit provide a basic framework for good lending and its principles hold true for lending to both small and large companies. Analyzing the business, financial and structural risks.
- There are many different sources of information that can assist in the analysis of credit risk of a company. However, the core source is the company's annual report and audited financial statements, although the "numbers" don't always tell the full story!

CREDIT RISK

4.1   Introduction to Credit Risk

Credit risk analysis encompasses various components that, in combination, offer the bank a way to measure the probability that a borrower may default on a contract—a debt, loan, or similar promise to perform—and how much value is likely to be recovered in the event of a default. **Credit risk** is most simply defined as the potential that a borrower, or counterparty, will fail to meet its obligations in accordance with agreed terms. **Default** is the failure to repay or meet existing obligations.

EXAMPLE

Growth Inc. provides goods and services that customers pay for after they receive the goods and services. The company provides the goods and services because it is confident its customers will make the payment when it is due. However, receipt of the payment is uncertain until it is actually made. Growth Inc. has taken on the risk that its customers may not honor their obligations. This is credit risk. In order to minimize its credit risk, Growth Inc. must evaluate its prospective customers in advance, determine if they are likely to honor their obligations, and decide whether to provide goods and services.

Counterparty risk is a common reference to the risk that another party to a contract or agreement will fail to perform under the terms of the agreement. This could mean the failure to provide promised goods or services, a refusal to provide promised loan facilities, or the failure to pay amounts owed.

EXAMPLE

On June 30, Bank A and Bank B entered into an agreement that contained the following terms:

Lender:	Bank B
Borrower:	Bank A
Amount:	USD 150 million
Term:	3 months from July 15
Interest rate:	5%

Bank B has incurred **counterparty credit risk**. Specifically, Bank B's counterparty credit risk is that Bank A will not repay the USD 150 million under the terms of the agreement and/or will fail to service the interest due on the loan. Conversely, Bank A has also accepted a counterparty credit risk—that is, the risk that Bank B may be unable to honor its agreement to lend funds on July 15.

This example illustrates that, in its most basic form, credit risk arises between two parties when there is a contractual obligation for one party (the lender) to provide funding to the other party (the borrower) in exchange for promised future payments. Earlier sections provided several examples of defaults, including how a default affects a bank's assets, liabilities, and equity (Section 2.2), and how banks seek to mitigate the effects of default through loan loss reserves (Section 2.2.4).

4.2   Lenders

Banks facilitate financial intermediation, the process by which one group in need of capital borrows funds from another group that has excess capital available for investment. In arranging this transfer of capital between the two groups, the bank uses deposits to finance the loan. Intermediation is critical to promoting economic development. Banks accept deposits from one group (depositors) and use those funds to provide credit products to another group (borrowers). Granting credit facilities (i.e., loans) creates risk. Banks accept this risk as a regular cost of business. Essentially, banks are in the business of managing risk. Banks continually attempt to expand their ability to manage all types of risks and, in particular, have gained considerable experience with credit risk analysis. Banks routinely evaluate their experiences and incorporate the lessons learned into their business practice by modifying or adding policies and procedures that mitigate credit risk. Despite these efforts, recent events in the banking sector highlight how challenging credit analysis and credit risk management can be.

Banking is essential to both the retail and the wholesale markets. There are thousands of local, regional, and global banks that offer a variety of products and services to meet the needs of the retail market (individual customers, shops, and small and medium-sized businesses). In the wholesale market (lending to other banks, large corporate entities, and large global institutions), only the larger banks are able to offer a diverse enough product range to meet the needs of the customers. Figure 4.1 describes the two major banking sectors.

Retail Bank	Wholesale Bank
Customers include:	Customers include:
▪ Individuals/Shops	▪ Other banks/Large corporations
▪ Small businesses	▪ Large global institutions

FIGURE 4.1 Major Types of Banks

Local and regional banks provide traditional and commercial banking operations such as lending to businesses, making loans to individuals, and accepting deposits. Examples of regional banks include Fifth Third Bank in the United States, Bankwest in Australia, Raiffiesen Bank in Central and

Eastern Europe, and Al-Ahli Commercial Bank in Bahrain. Global banks such as HSBC, ANZ, JPMorgan Chase, and the Royal Bank of Scotland are well placed to undertake both commercial banking and investment banking activities.

4.2.1   Investment Banks

Investment banks often act as an agent or financial intermediary to companies. Although they may have their own brokerage operations, provide investment advice to their customers, and provide loans and credit to commercial customers, their core activity is to arrange equity and debt financing on behalf of their corporate customers. Investment banks typically do not accept deposits from customers or provide loans to retail customers, and they are not often directly regulated by bank regulators unless the investment bank is part of a bank that is otherwise regulated by bank regulators.

As mentioned in Chapter 1, in late 2008, some large U.S. investment banks, including Goldman Sachs and Morgan Stanley, converted to banks regulated by the government. The change was considered necessary in order to allow these entities to increase their capital by collecting customer deposits and also, crucially, gave them access to the Federal Reserve's Emergency Lending Facilities. Given the severity of the global financial crisis of 2007–2009, it would appear that the investment banking model that has existed in the United States since the mid-1930s is becoming obsolete in a globally connected and capital-intensive financial world.

4.3   Borrowers

Both retail and wholesale banks differentiate between different types of borrowers based on a variety of factors, including size and financing needs. On the retail side, one broad distinction is typically drawn between individual borrowers and small business borrowers. On the wholesale side, however, the differentiation tends to be more complex.

4.3.1   Retail Borrowers

Retail borrowers include consumers (individuals) who borrow money to purchase homes, cars, and other goods (in many countries, consumers also borrow to finance education and similar expenses). Generally, consumers with high income, low levels of debt, and solid loan repayment records are considered less risky borrowers, but a borrower's rating ultimately depends on a variety of criteria.

In today's banking environment, retail banking has become a commodity-like business. Most banks now group their retail borrowers into relatively homogeneous risk groups based on standard criteria. This process allows banks to analyze repayment and default characteristics based on standardized borrower characteristics. One aspect of this process is credit scoring, which allows the common characteristics of loans and borrowers to be grouped and analyzed. Scoring in groups enables loans and borrowers to be dissected and analyzed to more accurately assess a portfolio's probability of loss. Standardization and credit scoring allow the assessment process to be completed more cheaply, making relatively small loans profitable. It has also facilitated securitization, the bundling or packaging of portfolios of loans, against which debt instruments can be issued. Securitization is covered in more detail in Section 5.2.3.

Each bank has developed credit decision policies that delineate what types of loans—size, exposure, and business—need to be approved or ratified by senior management and/or the bank board committee. Generally, the larger and more risky a loan is, the more likely that the loan will pass through several levels of the bank's decision-making hierarchy.

4.3.2   Corporate Borrowers

Corporate borrowers include companies ranging from small local companies to large global conglomerates (see below). Each has different financing needs, and each should be analyzed on a stand-alone basis. Depending on the ease of access to capital (public markets, banks, private funding), companies may borrow capital or raise equity to finance growth and generate income. When borrowing, companies typically repay their obligations from the cash generated from the growth. Companies with steady profits, low debt levels, and solid management are considered to be less risky and are offered better contractual terms for their borrowings. Corporate borrowers are frequently differentiated by their size and global reach. The main differences are listed in Figure 4.2.

- *Local companies.* These companies are generally referred to as **small and medium enterprises (SMEs)**. SMEs are usually smaller corporate entities such as partnerships, sole proprietorships, owner-operators, mom-and-pop shops, and other small businesses. SMEs are generally privately or closely held and have a straightforward legal structure. Annual sales are generally below USD 1 million, EUR 750,000, or GBP 500,000, but business size does differ across institutions and regulatory frameworks, and SMEs in emerging markets are generally much smaller than those seen in more developed economies.[1]

■ *Regional companies.* Regional companies are commercial businesses, generally larger SMEs, and include chain stores, gas stations, and restaurants, with sales between USD 1 million and 100 million (EUR 750,000 to 75 million, GBP 500,000 to 50 million). Some would fall into the definition of SMEs according to the Basel II Accord. Further, their business activities usually expose them to one or more local markets or provide general exposure within a region. The legal and ownership structure of these businesses can be more complex, with multiple owners, several subsidiaries, and locations in different legal jurisdictions.

■ *International companies.* International companies conduct their business across country borders but generally limit their activities to a certain region around the globe (e.g., Western Europe, the United States, and Canada). They may also be listed or publicly traded companies on a stock exchange or other similar exchange, or may be large, privately held businesses that operate in different countries. International companies can have sizable annual sales (often in the billions) and need to borrow regularly from banks or the corporate bond market to finance their activities and growth.

■ *Universal companies.* These companies are generally considered global conglomerates with exposures around the world. They typically manage their businesses by being constantly aware of global business considerations and pressures. Most are publicly traded on an exchange. Examples include Siemens, Mitsubishi Heavy Industries, Procter & Gamble, BP, Royal Dutch Shell, and General Electric. All are considered **institutional borrowers** by banks and demand unique consideration for their financing needs. Hedge funds, international banks, and global insurers are also considered universal companies and institutional borrowers.

---

1. Definitions of SMEs and corporate sizes vary widely. For instance, the Basel II Accord in its Annex 5 defines loans to SMEs as loans to corporations with reported annual sales of less than EUR 50 million.

Borrower	Capital Needs	Ownership Structure	Operations	Financial Sophistication
Local companies	Small needs and simple loan products.	Simple ownership structure (proprietorships, partnerships, or closely held and family-based corporations).	Limited operations at one location with fewer than 50 employees.	Limited. Relies heavily on one bank for financial advice and solutions to financial problems.
Regional companies	Substantial needs met by a combination of simpler loan products.	Several partners or corporations with multiple owners. May have some subsidiaries. May be publicly traded on a limited or regional scale.	Operations focused on one or a couple of closely related businesses at several locations, possibly including international operations. Employs several hundred people.	Some financial experience and understanding. Ability to evaluate what combination of loan and other financial products would best fit their needs. Often have multiple banking relationships.
International companies	Large, varied, and complex needs that require a range of simple and more complex loan products.	Publicly traded with a large number of owners (shareholders). Several subsidiaries around the world.	Focused on multiple businesses worldwide. Employs several thousand people.	Highly sophisticated. Employs staff that focus on finding optimal financing alternatives for the company. Multiple banking relationships, with one lead bank.
Universal companies	Large, varied, and complex needs that require a wide range of simple, complex loan products and other innovative financial products.	Publicly traded at several exchanges with a large number of owners (shareholders). Multiple subsidiaries around the world.	Multiple, possibly disparate businesses worldwide. Employs tens of thousands of people.	Very sophisticated. Employees in different parts of the world focusing on finding optimal financing options. Multiple banking relationships in several countries support the financing of the business.

FIGURE 4.2 An Overview of the Differences between Borrower Types

4.3.3   Sovereign Borrowers

Sovereign borrowers are governments that raise capital through bonds or direct borrowing generally from the larger global banks. Amounts raised are often used for large capital investments (roads, railways) or to finance government spending. Governments often use tax revenues to repay these loans.

4.3.4   Public Borrowers

Public borrowers are primarily state, provincial, and local governments (municipalities) and their subentities (e.g., water and sewage companies, airport authorities, public hospitals, and school districts). Amounts borrowed at this level are normally used either for investments (streets, water supply) or general spending. Since most local governments have the ability to generate cash by taxing their constituencies, public loans are considered relatively low risk. Nevertheless, there have been times when strong local governments have defaulted on their loans. Indeed, there have been a number of high-profile local government defaults. For example, the city of Detroit, Michigan, filed for Chapter 9 bankruptcy in July 2013 for USD 18.5 billion, dwarfing the Jefferson County, Alabama, Chapter 9 filing for USD 4 billion in November 2011. Chapter 9 is the chapter of the U.S. Bankruptcy Code pertaining to municipalities.

Supranational institutions such as the European Investment Bank, Asian Development Bank, European Bank of Reconstruction and Development, World Bank, African Development Bank, Inter-American Development Bank, and Islamic Development Bank are also classified as public borrowers.

4.4   Characteristics of Credit Products

There is a wide variety of loan types. All were developed to meet specific business needs of different borrowers' unique situations. This section describes basic lending facilities and their differences. To understand which type of lending facility is appropriate for a borrower, lenders must understand the details of the borrower's financial status, especially how it relates to existing and anticipated conditions in the local, regional, or international marketplaces.

There are a number of ways a credit product can be classified:
- Maturity
- Commitment specification
- Purpose
- Repayment source
- Collateral requirements
- Covenant requirements
- Repayment characteristics

While not exhaustive, this list sets the stage to understand the complexity of the lending process and the unique nature of most loans. The following subsections explore each of these characteristics in detail.

4.4.1 Maturity

Credit needs range over different time periods, with the loans made to meet those needs generally classified by maturity. Maturity simply means the date the final payment on the loan or other financial instrument becomes due. For instance, a loan of a maturity of one year must be repaid in full within one year.

For business, regulatory, and accounting purposes, banks usually distinguish between three maturity bands for lending: short, medium, and long term. Descriptions of the different maturity ranges or maturity bands are given in Figure 4.3. As noted in the table, loans within a particular maturity band tend to have similar uses and characteristics. For example, **medium-term lending** is usually cash flow based or asset based. With **cash flow–based lending** the quality and sufficiency of the cash being generated by the company over the period are paramount. **Asset-based lending** is secured by corporate assets such as accounts receivable, inventories, or certain property or equipment (see Section 4.5.2).

In the last few decades, there has been an increasing shift toward the establishment of long-term strategic banking relationships between banks and their borrowers. Banks support these relationships by increasingly offering longer-term loans to meet a borrower's credit needs (needs that previously were fulfilled by short-term borrowings). Having diverse facilities helps to cement a bank's corporate relationships, retain customers for the longer term, and contain competition from other banks. It also means that, despite a borrower's deteriorating credit condition, a bank may be obligated to fulfill lending commitments made at a much earlier time. Proper credit analysis, therefore, must take the time horizon (the maturity) of a loan commitment into consideration.

The business motivation to distinguish among the three maturity bands is to allow the bank to group loans of comparable maturity. Grouping creates efficiencies by allowing banks to manage loans within the same maturity band similarly. Banks seek to have a balance of maturity bands in their assets (loans and securities in their portfolio) to correspond to the maturity of their liabilities (deposits and other borrowings). Part of this process is managed by the bank's treasury department within its asset and liability management (ALM) function. From an accounting perspective, the maturity bands allow the bank to classify the various loans as short-term or long-term; banks use different accounting treatments for short-term and long-term loans. Most medium-maturity loans, for accounting purposes, are treated as long-term loans.

The third pillar of the Basel II Accord mandates what disclosures banks must make to the public, financial markets, and regulators. From a regulator's perspective, loan grouping reflects regulatory concerns and allows supervisors to assess more readily how closely the maturity of the bank's assets matches the maturity of the liabilities.

Category	Short-Term Lending	Medium-Term Lending	Long-Term Lending
Maturity Range	Less than 12 months	1 to 5 years	More than 5 years
Typical Use	Used for temporary or seasonal financing needs	Generally used for ongoing financing of investments in machinery and equipment or facilities for short-term projects, but not major capital expenditures. This type of financing can also meet cyclical needs as investments of this nature are not expected to generate cash within a short period.	Provides finance for a company's long-term needs. Typically, this credit type will finance the construction of larger capital-intensive projects or major capital expenditures. The cash produced by the new equipment, product, or activity is the primary source of repayment.
Example	A toy manufacturer expects to increase its borrowing needs during the early summer as the company buys raw materials and builds its inventory for the end-of-year holiday season. The money borrowed is then repaid from the cash collected when the goods are sold.	The toy manufacturer also needs to purchase machinery and equipment for the manufacturing process. These assets will have an expected life of 3 to 4 years and contribute to finished goods. Purchase of these assets increases manufacturing capacity, but the funding of the machinery will require matching funding over a 4-year period, either asset based or cash flow based.	As the toy business grows, the company decides to build a new manufacturing plant in a different part of the world. Building a new factory and buying new machinery is a considerable expansion, and to finance this expansion, banks usually will offer long-term financing to be repaid from the revenues generated from the expansion or derived from the new equipment.

FIGURE 4.3 Short-Term, Medium-Term, and Long-Term Lending

Maturities also deliberately correspond to the way corporations choose to finance their businesses, and generally include a mix of short-term debt (to be repaid in less than one year), medium-term debt (to be repaid in five years or less), and long-term debt (to be repaid over more than five years).

4.4.2 Commitment Specification

Banking facilities are further classified as committed or uncommitted. Figure 4.4 outlines the differences between standard bank facilities.

- Committed facilities *are characterized by formal loan agreements, usually for one year or more.* Committed facilities earn a **margin** for the bank above its own cost of funds and include a facility fee, a commitment fee, and a fee for the amount of the loan the bank has actually extended to the borrower, whether or not the borrower uses the full amount of the loan. The amount of the loan not yet taken by the borrower is referred to as an undrawn commitment. The **cost of funds** reflects the prevailing interest rates in the market, the bank's own cost to secure the funds to be lent, and a margin to cover the costs of asset transformation. The **facility fee** is the fee charged by the bank for putting the loan into place (i.e., all the aspects of the program that allows the borrower to borrow the funds if and when needed). The **commitment fee** is the fee the lender charges a borrower for its commitment to make available a **line of credit** and to guarantee that a loan may be available to the lender at a certain future date, even though the credit in question is not being used at that particular time.
- Uncommitted facilities *are less formal arrangements but often include a facility letter stating that funds would be made available on demand but solely at the lender's discretion.* Uncommitted facilities provide a general framework for the terms of the lending without noting the specific contractual terms of that agreement, such as the amount of the loan or its duration, although such facilities are short term in nature (often *on demand* or *overdrafts*). There may be different contractual terms depending on when the facility is used. Uncommitted facilities are generally cheaper than committed facilities and priced on a margin above the bank's base rate. There may also be an arrangement fee charged at each renewal of the uncommitted facility.

A **banker's acceptance** is an example of an uncommitted facility. A banker's acceptance is similar to a postdated check, except that once the bank accepts the draft, it becomes obligated to disperse the funds on the date they become due. A line of credit is considered a short-term uncommitted facility. With a line of credit, the borrower is preapproved to draw from the bank funds up to a specified amount on demand. The borrower repays, in whole or in part during the term of the letter of credit, the full amount plus any interest due when the letter expires. The borrower may or may not use the credit line, but is charged by the bank for making it available.

Both lines of credit and banker's acceptances are generally considered short-term methods of financing characterized by a three- or six-month time horizon.

Uncommitted Facility	Committed Facility
▦ Less formal arrangement	▦ Formal loan agreement
▦ At lender's discretion	▦ Lender is legally bound to extend the
▦ Usually short term in nature	credit to the borrower when the borrower
▦ Often "on demand"	so requires
▦ Generally cheaper than a	▦ Usually for one year or more
committed facility	▦ Borrower charged to ensure loan is
▦ *Example: line of credit*	available at future date
	▦ *Example: mortgage loan*

FIGURE 4.4 Committed and Uncommitted Facilities

Banks can also generate income through compensating balances. When a bank extends a committed or an uncommitted facility, it may require the borrower to deposit certain amounts of money with the lending bank for the duration of the loan commitment. These funds are referred to as **compensating balances**. This arrangement provides the bank with funds to be used for other purposes, thus allowing it to earn a return on those funds in excess of the costs of the services being provided to the borrower. The borrower may also receive a credit for the compensating balance through an offset of the fee for the banking facility.

Compensating balances serve several functions:
- They serve as collateral in case the borrower defaults.
- They reduce the bank's interest expenses. Since the deposit usually carries a very low interest rate, sometimes as low as 0%, it allows the bank to secure additional deposits effectively at a very low cost, providing the bank with cheap financing through low-cost deposits. Borrowing at a low rate while lending at a higher rate increases the bank's potential earnings.

■ Compensating balances also indirectly increase the interest the borrower pays to the bank and are consequently considered as a charge to the borrower, as interest is charged for the extension of a loan.

EXAMPLE

Bank C has extended a five-year, USD 1 million loan to Growth Corporation, a small swimwear company. The loan carries an interest rate of 10% per year. In the first year, the bank would receive USD 100,000 in interest income. However, the bank requires Growth Corporation to deposit 5% of the amount borrowed into an account with the bank that pays 0% interest. Thus, the bank effectively lends only USD 950,000 to Growth Corporation, but receives USD 100,000 in interest, which can be calculated as an effective interest rate of 10.53%. In addition, Bank C is likely to have collected a set-up or facility fee and has the ability to channel the USD 50,000 in deposit to generate additional revenue.

4.4.3   Loan Purpose

The use of loan proceeds can vary widely and can impact a lender's credit decision. A loan used to finance inventory, to purchase equipment used in the production process, or to address some other type of working capital need may be viewed as facilitating the normal course of business or perhaps making possible the exploitation of a perceived strategic opportunity. Typically, there is little credit quality decline inherent in these transactions. Loans, however, can also be used to buy back stock, to finance a leveraged buyout, to pay a dividend, or to fund other shareholder-friendly activities. These loans are typically considered riskier, as they tend to benefit shareholders at the expense of creditors.

4.4.4   Repayment Source

Another way to distinguish between the different loan types is to consider how the borrower generates funds to repay the loan.

Asset conversion loans, also known as self-liquidating loans, are loans that are repaid by converting the asset that is used to collateralize the loan into cash. The assets used for this type of loan are typically inventory and work in progress (partly completed jobs). The asset conversion loan is normally considered short-term or **temporary financing** with the asset later being sold on credit terms or for cash that ultimately will be used to repay the loan. Note that these loans are different from **asset-based loans** in that the asset used as collateral is being sold to repay the loan versus being used simply as collateral for the loan. Agricultural loans (see Section 4.5.1) are asset conversion loans.

With **cash flow–based loans,** a bank provides funds that are repaid with the cash flow from the company's operations. With asset-based loans, a bank extends a loan after a specific asset or a combination of assets is pledged as collateral or security (see next section on collateral) to cover the loan. Collateral for this type of loan typically includes inventory, machinery and equipment, leases, furniture and fixtures, or other tangible assets.

4.4.5   Collateral Requirements

Assets pledged by a borrower to secure a loan are called **collateral** (or security). Collateral is used by the bank to safeguard its capital and acts as insurance in case the borrower cannot repay the loan. In the event of default, the bank has the option of accepting the collateral as full or partial repayment of the loan's principal, accrued interest, fees and costs, and expenses. As such, collateral plays a major role in a bank's lending policies—it reduces the potential loss the bank can suffer when a borrower defaults. Collateral can come in many forms. Cash is the most obvious and most secure form of collateral since it is already liquid. Property is the most common form of collateral, but is unpredictable because its value fluctuates with market conditions and the lender may or may not have access to it. Mortgage lending uses real estate as the collateral for the loan against the property (Section 4.5.9).

In the United Kingdom and other countries, a debenture is a loan that is secured by a fixed and floating charge over all of a company's assets and undertakings.[2] Debentures are useful to enable a company to meet its working capital needs by allowing additional borrowing to be secured on its **circulating assets,** particularly in the case where there is not enough security over property alone for a bank to feel comfortable.

EXAMPLE

A company decides to build a new manufacturing plant. To finance the plant, it borrows from Bank C against the property itself (mortgage). To finance the purchase of machines and other equipment used for manufacturing, the company pledges these as collateral.

---

2. Note: In the United States a debenture is defined as an unsecured loan certificate issued by a corporate entity.

The bank also has to consider the changes in the value of the collateral and must ensure that the collateral will retain as much value as possible in the event of default.

The **loan-to-value (LTV) ratio** is a very important indicator for lending and credit risk management. Historically, banks very rarely underwrote loans when the LTV ratio exceeded 75% to 80% unless there was considerable collateral support or the borrower—due to superior financial strength, access to funds, and capital in general—presented limited risk to the lender. Pledges of very high-quality collateral, such as government bonds (e.g., U.S. Treasuries) or deposits with the bank, would often make higher LTV ratio loans possible. LTV serves as a critical benchmark in residential and commercial real estate lending (see Sections 4.5.9 and 4.5.11). Banks and other real estate lenders have long established LTV-based lending rules designed to prevent lending above the 80% LTV threshold that emerged over the years as a basic standard of lending.

Before the global financial crisis, however, financial innovation led to the creation of ingenious mortgage products designed to help individuals who could not afford to purchase a home. One such product was a mortgage with an LTV in excess of 100% and, in certain cases, up to 125%. Essentially, a borrower could purchase a property for USD 300,000 and finance the purchase with a mortgage of USD 360,000 (an LTV ratio of 120%). The USD 60,000 that the borrower received above the purchase price could be used to refurbish or improve the value of the property by adding features such as additional bedrooms, bathrooms, or landscaped outside areas. This approach assumed that home prices never went down, and lenders counted on the overall appreciation of real estate values to result in a declining LTV as a means of properly collateralizing the loan.

Lenders were willing to extend such highly risky, but inventive, mortgages because they allowed borrowers to acquire homes they otherwise could not have afforded. Some lenders went even further and promoted these loans to potential borrowers who were considered to be at high risk of default—termed subprime—due to either previous defaults or foreclosures or otherwise inadequate financial strength. Reaching out to this high-risk segment magnified the innate risk of the high LTV mortgages. Therefore, not only were lenders willing to lend against expected future price appreciation on property, but they were also willing to assume the added risk of a high-risk borrower. When real estate prices started to decline in 2006 in the United States and elsewhere, many borrowers who had used high LTV loans to acquire properties in anticipation of future price appreciation suddenly found the value of their property eroding, causing the LTV to increase to dangerously high levels. Buyers who were forced to sell their homes to cover their mortgage indebtedness were not able to sell their property in a rapidly deteriorating housing market at a price that exceeded their investment—the original purchase price plus value-increasing improvements. In many cases, houses would sell only with significant price concessions.

Since the financial crisis, such high-risk loans have been restricted either by retail regulatory oversight or by increased caution on the part of lenders.

EXAMPLE

In the US during the years 2006 - 2011 during a declining home market, LTV ratios exceeding 100% were not uncommon, and in fact became a major issue for lenders. With homes worth less than the loan, borrowers were starting to walk away from their homes irrespective of their contractual obligations. This problem led to many banks having to increase their provisions for bad debts, with some banks holding material positions in real estate on their balance sheets.

4.4.6   Covenant Requirements

Covenants are one-way commitments or promises by the obligor to honor an obligation. The essential purpose of covenants in the financial marketplace is to protect the lender by attempting to prevent events and/or processes that could result in a potential deterioration in the borrower's financial or business condition.

EXAMPLE

Bank D requires the borrower—a construction company—to build no more than 10 houses on a tract of land. The reason the bank may require such a covenant is if it is concerned that the company would overextend itself and then be unable to repay the loan.

Covenants are a control mechanism and typically restrict or affect the borrower's ability to manage its business. For example, as a condition of loan approval, a lender may require that the borrower agrees to establish a board committee consisting of individuals possessing certain skill sets to oversee a specific project for which a loan is given.

Covenants may also include additional features such as caps on dividend payments to shareholders or limits on owner and management compensation. They may restrict other corporate actions and may prevent a company from disposing of certain assets or require the company to purchase particular assets.

EXAMPLE

After suffering significant losses, Fly-By-Night Airline was forced to arrange a credit facility from its bank that would allow it to meet its cash flow needs. The borrowing (credit) ceiling was set at GBP 350 million, and covenants were agreed to by the airline as a part of the financial deal. The lender required covenants to monitor the progress of the company and ensure that management's decisions would not compromise the value of the lender's investment.

One of the covenants allowed Fly-By-Night to pay dividends to its shareholders only if the company could achieve eight consecutive profitable quarters. Another covenant linked the amount of the credit facility to the airline's assets, which, at the time of the agreement, were valued at GBP 450 million. One year later, the covenant that linked the airline's assets to what it could draw on from the credit facility became an issue when it was determined that the aircraft it owned were worth about GBP 50 million less than originally estimated because of an oversupply of planes in the marketplace. As a result, Fly-By-Night's borrowing line was reduced from the original GBP 350 million to GBP 300 million.

In addition, the airline also reported losses of approximately GBP 10 million each quarter that year, which further reduced the airline's assets, and therefore its borrowing ability, as defined under the covenant, fell even further, to around GBP 260 million. Fly-By-Night's management was unable to secure additional funding to support its operations and was forced to seek financing for its daily operations elsewhere. Given its poor operating history, entering into a new credit facility proved to be difficult. With limited options, Fly-By-Night was eventually acquired by a larger airline.

The previous example shows how covenants are an important tool banks use to limit their counterparty credit risk. It is also crucial that the borrower thoroughly understands the ramifications of the covenants to which the borrower has committed.

4.4.7   Loan Repayment

Loan products are also differentiated by the method of repayment. The stipulated payments that borrowers make to the lenders throughout the loan period—from the day the loan is funded until the day the loan is repaid in full—include both the contractual interest payments and the repayment of the amount borrowed, or the **principal**.

Interest rates on loans can be either fixed or floating. In a **fixed rate loan**, the interest rate charged on the loan does not change during the maturity of the loan. In a **floating rate loan**, the interest charged on the loan is tied to or follows a base rate, set by an independent third party, or an index. The bank will add a charge on top of the base rate or index to earn a profit.

EXAMPLE

On January 1, Bank E extends a floating rate EUR 100,000 loan with a three-month maturity to Centre Corporation. The monthly interest rate is tied to an index and is set on the first day of each month following the issuance of the loan.

The index on January 1 was 1.25%; on February 1, it increased to 1.50%; and by March 1, it was 1.75%. The monthly interest payments on this loan are as follows:

January	EUR 100,000 * 1.25%	=	EUR 1,250
February	EUR 100,000 * 1.50%	=	EUR 1,500
March	EUR 100,000 * 1.75%	=	EUR 1,750

Three general approaches are common for repayment: the sinking-fund amortization, the level amortization, and the balloon payment.

Under **sinking-fund amortization**, the borrower pays a predetermined amount of the principal as well as interest on the outstanding balance of the loan. Initially, the payments on sinking-fund amortization loans are large, but as the principal is reduced, the interest payment accruing on the outstanding balance is reduced. If the loan is a fixed-rate loan, the proportion of the loan repayment that reflects the interest payments will decline over the life of the loan; if it is a floating-rate loan, the interest payments will fluctuate.

Under **level amortization**, the borrower, at each payment date, pays a predetermined amount consisting of principal repayment as well as interest on the outstanding balance of the loan. The payments for a fixed-rate loan do not change over time: the amount to be paid is the same each month, but the proportion of interest payment and principal repayment does change. Initially, the proportion of interest payments is considerably larger than the principal repayment, but over time, the proportion of principal repayment increases. With a floating-rate loan, the interest payments will change as the index or base rate is reset, and the amount to be paid changes, requiring the level payments to change to accommodate the interest rate changes.

The distinguishing feature of **balloon payments**—also called bullet payments—is that there is a large payment at maturity, which usually includes full repayment of the principal. A large balloon payment structure can also include all the accumulated interest on the loan, but the borrower typically pays interest on the outstanding loan periodically and repays the principal fully at maturity. In a floating-rate balloon loan, the payments will be determined by the index and will change over time. Since the loan has not been amortized over the life of the loan, it is imperative that the borrower has the resources to either repay or otherwise refinance the full amount of the loan at maturity date.

4.5   Types of Credit Products

This section explains the most common commercial and retail credit products that combine the key credit product characteristics covered in the previous section. The credit products are listed alphabetically.

4.5.1   Agricultural Loans

Agricultural loans support lending for farming and other agricultural production. Clients borrow money to finance the purchase of fixed assets such as land and equipment, or to cover their cash flow requirements for the growing season until the farm has had time to sell its goods. Facilities are generally medium to long term but can also be short term in nature (to finance seed, feed, and cattle for rearing). The types of loans used may range from asset-based to simple revolving facilities.

EXAMPLE

Bank F provides funds to a farmer for the planting season; the loan is to be repaid after the crop has been harvested and sold. If the farmer delays the sale of crops by storing them in the hope of achieving a higher market price, the bank would most likely offer additional financing to carry the unsold crops (inventory) over the extended term. Farmers also need to replace or expand upon existing equipment. Increasingly sophisticated, and therefore more expensive, new farming machinery is driving demand for longer-term loans, giving the farmer a longer time period to pay off the loan.

4.5.2   Asset-Based or Secured Lending

Asset-based or **secured lending** involves a bank or commercial finance company lending specifically against the borrower's assets. Commercial bankers will generally lend against inventory (also called stock, stock-in-trade, or items for sale) and receivables (factoring). Asset-based loans generally require a company to be able to repay a loan out of operational cash flow. Thus, the value and marketability of the collateral are important. **Asset-based lending** can be extended to both commercial and retail customers.

EXAMPLE

Growth Corporation is a small manufacturer, with almost 60% of its assets in receivables and inventory and an additional 35% in fixed assets. It turns to Bank G to see how it can use its inventory and receivables to raise the financing necessary to support future growth. With sales almost doubling in the last year, Growth Corporation appears to be a strong candidate for asset-based lending.

Rapidly growing companies are likely to experience cash shortages due to cash collections from sales not being fast enough to cover cash requirements for inventory and operating expenses. Repayment of the loan could be tied to the sale of inventory, one of Growth Corporation's largest assets. Asset-based financing would increase the company's interest expense, but it would also provide the cash needed to support sales growth.

4.5.3   Automobile Loans

Automobile or **car loans** come either as **direct automobile loans** that finance the purchase of a car between the bank and the customer, in which the bank secures the loan using the car as collateral, or as **indirect automobile loans,** which are loans arranged between an automobile dealer and the customer. In an indirect automobile loan, the customer applies for a loan through the dealer, who then forwards the borrower's information to the lending bank. In some instances, this type of loan is thought to allow the borrower (automobile purchaser) the ability to obtain a lower interest rate on the loan if the dealer and the bank have an arrangement. The bank may offer a lower interest rate to customers introduced by the dealer.

Automobile loans are predominately retail loan products. However, in some cases, banks provide fleet financing for companies that need to build up a fleet of cars—such as distribution and transportation companies. In these cases, the financing is considered commercial and is usually priced at a lower rate than a retail or individual automobile loan.

EXAMPLE

To increase its distribution network, Growth Corporation decides to acquire a fleet of vehicles that it finances using a program provided by Bank H. The bank lends against the vehicles—they serve as the collateral—and instead of committing a large proportion of its cash reserves, Growth Corporation extends the payments for these cars over several years.

4.5.4   Commercial Paper

Commercial paper refers to very short-term, unsecured notes generally issued by large and financially strong companies. The funds received by the companies are generally used to purchase inventory or manage everyday capital needs. Maturities range from three weeks to nine months, and the bonds usually benefit from a traditional credit line, which is known as a **backstop**—credit support or backup funds that provide a secondary source of repayment. The commercial paper market is primarily used by large, publicly traded corporations, such as Apple, General Electric, or Wal-Mart.

4.5.5   Corporate Bonds

Corporate bonds are debt securities issued by companies and sold to institutional investors such as pension funds or in some cases individuals. Corporate bonds represent a major source of financing, especially for large companies. When corporate bonds are first issued, they are issued in what is called the primary market. But once the bond has been issued and allocations have been made, investors may then trade the bonds in what is called the secondary market. The secondary market brings together buyers and sellers, allowing investors to manage their **investment portfolios** (e.g., selling the bond of a particular company if its operating performance deteriorates). Many corporate bonds are independently rated by credit rating agencies (see Chapter 5). Bonds typically pay a **coupon** on a semiannual basis, and the interest rate may be fixed or floating. The maturity (or tenor) of a corporate bond depends on the credit quality of the issuer and the bond issuer's location.. Corporate bonds in emerging markets tend to be shorter term—three to five years—while those issued in developed markets may range from five to 20 or more years. Corporate bonds with very long-dated maturities, irrespective of where the company is located, are usually reserved for those companies perceived to be of the highest credit quality.

4.5.6   Covered Bonds

Covered bonds are bank issued corporate bonds backed—or covered—by a pool of mortgages or public sector loans and are similar to **asset-backed securities** created in securitization (Section 5.2.3). However, a critical difference is that if the mortgages or loans in the pool underlying the covered bond are unable to repay the covered bondholders, then the covered bondholders have a general claim on the assets of the bank in addition to the bond's assets. This is called "dual recourse." In contrast, holders of securitized bonds have a claim only on the securitized assets that comprise the bond and not on the bank that has arranged the transaction or originated the assets. Covered bonds are always shown on the bank's balance sheet, whereas securitized assets are sometimes kept on the balance sheet but more often off the balance sheet.

4.5.7   Factoring

Factoring is a service that a specialist financial institution or bank offers to help a company meet its cash requirements and reduce its potential credit losses. There are different types of factoring approaches that can be used separately or in combination. All assure the company of earlier receipt of cash payment. The advantage of factoring is that the company is better able to manage its assets, particularly its cash position. The major disadvantage is that the company will not receive the full amount of the money due, as the bank or the organization providing the factoring services charges a percentage of the assets as a fee for providing the service, typically called a **haircut**. The following is a listing of the various types of factoring services available to companies:

- *Maturity factoring.* The bank will effectively take over the company's receivables, work to collect on them, and take a commission from whatever is collected. The company receives the funds when due on the invoice, minus the commission.
- *Finance factoring.* The bank will advance funds to the company using the goods and services to be produced with the funds as collateral.
- *Discount factoring.* The bank will advance funds to the company, usually representing no more than 85% of the receivables, and then take full responsibility for collecting the funds owed.
- *Undisclosed factoring.* The bank will take full responsibility for the invoices due, pay the company up to 85% of that amount, and then appoint the company its agent to collect the invoices. In this arrangement, outsiders do not perceive the company as needing the funding, and it appears as if the company is conducting its business in a normal manner.

Among the various factoring arrangements, different parties are exposed to credit risk if a creditor defaults. If the bank takes over collection on the receivables and assumes full responsibility for the potential losses, then the bank bears the risk of the losses. In this case, the bank has a major incentive to collect the funds.

In the case of maturity and finance factoring, the bank does not assume full responsibility for the potential losses; these losses continue to be borne by the company that sold the receivables to the bank. However, in the case of discount and undisclosed factoring, the bank assumes full responsibility.

In discount and undisclosed factoring, the risk of collecting payment is transferred to the factoring entity. In return, the company selling the receivables ensures its cash flow and eliminates its credit risk at a cost of reducing its potential profitability.

EXAMPLE

Growth Corporation needs to improve its cash flow and quickly raise cash, so it enters into a factoring relationship with Bank I whereby, at the end of each month, it agrees to sell its invoices to the bank (representing approximately USD 250,000). The bank agrees to buy the invoices at a 2% discount (i.e., for each USD 100 in invoices, the bank pays the company USD 98). In addition, the bank is willing to offer immediate financing on the invoices by advancing 85% of the amount owed. By selling the USD 250,000 invoices at a 2% discount, the company receives USD 245,000 million, and the bank advances 85%, or USD 208,250, of the total amount due. The remaining USD 36,750 is paid to the bank for collection services. Selling the invoices improves Growth Corporation's cash flow and, in turn, earns the bank a monthly profit.

4.5.8   Leasing

Leasing allows an individual or a firm (called the **lessee** in leasing transactions) the right to use an asset that it does not own. In exchange for the right to use an asset, the lessee will make regular contractual payments to the lessor. The **lessor** owns the asset and provides the lessee the right to use the asset.

Leases are both retail and commercial products. As a retail product, leases are often used to finance cars and other expensive consumer products. Retail leases offer flexibility over the time during which lease payments may be made and may even offer lower payments that fit with the lessee's ability to pay. For example, the longer the lease term, the lower the payment made on the lease; however, the longer the term on the lease, the more interest payments the lessee will pay.

As a commercial product, leases are widely used to finance expensive equipment. One of the main reasons for this is that leasing does not require the large capital outlay required to purchase the equipment. This approach is especially beneficial to small and/or rapidly growing firms, where access to cash and the availability of capital may be limited.

Many leasing arrangements include a provision that at the end of the lease the lessee has the right, but not the obligation, to purchase the leased asset at a price negotiated or set when the lease is first signed. This option provides considerable flexibility to the lessee, and may be particularly useful to finance the acquisition of equipment that does not become quickly obsolete. In other instances, the lessee at the end of the lease simply returns the equipment to the lessor, who then must determine what to do with the old equipment. The lessee can then negotiate the leasing and/or acquisition of newer equipment.

A lease where the lessee pays a fee for using the equipment and then returns it to the lessor at the end of the lease's term is called an **operating lease,** and a lease that may entail the lessee acquiring the equipment at the end of the term is called a **financing lease.**

EXAMPLE

Growth Corporation is considering purchasing a new telecommunications and computer network infrastructure system for its rapidly growing operations. Currently, it does not have the cash or the capital to purchase the system outright. Additionally, the company is concerned about the speed with which technological advances result in the obsolescence of communications systems such as the one being considered, and the company is not confident that the system will be sufficient to meet its needs over the next several years.

The company faces a choice: It can purchase the communications system outright for USD 150,000 or enter into a lease.

- If the purchase is financed through a loan from Bank J, the bank would mandate interest payments as well as the repayment of the principal, of USD 150,000. Depending on the repayment structure, the company could face monthly payments that include both repayment of the loan and payment of interest on the loan. For a three-year loan at 8% annual interest rate, the monthly payments that include both interest payment and principal repayment are around USD 4,700.

- If the purchase is financed through a lease from Bank J, the bank would mandate payments that include interest payment as well as partial repayment of the principal. Depending on how the lease is structured, the company could face monthly payments and have the option to purchase the equipment at the end of the lease. If the bank mandates the purchase of the equipment at the end of three years for USD 80,000, then the monthly cash flows at an 8% interest rate would be around USD 2,700. Figure 4.5 shows the size of the cash flows for both alternatives.

Since the purchase price of the equipment at the end of the lease will include the delayed repayment of the cost of the system, the lease payments are less than comparable payments on a loan. Lower regular cash payments, coupled with the option of buying the equipment at the end of the lease—further delaying the cash outflows—make leases an attractive alternative for a company such as this.

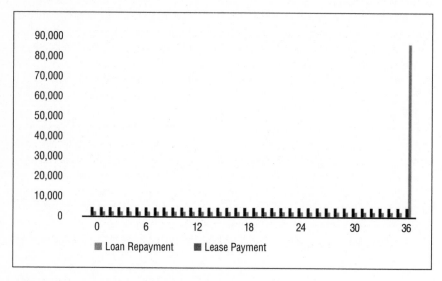

FIGURE 4.5 Loan and Lease Cash Flows (in USD)

Growth Corporation ultimately decides to lease the communications system from Bank J for three years. Growth Corporation will have the use of the system for three years and in return will pay a monthly fee to Bank J. If at the end of the three-year period the communications system does not meet the needs of the company, Growth Corporation can simply give it back to

Bank J and invest in a new system that better fits its needs. Also, if the system has dropped in value, that problem would not be handled by Growth Corporation, but by Bank J, since it is the bank that owns the equipment. In this case leasing offers a very good business solution, given Growth Corporation's limited access to capital and its concerns about the future viability of the communications system.

In general, there is no ready answer to whether a company or a person should purchase or lease. The factors to consider are numerous and highly individual. Even after a careful analysis, the final decision may rest with the company's or individual's simple business judgment, rather than be the result of a financial calculation.

4.5.9 Mortgages

A **mortgage** is a financial arrangement that enables a borrower to acquire a real estate asset and to use the real estate as collateral for the debt. Mortgages are extended to both commercial and retail customers. The real estate being purchased is used as collateral or security for the loan.

Mortgages can be divided into commercial and residential mortgages. **Commercial mortgages** predominantly finance office buildings, factories, and any other type of real estate that is used for business or industrial purposes. The main users of commercial mortgages are businesses that consider this as an advantageous source of financing because of the lower rate the bank offers in exchange for having the real estate as collateral. **Residential mortgages** exclusively finance purchases of residential real estate, such as houses and apartments.

Almost every jurisdiction in the world offers a security interest in real estate that is, or is highly comparable to, a mortgage. Consequently, different jurisdictional areas' legal and procedural rules and commercial conventions determine the extent of mortgage financing.

EXAMPLE

To support its expansion, Growth Corporation's management decides to purchase a new warehouse facility and retail distribution center. Bank K provides a USD 5,000,000 mortgage to finance the purchase. In exchange for the loan, Growth Corporation pledges the warehouse as collateral against the loan. Should Growth Corporation fail to make payments on the mortgage, it may lose the facility to the bank.

4.5.10 Overdraft Facilities

Overdraft facilities allow borrowers to borrow funds in excess of those they have deposited into their checking accounts. Overdraft facilities offer a flexible type of financing, but the interest rate is usually significantly higher than other financing options, making it a relatively expensive option. As deposits are received on the account, they are first applied to any borrowed amount outstanding from the overdraft facility. Once the overdraft is repaid, any remaining funds would then be applied to the borrower's account as a deposit. For the business customer, this can be an efficient (but expensive) way to finance short-term business needs. Overdraft facilities are extended to both commercial and retail customers.

EXAMPLE

Growth Corporation arranges a USD 100,000 overdraft from Bank L to ensure it is able to meet its regular expenses on a timely basis. There is no specific purpose stated other than to satisfy working investment requirements (this may include the financing of additional inventory and **trade receivables**, as well as expense items to be found in the income statement). Growth Corporation can draw down on the USD 100,000 at any time but must first use the funds in its checking account; only then will it be able to access the overdraft facility.

Banks, however, have no real control over whether, when, or how long the funds are used, so they assume a greater risk in providing overdraft facilities than with a conventional loan. This is accentuated when financially stressed borrowers with access to overdraft facilities start to use these facilities as a source of financing, which for a number of reasons increases the bank's exposure as well as credit risk. This is an inherent risk of overdraft facilities.

4.5.11 Home Equity Credit Lines and Home Equity Loans

Popular in the United States, **home equity credit lines** or loans allow homeowners to borrow against the value of their property in a way similar to mortgages (see Section 4.5.9 for a discussion on mortgages). Generally, there are two different types of home equity credits.

Home equity credit loans are personal revolving credit facilities (see Section 4.5.13 on revolving lines of credit) collateralized by the borrower's property. The bank issuing the home equity loan limits the amount of the loan to a certain percentage of the equity the homeowner has in the home. The loan-to-value (LTV) ratio, the ratio of the value of the property to the amount of money borrowed (see Section 4.4.5), is an important analytical tool to determine a home equity loan. The holder may draw down on the home equity loan at any time during its term up to the amount of the line of credit. Interest on the loan is usually tied to a major index such as the U.S. prime rate or **LIBOR** (London Interbank Offered Rate), plus a set interest percentage.

A home equity credit line is different from a mortgage. A home equity credit line allows the homeowner to borrow up to a certain limit that reflects the value of the home and the existing mortgage on the home. These credit lines offer the homeowner the convenience of on-demand financing, essentially tapping the equity built up over time in the home in exchange for cash. Many compare these lines to withdrawing a deposit from the bank.

Home equity credits—both credit lines and loans—can be secured through second mortgages. In case of foreclosure or default, the first mortgage will be repaid first from the disposal of the foreclosed property. After the first mortgage has been satisfied, any remaining funds are allocated to the second mortgage. This makes a loan secured by a second mortgage considerably more risky than a first mortgage. Due to this added risk, many lenders restrict the amount borrowed against home equity to 80% of the property's value, less other existing mortgages. The combination of two or more mortgages encumbering the same property may lead to potential problems for the homeowner if payments are not made on the mortgages. While specific details differ across jurisdictions, in general, nonpayment of a mortgage starts the foreclosure process, which legally transfers the ownership of the property to the lender to satisfy the unpaid balances on the mortgage in question.

4.5.12 Project or Infrastructure Finance

Project or **infrastructure finance** funds long-term infrastructure and industrial projects, usually by combining the resources of several banks or other financial institutions to provide the necessary capital. The project itself provides the security for the loans, and the loans are repaid from the cash flow generated from the project.

EXAMPLE

AcmePower Company produces and sells electricity to customers. Its main power plant is fueled with natural gas. BigGas Company wants to sell its natural gas to AcmePower. The two companies agree to build a pipeline from BigGas Company's gas fields to AcmePower's power plant. The pipeline project is expected to cost hundreds of millions of USD. To finance the project, the two companies turn to a consortium led by Bank M to provide the necessary development funding. The consortium's underwriting analysis concludes that building the pipeline will take several years, with the pipeline's expected life to be several decades. It also finds that the market for AcmePower is expected to increase over the years and that BigGas's natural gas will be an important part of allowing AcmePower to expand and service its growing market. The banking consortium agrees to tie the loan's repayment terms to the revenues generated from the pipeline when it begins operating and to delay starting repayment of the loan until the pipeline is built and operational.

4.5.13   Revolving Lines of Credit

With a **revolving line of credit** the customer is free to borrow funds and pay back when needed, subject to a pre-agreed credit limit. These lines are generally provided to businesses with a temporary or seasonal borrowing requirement (these are considered commercial loans). Credit cards and home equity lines of credit are examples of retail forms of a revolving line of credit.

EXAMPLE

Growth Corporation is quickly expanding and wants to be assured that it has the financing to continue this process. It negotiates a USD 1 million three-year revolving line of credit with Bank N. During the first year, it draws down USD 550,000 of the loan, which it repays, with interest, by the end of the year. Because it has a commitment from the bank for another two years, it can continue to draw down and repay as often as it likes until either it reaches the USD 1 million loan limit, or the three-year maturity period expires. Each time it draws down and repays that amount, the repaid funds become available for borrowing. For example, when Growth Corporation repaid the USD 550,000, the full USD 1 million was again available for it to use.

Credit card lending is an example of revolving consumer loans and is based on preauthorized lines of credit that can be drawn down as the consumer wishes, through either purchases or cash withdrawals. Credit cards, which are used to access the revolving consumer loans, have one of the highest consumer credit growth rates. The rapid increase in credit card debt has been facilitated by the use of EFTPOS (electronic funds transfer at point of sale) and ATMs (automatic teller machines) in many countries.

EXAMPLE

Credit cards are ubiquitous in modern life. Initially, credit cards were used as a convenience by executives to pay for corporate travel. Having access to credit cards reduced the need to carry large amounts of cash and reduced the likelihood that executives would be robbed. Soon, credit cards migrated to wider use and today offer consumers immediate and instant access to funds.

The bank extending a revolving line of credit has no real control over whether, when, or how long the funds are used and assumes a greater risk in providing revolving lines of credit than a conventional loan. When financially stressed borrowers with access to revolving lines of credit start to draw on their lines of credit, the bank's exposure and credit risk increase. This is an inherent risk of revolving lines of credit, and this risk is similar to that of overdraft facilities.

4.5.14 Syndicated Loans

Syndicated loans are loans provided to a borrower through the combined activities of several banks. Banks working together to provide the loan are called a **consortium**. Syndicated loans provide capital to a company when the ability or desire of an individual bank to meet the financing need(s) of the company is insufficient. There are a number of benefits to banks for working as a consortium that include but are not limited to:

- Allowing a bank to participate in a lending transaction where it may not otherwise have the opportunity because of the bank's balance sheet or other constraints
- Allowing a bank to reduce its overall risk exposure for the transaction, as any potential loss will be borne by all the bank consortium members

In a syndicated loan, usually one of the participating banks will act as the agent for the transaction on behalf of all the banks, coordinating their efforts to get the transaction done.

Big Sky Builders wants to build the world's tallest building to house apartments and offices. The estimated cost of the project is EUR 4 billion. Big Sky does not have the capital to construct the building, so it decided to contact its bank, Bank O, for a loan. Bank O analyzes the transaction and considers it a good project with an above-average chance of success, but does not want to finance the project alone. Bank O arranges a loan syndication with six other banks to provide the capital for Big Sky Builders' project. Each of the banks will participate in proportion to the risk of the transaction it is willing to take. For example, Bank P, the leading bank in the consortium, commits to lending EUR 1.5 billion. The other banks in the syndicate provide the remainder of EUR 2.5 billion for the project. The extent of each bank's participation depends on its ability and willingness to contribute. Bank Q is large, so it commits EUR 1 billion, and the remaining five banks provide EUR 300 million each. Because Bank O arranged the consortium, it receives compensation for the managerial work it undertook. Bank O will also earn fees from disbursing payments to the borrower, collecting payments from Big Sky Builders, and distributing payments to the consortium banks.

4.6   The Credit Process

Credit analysis or credit assessment is the process of assessing risk as measured by a borrower's ability to repay the loan. Within the credit analysis or assessment process, analysts also consider possible recovery in the case of default and evaluate the support collateral and other credit support tools that bear on the bank's final decision to develop a creditor relationship. Having assessed the possibility of repayment, the decision to proceed with a loan is then, effectively, a commercial decision: Is the risk of repayment acceptable, given the exposure to the borrower, and do the terms sufficiently mitigate the bank's risk?

Credit assessment is not an exact science, and no one factor, ratio, or other indicator alone determines if a particular loan is a suitable risk. The banking industry has developed numerous methods to help structure the credit process and improve financial results and profitability. Some methods include internal scorecards and facility and borrower ratings; cash flow analysis; computer sensitivity models; and external ratings such as those issued by Moody's Investors Service, Fitch Ratings, and Standard & Poor's. Whatever methods are used, credit analysts must balance all the available information and deliver an objective and well-reasoned opinion of the overall risk associated with a particular loan or credit product. Figure 4.6 shows the steps involved in the credit process.

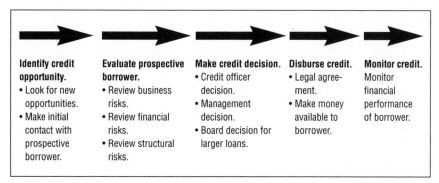

FIGURE 4.6 Steps in the Credit Process

4.6.1 Identifying the Credit Opportunity

In the credit process, the loan officer or relationship manager initiates contact with the potential borrower. In many banks, the chief function of the loan officer is marketing: to seek out new business opportunities and present them for evaluation.

4.6.2 Credit Evaluation—Companies

After a loan officer identifies an opportunity, the officer will gather all required information from the borrower and present it to the credit analyst. The credit analyst then analyzes the creditworthiness of the potential borrower by evaluating the proposed loan type and the potential risks (business risk, financial risk, and structural risk), and then makes a recommendation to proceed with the loan or not and, if so, on what terms (e.g., amount to be lent, the interest rate for the loan, use of collateral or other security, maturity, etc.). The credit analyst's evaluation is often accompanied by qualitative factors, including site visits to the customer, evaluation of the current business and the potential for continued business, the availability of collateral to support the credit, and other relevant information.

The credit analyst collects and reviews information about the potential borrower, including:

- Internal bank records and account performance
- Historical and current financial accounts
- Management accounts and projections

- External ratings of the borrower as provided by independent rating firms such as Dun & Bradstreet or similar (for smaller businesses), and Moody's, Standard & Poor's, or Fitch Ratings (for larger firms)
- Company websites and brochures
- Group structure, ownership, and management information, including information on the board of directors

4.6.3   Credit Decision Making

Often, routine credit decisions are made by the loan officer in conjunction with the credit analyst or by a committee. Loan officers are generally compensated by the number of loans generated. This creates a potential conflict of interest and, therefore, poses a risk when the loan officer makes the loan decision. It is in the interest of a loan officer to underwrite as many loans as possible, which may result in the loan officer ignoring signs that would counter the decision to extend the loan. To guard against this problem, banks implement processes that require all loans to be reviewed by an independent senior manager or credit analyst. Each bank has developed credit decision policies that delineate what types of loans—size, exposure, and business—need to be signed off or ratified by senior management and/or the bank board committee. Generally, the larger and more risky a loan is, the more likely that the loan passes through several levels of the bank's decision-making hierarchy.

A core consideration in credit decision making is the pricing of credit—the fees and interest rates the bank charges the borrower. This interest rate may be determined by a loan pricing model that sets the minimum rate the loan should carry and incorporates various pricing factors. Generally, the greater the risk the bank takes when lending to the particular borrower, the higher the price—interest rate—it charges. The accuracy of the loan pricing model is essential. In many cases, the margin between what banks earn on a loan and its costs associated with analyzing, funding and monitoring the loan is extremely small. If the loan is underpriced, then the bank is unlikely to receive sufficient compensation for the risk it assumed. Overpricing the loan may drive the potential borrower to another lender for the needed funds.

Loan pricing models can be quite complex. Even the simplest of these models take the following factors into consideration:

- The risk rating of the borrower
- The bank's underlying funding cost
- The loan's administrative and processing expenses

The higher the risk of default, the higher the rate the loan should carry. As a result, more risky borrowers pay higher rates than less risky borrowers. In many cases, the bank prices the risk in the loan so that as the fortunes of the borrower improve, the price of the loan declines. Some are also structured to penalize borrowers through higher interest rates if their credit quality declines. This type of pricing structure offers the borrower a strong financial incentive and, when correctly used, reduces the risk to the lender.

- Maturity is the date when the principal of the loan must be paid in full. Generally, the longer the maturity of the loan, the higher the interest rate the loan carries.
- Banks profit on the interest rate differential between their assets (loans made by the bank and securities held by the bank) and their liabilities (deposits in the bank and the bank's own debt) (see Section 2.1.4). Both lending and borrowing interest rates are usually set by the market and can be readily captured by an index. In many cases, banks set the price they charge on loans as a markup to an index. The **prime lending rate**— the rate banks charge their best customers—is an example of a common benchmark used as a base rate for a loan, with a margin added to enhance risk-adjusted profitability.

4.6.4   Credit Disbursement

Once the credit request has been approved, the loan agreement is prepared for signature. The loan agreement is a legal contract between the bank and the borrower and includes a description of undertakings and understandings, such as the principal, the stated interest rate and its calculation, the schedule of payments and repayments, the use of collateral, covenants, and so on. Once the contract is signed, funds are made available to the borrower.

4.6.5   Credit Monitoring

After the credit is underwritten and the funds have been made available to the borrower, the bank continues to monitor the financial performance of the borrower. The contract usually has hard and soft covenants or provisions (Section 4.4.6). An example of a hard covenant is a requirement that the borrower maintains certain key financial ratios throughout the life of the loan. An example of a soft covenant is the requirement that the borrower delivers its financial statements to the lender in a timely manner.

4.7 The Credit Analysis Process

As previously noted, despite the emphasis on quantitative modeling and vigilance, credit analysis is not an exact science, as there is no single formula, ratio, or tool that will determine if a company is an acceptable credit risk. Therefore, it is important to follow some basic principles and practices of good lending as illustrated by the frameworks outlined next.

4.7.1 The Five Cs of Credit

The **Five Cs of Credit** provide a basic framework for good lending, which is particularly relevant to small business lending and to the small and medium enterprise (SME) sector. Bank financing is the primary option for small or recently established firms because these firms do not have access to the financial markets—to issue stocks or bonds—in the same way large, established companies with an established financial history do. Figure 4.7 depicts a schematic of the Five Cs.

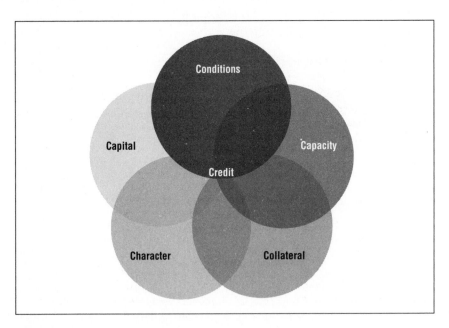

FIGURE 4.7 The Five Cs of Credit

The Five Cs of Credit: No. 1—Character

In analyzing **character,** the bank seeks to answer the following question: What is the reputation of the company's management in the industry and in the greater business community?

Bankers will always look to lend money to those with immaculate credentials and references. Credit analysts should determine the quality of management's relationship with its employees as well as with its customers and how these relationships are managed through the company's obligations. These characteristics afford insight into management's character.

EXAMPLE

The three owners of Good Impressions Inc., a well-established business, have approached Bank R for credit. To assess the character of the company's management, the bank analyst would necessarily rely on his or her impressions from interviews of the company's management at the company's premises. The high quality of the products, the generally appealing appearance of the premises, and the good relationship management has with its employees all suggest positive character traits. However, it is subsequently discovered that the company has repeatedly overdrawn its bank accounts and regularly paid invoices late. The latter two issues raise the bank analyst's concerns, and the analyst includes this information in the risk analysis. The result of the analysis is a conclusion that doing business with the company would be riskier than originally thought.

Associated with character is management's ability to administer the company's future. Indicators of management capabilities include the level of engagement in day-to-day operations, flexibility in embracing current technologies, understanding prevailing industry trends, and, most importantly, its ability to contain costs and seek efficiencies.

The Five Cs of Credit: No. 2—Capital

When analyzing **capital,** the bank seeks to answer the following question: How is the company currently financed? The relationship between equity and debt is critical, and the higher the level of equity relative to debt, the healthier the company will appear from a credit risk perspective. It also reveals the financial commitment of the company's owners and indicates how much they have put themselves at risk. Particularly in small and medium-sized businesses where the owners' wealth is very closely linked to the fortunes of the business, it is not only the company's financial statements that should receive scrutiny, but also the owners' personal financial standing, assets, and credit quality.

EXAMPLE

In further analyzing Good Impressions Inc., the analyst at Bank R notes that the three owners of the company have invested USD 250,000 each of their own money into the business—a positive factor. However, the analyst also finds out that collectively the three owners have personally borrowed approximately USD 14 million using their ownership interest in the company as collateral for those loans and are now seeking an additional USD 2 million loan from the bank to support the company's ongoing operations. After taking into account the owners' cumulative capital invested (USD 750,000) in view of their current borrowings (USD 14 million) using their interest in the company as collateral, the analyst can easily come to the conclusion that the risks of lending the USD 2 million to the company are too great to move forward with the loan application.

Should a borrower default, a lender loses more than just the funded obligation or capital (principal plus interest). For instance, reputational risk is important because banks have a responsibility to shareholders and are entrusted by depositors to conduct business in a responsible and profitable manner. Significant defaults also use up a disproportionate amount of managerial time, diverting scarce resources that the bank's management would prefer to use in business development to manage complex negotiations with the borrowers and other lenders. Defaults could also negatively affect potential borrowers who would be less likely to use a bank with a reputation for foreclosing and forcing customers out of business during tough economic times.

The Five Cs of Credit: No. 3—Conditions

When analyzing **conditions**, the bank seeks to answer the following questions: What is the economic situation in the country or countries in which a company operates, and what are the economic conditions of the industry in which it operates?

The credit analyst must determine what outside risks might cause the company's financial condition to deteriorate.

EXAMPLE

In a further review of Good Impressions Inc., the analyst at Bank R discovers that the largest single market for its products is Malaysia, where more than 80% of its sales are made, bringing in nearly 90% of its profits. A business that generates income and cash flow in a currency different from the lender introduces considerable risk. One risk is the potential decline in the value of the Malaysian ringgit relative to Good Impressions Inc.'s home currency, the U.S. dollar. If Good Impressions Inc. does not reduce—or hedge—this risk, the cost of the loan to the company could ultimately be much more than anticipated, perhaps making it so costly that the company would default on either its interest payments or repayment of the loan principal. The analyst making the lending decision must examine the economic conditions under which the company operates (in this case Malaysia and the United States) to determine the potential not only for the direct counterparty credit risk that Bank R would assume with the company, but also for the risks associated with the company's dealing in a foreign currency and in that particular country.

The Five Cs of Credit: No. 4—Capacity

When analyzing **capacity,** the bank seeks to answer the following questions: How much cash does the company generate, and are the cash flows sustainable, repeatable, and predictable? The credit analyst must evaluate the company's ability to generate sufficient cash flows as well as management's ability to run its operations efficiently and effectively. The credit analyst works from cash flow projections to determine the debt or exposure a company can incur.

EXAMPLE

The bank analyst at Bank R, evaluating Good Impressions Inc., will investigate the sources and uses of the company's income to determine if the company will generate enough funds to repay the loan as well as cover the company's ongoing expenses. The analyst will usually build a quantitative model to attempt to predict the income-generating capacity of Good Impressions. In particular, it is important for the analyst to identify the factors that can easily and rapidly deteriorate, those that would have a negative impact on the future of the business's cash flow, and the business itself. Good capacity to generate cash is one of the first quantitative factors to analyze and probably the most important one.

Financing needs differ from company to company and can be affected by timing, economic conditions, and business circumstances. For some companies, cash flow will follow a stable path, although subject to some predictable seasonal deviations. Such companies will in general find it easier to negotiate a **permanent financing** facility, as the bank will be better able to judge the company's creditworthiness based on historical information. However, other businesses may experience material cash flow volatility, especially where sales and costs are unevenly matched. In this case, cash flows are more difficult, but not necessarily impossible, to project. Business models with random cash flow volatility will likely find it difficult to establish a permanent financing facility with a bank because of the risk associated with their cash flows. In these cases, various combinations of temporary financing are usually suggested to the borrower. It is critical to understand a company's cash flow volatility since it may impact the amount or type of financing facility offered by the bank. However, a key factor in the loan decision remains the adequacy and predictability of the cash flows.

Banks distinguish between seasonal, cyclical, and permanent financing. Seasonal financing and cyclical financing are considered to be temporary financing.

- **Seasonal financing** is usually provided to pay for a substantial increase in inventory and work in progress. For example, seasonal loans may be sought by a swimsuit manufacturer limited to summer sales or for the purchase of goods by retailers and buildup of inventory by toy manufacturers prior to a peak selling time (e.g., major holidays). Seasonal credit needs are usually quite predictable and follow well-established patterns.
- **Cyclical financing** is similar to seasonal financing, except that the cycle is generally a business cycle rather than a more predictable change in seasons, and repayment is more dependent on random changes in the long-term macroeconomic environment in which the business operates. Since banks typically consider cyclical needs to be more difficult to predict, they consider cyclical lending to be riskier than seasonal lending. An example of a cyclical loan is a dedicated loan that supports the development and production of a new product with the financing provided incrementally throughout the product cycle.
- **Permanent financing** is usually long-term financing of 15 years or more and is provided in the form of a mortgage (e.g., an individual borrowing to purchase a home with a 30-year mortgage) or bond issuance for a company. Permanent financing is often used for investment in buildings or other types of real estate projects.

Figure 4.8 shows the relationship between asset growth and financing needs. There is a strong relationship between sales and assets and the financing of the assets. As a company's sales grow, its assets also increase and the company will need to finance this increase in assets, either through its own liquidity or from external financing. Part of the increase in assets reflects a permanent increase and includes the new factories, facilities, machinery, and production infrastructure a company has created. It also reflects the increasing level of inventory the company has and accounts receivable that the company collected. A company will usually seek to finance most of its permanent increase in assets through medium- and long-term financing, although these needs may also be met through equity financing.

Variations in sales and assets are characteristically cyclical or seasonal. Cyclical asset changes reflect the fluctuating fortunes of companies throughout the business cycle. As the economy goes through cycles—expansion, contraction, and recession—a company's sales or revenues and its assets are affected. During expansion, sales and assets increase and borrowing needs rise. Conversely, during contraction or recession, sales drop and the need for assets declines, thereby reducing a company's financing needs. To meet such changes in the demand for capital, many banks provide medium-term financing that roughly corresponds to three- to five-year business cycles.

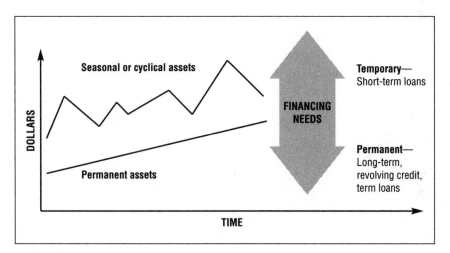

FIGURE 4.8 Asset Growth and Financing

Seasonal changes in assets have shorter-term effects on sales, revenues, and assets. These financing needs are met with short-term loans that have maturities of around one year.

Assessing the quality of the borrower's assets is also part of capacity analysis and is particularly useful when the company has significant trade receivables that can be used for asset-based lending or converted into cash after collecting on the receivables.

Trade receivables result from credit sales, where the company extends credit to its customers to purchase its products or services in anticipation of payment. In many small and medium-sized businesses, a listing of all debtors and the aging of all invoices due from each provides important information of not only what is due and owed to the company, but also the company's ability to collect on its debts, implement its policies, and assess whether a buyer is truly creditworthy. In economic downturns, assets could be increasing as customers either use more trade financing or slow their payments. Therefore, asset growth (mentioned earlier as a good thing) needs to be critically analyzed and good asset growth differentiated from bad asset growth.

Credit analysts also evaluate a company's **inventory**. Inventory has to be of salable quality reflective of the company's intention to continue business, and, should there be a default, the company's assets—including its inventory—should be of satisfactory quality to pay debts when sold.

The analyst must also assess the borrower's **liquidity**. A business that has enough cash is more likely to pay what it owes when payment is due. Illiquid businesses, which can include businesses that are profitable but lack sufficient cash flows, present potential credit risks.

The Five Cs of Credit: No. 5—Collateral

When analyzing **collateral,** the bank seeks to answer the following question: In the event the borrower cannot honor its obligations, what assets does it have that the bank can lay claim to in order to satisfy the debt? Section 4.4.5 discusses the role of collateral.

The analyst should confirm that the company's primary source of loan repayment, cash flow or assets are, and will be, sufficient to meet all its obligations as they fall due. But a lender has a responsibility to its shareholders and depositors to ensure a secondary or complementary source of repayment. The secondary source of repayment is other assets owned by the borrower (most commonly referred to as collateral). In the event of a **default**, the bank should be able to assume control over these assets and organize an orderly sale to satisfy the loan's terms. In loans to lower-rated companies, where the risk of default is greater, the company will typically pledge all of its assets as collateral.

EXAMPLE

In the loan evaluation process, the bank and Good Impressions Inc. discuss what collateral appropriately covers the terms of the loan. The bank and Good Impressions decide that in exchange for the credit to finance the purchase of machinery, some of the company's machinery will be pledged as collateral. At the time the loan is approved, the bank's loan officer is confident that, should Good Impressions default on the loan, the bank could recover the loan by selling the collateral to other companies. Several months after the loan is granted, however, the business starts to worsen. Within a year, Good Impressions falls on hard times and is unable to repay its loan, and the bank repossesses the collateral. However, the analyst failed to take into account the fact that Good Impressions had several local and international competitors. So, when the bank tries to sell the repossessed machinery, there are no buyers. Eventually, the bank has no choice but to write off the loan, taking a loss on the transaction. The lesson: Always investigate the future value of the assets offered as collateral should they have to be sold in a hurry or in an unfavorable market. In such circumstances, the assets usually will not have much value, if any.

4.7.2   The Credit Analysis Path

The Five Cs of Credit just outlined provide a sound framework for analyzing small businesses, and the principles hold equally true for lending to larger companies. However, the credit analysis path described next provides an alternative framework for a more detailed credit analysis or for lending to larger or more complex companies.

The credit analysis path depicted in Figure 4.9 requires the analysis of the key business, financial, and structural risks of the credit proposal.

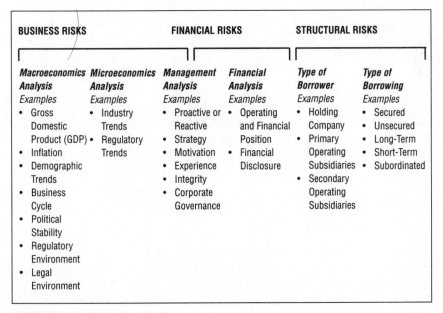

FIGURE 4.9 Credit Analysis Path

In the credit analysis path, the focus is to analyze the various risks that may impact the borrower. The overall analysis encompasses business—or macroeconomic—risks, financial—or microeconomic—risks, and structural risks. These risk areas overlap, as the factors that impact them are closely related and interdependent. The three areas of analysis are separated into several general layers, or components, and are shown in Figure 4.10.

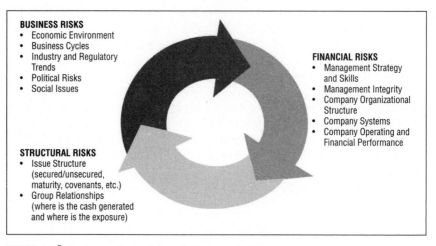

FIGURE 4.10 Business, Financial, and Structural Risks

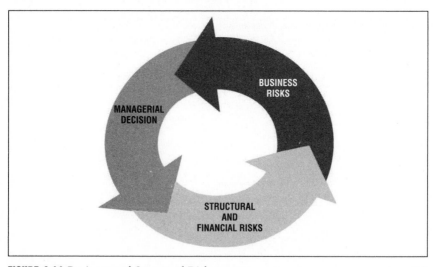

FIGURE 4.11 Business and Structural Risks

The credit analysis path shows that the company's decision-making process will directly impact the risks the organization takes, and that management's decisions are influenced by the industry's macroeconomic and microeconomic trends. The relationship between business risks and structural risks is illustrated in Figure 4.11.

4.7.3 Business or Macroeconomic Risks

Business—or macroeconomic—risks reflect both the bank's and the borrower's respective environments. Analysis of the bank's operating environment helps the banks' management determine the appropriate loan allocation. Banks usually select loans where there is an appropriate risk/return trade-off. A requirement for higher returns on loans necessitates an appetite for elevated exposure to credit default risks. In other words, considering the risks associated with a credit proposal, does the return offered by the credit provide appropriate compensation to the bank?

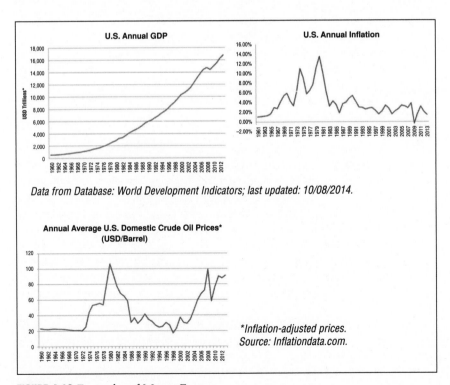

FIGURE 4.12 Examples of Macro Factors

Analysis of the borrower's operating environment reflects a market risk assessment. After reviewing the borrower's overall market (i.e., macroeconomic drivers, competitive factors, etc.), the credit analyst is able to determine the borrower's challenges and opportunities. Figure 4.12 shows some of the business, or macroeconomic, factors that analysts consider. These macroeconomic factors are trends that impact all industries, companies, and firms. There are numerous macro factors; typically, they are likely to include long-term trends:

- Level of economic activity—measured by changes in the global GDP
- Global changes in inflation (the decline in the purchasing power of money)
- Worldwide price of energy (the price of crude oil, an important commodity that, when refined, powers machinery, etc.)

EXAMPLE

Bank S evaluated a complex credit proposal submitted by XYZ Corporation. The loan officer's credit analysis detailed that XYZ Corporation was a manufacturer of complex and expensive machinery used in manufacturing. It was a global business, but approximately 80% of its sales were generated in several developing countries. Moreover, many of the countries to which XYZ was most exposed were suffering from high interest rates and consequentially unfavorable exchange rates. These adverse economic conditions were expected to continue over the coming years.

The loan officer cited concerns that XYZ's strategy to maintain its sales growth was to provide cheap financing—using low-interest borrowings from developed countries—to its customers as a means of making their products more attractive than those of their competitors. Furthermore, XYZ's management appeared unconcerned by weakening exchange rates, instead maintaining that the additional earnings generated by these sales would be sufficiently profitable to repay the loans even if exchange rates were to deteriorate further.

In contrast to its sales, XYZ's production was concentrated in a few developed countries that had low interest rates and strong economic fundamentals. However, cost inflation in these countries was causing XYZ's production costs to increase to the point where its products were becoming too expensive and were impairing its ability to retain existing customers or win new orders.

The component costs of the goods it produced were overly sensitive to negative exchange rate changes (it had overlooked the macroeconomic impact of both the interest rate and exchange rate changes together). As a result, XYZ's management would be unable to control a deteriorating long-term outlook, increasing its risk of loss, and possible failure.

The loan officer recognized the weaknesses in XYZ's strategy: There was a lack of focus on mitigating the long-term negatives along with dealing with the short-term impact of the increase in interest rates. As a consequence and on the advice of the loan officer, Bank S did not extend credit to XYZ Corporation.

An analyst's evaluation of the business includes how the client's management team deals with competition. There are a number of ways to analyze competitive forces. It is vitally important to identify and understand how competitive forces can influence the company's risk drivers, which, in turn, will impact its liquidity and solvency. These competitive forces can include government regulation, changes in technology and technological advances, and the environment, all areas where matters can and do change dramatically and quite swiftly. Such changes can prove very costly and can either open up or close down markets.

EXAMPLE

Disruption to a market by the introduction of a substitute product or technological advance has the potential to destroy existing business models. The printed yellow pages industry is one such example.

The yellow pages businesses typically benefited from either monopolistic or oligopolistic market positions in SME advertising. Retention rates were typically very high, leading to lucrative profit margins and strong cash generation with the added benefit of little capital expenditure requirements. As such, these businesses lent themselves well to the model of utilizing future operating cash flows to pay down debt taken on to support and grow the business.

Unfortunately, many yellow pages publishers expanded using debt-funded acquisitions and found themselves overleveraged with falling sales and weakening margins as the global financial crisis unfolded and their customers cut advertising spending. This trend was exacerbated by increasing Internet usage—first on computers and then on smartphones or other devices—which removed the need for paper-based directories. Internet listings were more convenient for users and a cheaper and increasingly more effective advertising medium for SMEs. Directory companies such as Yell, Pages Jaune, R.H. Donnelley, and others found themselves having to restructure their debt or worse—**file for administration** or **Chapter 11 bankruptcy**, resulting in severe losses to their creditors.

4.7.4   Financial or Microeconomic Risks

The financial risk assessment reviews the company's management and especially how it handles the company's operating and financial environment. Credit analysts primarily focus on management strategies and their ability to manage the business in conjunction with an in-depth analysis of the company's historical, current, and pro forma financial statements. The overall assessment and results are then compared to the company's peers. Figure 4.13 shows several financial, or micro, risks that analysis would typically consider. This information reflects comparative factors in a distinct part of the economy affecting only a handful of businesses and could include production, capacity, and sales growth over several years. The following graphs show some micro factors from the top five companies in the steel industry:

- Revenue growth (measured by annual sales growth between 2009 and 2013)
- Annual operating margin, 2009–2013
- Crude steel production measured in millions of tons in 2013
- Average annual capital expenditure/depreciation (2009–2013)

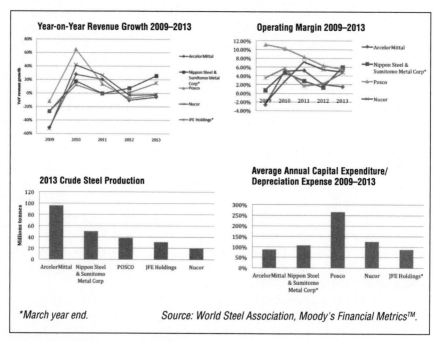

*March year end.   Source: World Steel Association, Moody's Financial Metrics™.

FIGURE 4.13 Microeconomic Factors

It is during analysis of financial, or micro, risks that the credit analysis focuses on the company's credit facilities and how those would relate to the company's future growth prospects, and whether they will require a substantial investment in order to sustain future growth. All these factors allow for the relative comparison of the different companies active in the industry. In financial risk analysis, the company's operating conditions are important, and the lender must also assess third-party credit and trade references to determine if the company has solid relationships—including payment relationships. This process involves looking at the business partners of the potential borrower to obtain a holistic assessment about how its business relationships are being managed.

Most banks use credit-scoring models in their credit assessment process for retail credit products such as mortgages and credit card applications, and many use models for corporate credit products also. These models are tools that help predict the probability a loan might default. The **probability of default** is communicated as a **credit score**. The credit score relates the strength of each borrower relative to all borrowers. The higher the prospective borrower's credit score, the less the chance of defaulting. Credit-scoring models may use more than 100 different factors in their calculation. The models follow a consistent approach developed from years of experience. Thus, models reduce the cost of credit evaluation and increase the speed and accuracy in the credit decision-making process. They also improve on consistency and accuracy because the results are more standardized and can be compared against the results of other prospective borrowers. This allows managers to better assess the true quality of their credit loan portfolios.

More advanced assessment models are used to predict the probability of default for large corporate borrowers, which may also include quantitative analytics such as data on the price and volatility of the company's publicly traded shares and bonds.

4.7.5 Structural Risk

In this assessment, the credit analyst must understand the legal structure of the borrower, the various subsidiaries, intracompany transactions, and ownership and partnership linkages. All are analyzed to better gauge the true financial and potential economic exposure embedded in the proposed credit structure.

A simple framework for ensuring that the above information is collected should include answers to the following:

- Who—or which entity—is the borrower?
- Where—or in which entity—are the assets located?
- Who—or which entity—generates the cash flows of the business?
- Are there any intercompany linkages such as guarantees or significant related-party transactions?

Covenants, collateral, and pricing are critical in mitigating structural weaknesses. Structural enhancements such as guarantees (e.g., from a better capitalized parent or government or export trade body) should also be considered in the event of the loan being structurally subordinated to other creditors. Debt that is lent to an entity that is not the generator of the company's cash flows (i.e., a holding company) is said to be structurally subordinated to debt located at the company's operating subsidiaries, with the expectation that the claims of the subsidiary's creditors would be satisfied first in the event of a corporate default.

4.7.6 SWOT Analysis

A **SWOT analysis** is a useful tool for outlining the key issues that emerge from the analysis of the business, financial, and structural risks as detailed previously. SWOT stands for strengths, weaknesses, opportunities, and threats, and is illustrated in Figure 4.14.

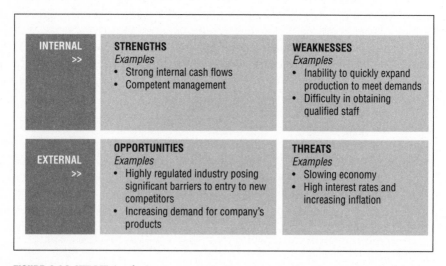

FIGURE 4.14 SWOT Analysis

A SWOT analysis is used to obtain an objective assessment of a company's internal strengths and weaknesses and the opportunities and threats presented by the external business environment in which the company operates. This information, coupled with an in-depth analysis of the company's current financial condition, allows for an objective and forward-looking determination of the potential borrower's creditworthiness.

4.8   Information Sources

There are many different sources of information used in the credit assessment process. A key source is the company's annual report and its audited financial statements. The company's financial statements are usually audited or independently evaluated by outside accounting experts who review the company's financial information to certify it is within a certain country's Generally Accepted Accounting Principles (GAAP) or within International Financial Reporting Standards (IFRS). Accounting principles/standards are part of a company's corporate governance procedures and ensure that all financial information is presented in a uniform way, thus allowing for greater ease of review by the credit analyst and other interested parties.

It is important to note that producing and subsequently providing this information to the credit analyst does not prevent companies from engaging in questionable or fraudulent activities. However, the information does serve as a check on the company's management, and an analysis of the audited financial statements provides a reasonable, though not complete, level of comfort to potential investors and bankers alike.

Note, however, that in most countries small businesses are not required to have their financial statements independently audited, and credit analysts will have to form their own judgment on the accuracy of the accounts.

Credit Risk Management

Chapter 5 takes a deeper look at how banks manage credit risk, starting with portfolio risks and credit exposure. Credit portfolio modeling is complex, and while some banks do build their own models, most use commercially available models; Section 5.3 provides a brief description of such tools. Credit monitoring was described in Chapter 4 in Section 4.6 on the credit process, but it features here again along with early warning signals, given their important role in the management of the portfolio credit risk profile. Section 5.8 explains remedial management and provides a framework of next steps in the event of distressed loans. The final section discusses the Basel III Accord's guidelines to measure and manage credit risk.

Chapter Outline

5.10 Practical Implications of the Default Process

5.11 Credit Risk and the Basel Accords

Key Learning Points

- **Portfolio management** involves determining the contents and the structure of the portfolio, monitoring its performance, making any changes, and deciding which assets to acquire and which assets to divest.

- Key portfolio risks are concentration risk, correlation risk, and contagion risk.

- Banks use various techniques to reduce the overall risk of their loan portfolios.

- Effective credit monitoring is an important part of the credit process and enables a bank to recognize changes in the creditworthiness of credits within the portfolio and to minimize migration risk.

- Credit rating agencies provide independent credit assessments, which can be used to independently verify a counterparty's creditworthiness and also to monitor credit.

- Market-derived ratings can identify where market sentiment may differ from an internal or external credit rating and may indicate a warning signal to a portfolio manager.

- Portfolio managers should learn to recognize the signals of increasing default risk.

- Portfolio managers should have an effective framework to limit potential losses.

- A portfolio manager needs a process of practical actions to manage the documentation and liquidation of assets in a controlled and prudent manner.

- Banks consider the legal, loan losses, and reputational risks of default.

- The Basel II Accord provides three primary approaches to measure the capital a bank has to hold against its loan portfolio: the Standardized, the Foundation Internal Ratings-Based, and the Advanced Internal Ratings-Based approaches.

CREDIT RISK MANAGEMENT

5.1   Portfolio Management

An **investment portfolio** held by a bank or an individual contains various investments that typically include stocks (equity), bonds, loans, financial derivatives (options, futures, etc.), investible commodities such as gold or platinum, real estate, or similar assets of value. The **investor** is the entity that holds the portfolio and may be a company, a bank, or an individual. **Portfolio management** involves determining the contents and the structure of the portfolio, monitoring its performance, making any changes, and deciding which assets to acquire and which assets to divest. Portfolio managers weigh both the expected risk and return characteristics of individual assets, the performance of the entire portfolio, and the investor's financial objectives in order to find an optimal combination of investments that provides the highest level of return for any given level of risk.

Banks use several approaches to measure portfolio performance and reduce credit losses. The approaches utilize quantitative assessment tools to predict the likelihood of a default and estimate the impact of the default.

5.1.1   Portfolio Management Terminology

- *Probability of default (PD)*. The likelihood that the borrower will default. PD is normally represented as a percentage.
- *Exposure at default (EAD)*. The total exposure the lender could have at the time of default. EAD is influenced by debt type, asset type, recourse, assignment terms, and payment delays. EAD is normally represented as an amount of money.
- *Recovery rate (RR)*. The assumption of the fraction of the asset value that will likely be recovered after a default. RR is normally represented as a percentage.
- *Loss given default (LGD)*. The actual loss the lender suffers in the wake of a default: a function of $(1 - RR)$. LGD is normally represented as a percentage. Gross LGD is used for bonds, whereas Blanco LGD is used for loans where bankers include the effects of collateral, if any.
- *Expected loss (EL)*. The loss given default multiplied by the probability of default multiplied by exposure at default.

EXAMPLE

In 2012, XYZ Corporation arranged a facility to borrow EUR 10 million from Bank A for a five-year period at an annual interest rate of 7%. After two years, XYZ had repaid EUR 4 million, but still owed the bank EUR 6 million plus EUR 300,000 in interest. Bank A made the following assessment about XYZ Corporation in January 2014:

- If XYZ Corporation defaulted in 2014, Bank A's exposure at default (EAD) would be EUR 6.3 million: EUR 6 million in principal and EUR 300,000 in interest.
- Bank A is assuming a recovery rate (RR) in the event of a default in 2014 of 90% or EUR 5.67 million (90% of EUR 6.3 million).
- The actual loss Bank A would suffer in default (LGD) would be (1 − 0.9), or 10% of the actual exposure. Applied to the EAD of EUR 6,300,000, this gives EUR 630,000.
- The probability that XYZ Corporation would default during 2014 was 1%.
- Therefore, the expected loss (EL) is EUR 630,000 * 1% = EUR 6,300.

In addition to finding the best combination of investments that delivers the optimal return for the allowable risk profile of the portfolio, the portfolio manager must also seek to minimize specific portfolio risks, namely concentration and default correlation risks.

5.1.2   Concentration Risk

An inherent risk in lending is that a bank can become skilled in lending to, for example, one geographical area or to one industry (e.g., shipping) and will then tend to focus the majority of its underwriting efforts on that area or sector. This can lead to a highly concentrated, or not suitably diversified, credit portfolio, which will increase the bank's exposure to potential losses in the event of deterioration in that particular area or industry.

A diversified loan portfolio will be diversified by geography, industry type, demographic profile, or other indicators and should reduce the impact to the bank of a severe market disruption. Although development of a core competency in lending to a specific market or industry might lead to concentration risks, its effects might be mitigated somewhat by the possibility that the bank's expertise in that specific sector helps it avoid the weakest credits.

Reducing concentration risk may require active management of a bank's loan portfolio. For example, a bank might sell some of its loans to third parties, thereby removing those risks from its banking book. Or it might introduce diversification into its portfolio by buying nonsimilar loans from other banks.

EXAMPLE

Bank B, a small rural bank, has made approximately 60% of its loans to area businesses that are all active in or closely related to coal mining. Most of the mining-related companies are well established with very good credit histories. Because Bank B is closely related to the fortunes of the coal mining industry, bank management decided to reduce its concentration risk and implemented the following plan:

- First, it sold some of its highest-quality loans to banks in a different part of the country. Many of those banks do not have exposure to the mining industry and, interested in their own diversification, wanted to increase their credit exposure to that industry segment.
- Second, it purchased technology-related loans from other banks to increase its exposure to businesses unrelated to mining.
- Third, it started to offer different types of loans. Previously, the bank had not offered any residential mortgage loans. By offering residential mortgages through its correspondent banks to finance purchases outside the bank's home business area, it expanded its loan portfolio to retail customers and reduced its exposure to its home market.
- Fourth, it started to offer loans to businesses in industries it had previously avoided due to weaker credit quality. The new loans, while carrying more risk exposure, effectively helped diversify the risks in its portfolio and increased the portfolio's return—it would earn a higher return on those loans because of their riskier nature.

5.1.3   Default Correlation Risk

Default correlation risk refers to the likelihood that the default of one borrower is affected by the default of another borrower.

An example of positive correlation would be two companies that are not part of the same corporate or group structure but are trade creditors to each other. An example of negative correlation could be two competitors, the default of one of which takes capacity out of the market, possibly providing some pricing or volume improvement for the remaining company.

The key drivers for default correlation risk are the macroeconomic climate in general and specific industry factors such as timing with respect to an industry cycle.

EXAMPLE

Utility firms are typically considered to have low credit risk, given their regulated and often monopolistic market positions that result in highly predictable cash generation. Nevertheless, utilities often exhibit high default correlation to the sovereign's or country's macroeconomic condition. In the event of recession, a government might impose higher taxes on industries such as utilities, and at the same time the utilities might find themselves with lower sales due to reduced manufacturing output or increased austerity on the part of their customers.

5.1.4   Contagion Risk

Contagion risk refers to a ripple effect of defaults that may occur in a particular industry or country or between countries where the default of one borrower—or counterparty—has a negative impact on other borrowers. The sudden default of Lehman Brothers in the United States in September 2008 sparked a liquidity crisis due to fears of counterparty risk among financial institutions. Another example of contagion risk could be the higher likelihood of default of other firms in the event of the default of a major customer or supplier. An example of macroeconomic factors driving contagion risk include the European sovereign debt crisis starting in 2009, which led to a crisis in investor confidence that affected all borrowers through increased borrowing costs or in some instances sharply reduced access to capital.

5.2   Techniques to Reduce Portfolio Risk

5.2.1   Syndication

The loan syndication process (Section 4.5.14) provides a useful mechanism to enable a bank that has developed strong relationships or expertise in a particular market or industry sector to reduce its exposure by syndicating portions of the loan to other financial institutions. The other syndication members, for their part, may be looking to diversify their own portfolio holdings by adding transactions that meet their risk-adjusted investment criteria.

5.2.2   Whole Loan Sales

Whole loan sales enable a bank to reduce its exposure by selling a specific loan to another financial institution. An example would be the sale of a mortgage from one bank to another. The loan originator—the bank that arranged the original mortgage—may not want to have such a long-dated loan in its portfolio. Selling the loan will allow the originator to remove it from its books and receive funds in return for the loan, providing it with capital to make other loans.

EXAMPLE

The mandate of the U.S. government-sponsored enterprise (GSE) Fannie Mae is to facilitate liquidity for the national mortgage market. Fannie Mae borrows at low rates and then buys whole loans or pools and packages of mortgages from financial institutions. Fannie Mae then repackages these loans into mortgage-backed securities.

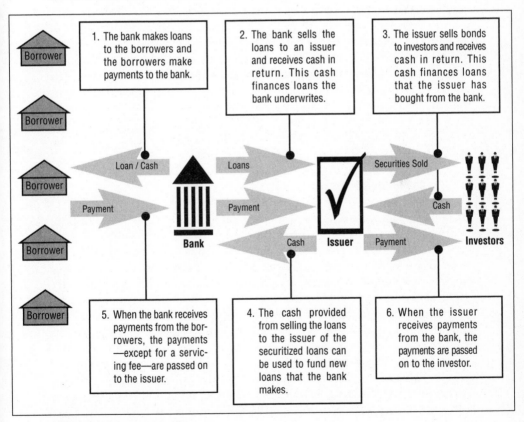

FIGURE 5.1 Securitization Process

From the originator's perspective, **securitizing** such credit products not only reduces potentially high levels of risk exposure, including concentration risk (Section 5.1.2), but the removal of such assets from its books also reduces the bank's capital requirements. Furthermore, as with whole loan sales, the securitization process earns proceeds for the bank from which it can generate new loans or conduct other business.

5.2.3   Securitization

Typically, the bank will transfer or sell the securitized loans to an issuer that may be affiliated with the bank. The issuer then bundles the assets (mortgages, credit card receivables, etc.) and sells securities backed by them. The payments on the pool of loans are used to pay off the securities. If the transfer or sale of securities is without recourse (that is, the selling bank is not liable to pay compensation to the buyer in case the loan defaults), this process then decreases the bank's default risk. Figure 5.1 illustrates a securitization process.

Another technique banks employ to reduce the effects of credit losses is to pool or bundle together assets such as mortgages or credit card receivables, and sell them to other financial institutions or into the capital markets. This is known as **securitization**. A pool of loans is more diversified than one individual loan—since not all loans will be expected to default simultaneously—and is therefore more attractive to investors seeking to achieve portfolio diversification. Many types of loan products can be securitized as long as they are associated with a cash flow.

5.2.4   Credit Default Swaps

A credit default swap (CDS) is a form of **credit derivative**. A CDS contract is similar to insurance—it is often referred to as default protection—and involves the transfer of credit risk between two parties. The buyer of the CDS (who may already own the underlying credit exposure—for instance, a specific reference bond) essentially sells or transfers its default risk to the seller of the CDS contract.

Through the use of the CDS market, a portfolio manager is therefore able to limit losses in the event of a default without actually having to eliminate the exposure by outright sale. This is also referred to as a hedge. If a negative credit event occurs—say a default on a specific corporate bond—then the seller of the CDS will have to deliver the value of the principal and interest on that bond to the CDS buyer. If no credit event occurs, the CDS seller receives a periodic fee from the CDS buyer over the life of the bond.

5.3   Portfolio Credit Risk Models

Portfolio credit risk models are used to quantify credit risk exposures by modeling factors that impact the credit of an asset and the value of the credit portfolio. Such factors include default risk—nonpayment of principal or interest; recovery risk—changing the value or recoverability of collateral; spread risk—changing the price of a credit without a change in the underlying rating; and migration risk—changing internal or external ratings. Portfolio credit risk models are complex because they model the likelihood as well as the potential value effect of a credit event. The outcome is usually articulated in a range of probability distributions of future potential losses.

Some banks develop their own proprietary models, and these have the advantage of customization to allow for more complex instruments or portfolios, the inclusion of region-specific correlation factors, and comprehensive stress-testing scenarios. However, given the complexity of such models and therefore the need for specialized expertise, most banks rely on one of a number of commercially available models.

There are a number of vendors that offer portfolio credit models that contain various underlying calculations, providing the user with a number of different options from which to choose. For example, models may include calculations around options pricing theory, asset volatility, different pricing frameworks, the ability to provide user-estimated recovery rates, interest rate simulations, default modeling, and other pricing theories.

Information from these models assists a bank in establishing credit limits across geographies, industries, and asset classes.

5.4   Credit Monitoring

Effective credit monitoring is an important part of the credit process. A robust monitoring process enables a bank to recognize credit deterioration in the portfolio and to take appropriate actions. Any decrease in headroom under a loan covenant package should be captured and highlighted by the credit monitoring team.

Migration risk occurs when the creditworthiness of a single credit or a whole portfolio begins to change—either through internal or external ratings—thus changing the risk profile of the portfolio. The critical nature of credit monitoring in protecting a bank's credit portfolios is enshrined in regulatory requirements such as Basel III.

5.5   Credit Rating Agencies

In some ways **credit rating agencies (CRAs)** play a role similar to that of lenders in that they both evaluate the creditworthiness of various borrowers. The clear difference between them, however, is the fact that CRAs do not lend money.

CRAs evaluate the creditworthiness of borrowers and publicly traded debt, and assign credit ratings to borrowers and the debt instruments they issue. Ratings are intended to provide an independent assessment of a borrower's general creditworthiness based on a wide array of risk factors. Ratings on individual debt instruments incorporate the creditworthiness of the issuer with relevant instrument-specific risk factors.

The ratings range from the highest credit rating (typically AAA or Aaa indicates a very high ability to repay the loan) to the lowest credit rating (typically C or D suggests the bond is about to default or is in fact in default). **Investment grade credit ratings** are generally from AAA/Aaa to BBB/Baa, and **non–investment grade credit ratings** generally fall in the BB/Ba to C/D range. Figure 5.2 contains a detailed description of the various ratings.

Letter ratings—such as AAA, BB, or C—are effectively letter summary representations of material information including quantitative, qualitative, and legal data about the borrower, and they communicate the results of the ratings process to the public.

Figure 5.2 shows the different grades (ratings) used by Moody's, Fitch, and Standard & Poor's. The plus and minus signs following each grade are modifiers indicating relative differences between various issues within the same rating category. A positive or plus sign indicates that the issue is better than the average issue in that rating category. A negative or minus sign indicates that the issue is worse than the average issue in that rating category. These ratings may change as the issuer's credit quality changes. Ratings can also be qualified by rating "watches" and "outlooks" that could provide some forward-looking guidance for a credit analyst.

Credit analysis by CRAs is similar to the credit analysis process described in Section 4.7. CRAs examine the borrower's fundamental and vital characteristics, including the borrower's industry, prospects for growth, risks, threats, and weaknesses.

Rating agencies evaluate different criteria for different borrower types. For instance, when rating sovereign borrowers, rating agencies analyze a country's ability and willingness to repay a debt, and consider relevant and substantive information on the economic and fiscal strength of the country, the stability and viability of the political and social system, and susceptibility to event risk.

	Description	Fitch & S&P		Moody's		Explanation
Investment grade	Highest credit quality —lowest risk	AAA		Aaa		Exceptionally strong capacity for timely payment of financial commitments, which is highly unlikely to be adversely affected by foreseeable events.
	Very high credit quality —low risk	AA	AA+ AA AA–	Aa	Aa 1 Aa 2 Aa 3	Very strong capacity for timely payment of financial commitments, which is not significantly vulnerable to foreseeable events.
	High credit quality —low risk	A	A+ A A–	A	A 1 A 2 A 3	Strong capacity for timely payment of financial commitments, which may be more vulnerable to changes in circumspectness/economic conditions.
	Good credit quality —medium risk	BBB	BBB+ BBB BBB–	Baa	Baa 1 Baa 2 Baa 3	Adequate capacity for timely payment of financial commitments, but adverse changes in circumstances/economic conditions are more likely to impair this capacity.
Speculative grade	Speculative —high risk	BB	BB+ BB BB–	Ba	Ba 1 Ba 2 Ba 3	Possibility of credit risk developing, particularly due to adverse economic change over time. Business/financial alternatives may be available to allow financial commitments to be met.
	Highly speculative —high risk	B	B+ B B–	B	B 1 B 2 B 3	Significant credit risk with a limited margin of safety. Financial commitments are currently being met; however, continued payments are contingent upon a sustained, favorable business and economic environment.
	High default risk —higher risk	CCC		Caa		Default is a real possibility. Capacity for meeting financial commitments is solely reliant upon sustained, favorable business or economic developments.
	Probable default —very high risk	CC		Ca		Default of some kind appears probable, and the issue is vulnerable to worsening in the issuer's conditions.
	Likely default —highest risk	C		C		Default is imminent and highly vulnerable to any worsening in the issuer's conditions.
Default	In default	D				Defaulted issue. Payment of interest and repayment of principal have not been made on the due date, or it is highly uncertain that such payment will be made, or the issuer enters into bankruptcy, reorganization, or similar procedure.

FIGURE 5.2 Credit Ratings and Their Interpretations

The review of sovereigns also includes their ability to deal with internal as well as global economic, political, interest rate, and commodity changes.

The sovereign rating is often—though not always—the highest rating in a given country. However, it is important to note that although corporates or financial institutions may be rated higher than their sovereign, the existence of strong linkages and default correlation factors between them means the ratings may not be more than a few notches apart.

Like corporations or financial institutions, sovereigns can expect their debt creditworthiness to be subject to upgrades as well as downgrades. Indeed, the European sovereign crisis resulted in four European countries— Portugal, Ireland, Greece, and Cyprus—being downgraded to non-investment grade, with the latter two defaulting in 2012 and 2013, respectively. Indeed, over the years, there have been a number of sovereign debt-related defaults, and in fact some sovereigns have defaulted more than once. Figure 5.3 provides a timeline of some recent sovereign defaults.

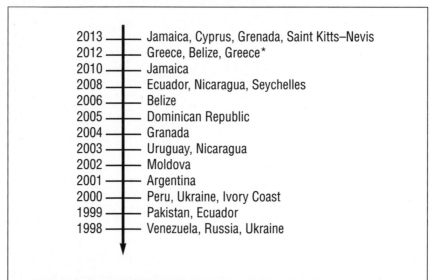

2013	Jamaica, Cyprus, Grenada, Saint Kitts–Nevis
2012	Greece, Belize, Greece*
2010	Jamaica
2008	Ecuador, Nicaragua, Seychelles
2006	Belize
2005	Dominican Republic
2004	Granada
2003	Uruguay, Nicaragua
2002	Moldova
2001	Argentina
2000	Peru, Ukraine, Ivory Coast
1999	Pakistan, Ecuador
1998	Venezuela, Russia, Ukraine

*Greece bought back EUR 31.9 billion of debt, including previously restructured Greek government bonds, for EUR 11.29 billion, implying a net present value loss of over 60%, and Moody's clarified this debt buyback as a distressed exchange and hence a second default.

Source: Moody's Investors Service, "Sovereign Default and Recovery Rates, 1983–2013," April 11, 2014.

FIGURE 5.3 Timeline of Sovereign Defaults—1998 to 2014

In the United States, CRAs registered with the Securities and Exchange Commission (SEC) as nationally recognized statistical rating organizations (**NRSROs**) are regulated by the Dodd-Frank Wall Street Reform and Consumer Protection Act and overseen by the Office of Credit Ratings at the SEC, which holds CRAs accountable for their actions. In August 2014, 10 CRAs, including the three largest CRAs—Moody's Investors Service, Standard & Poor's, and Fitch Group)—were registered NRSROs. Figure 5.4 lists the NRSROs as of August 2014.

Early in 2011, the European Union established the European Securities and Markets Authority (ESMA), which is charged, inter alia, with regulating CRAs relative to EU standards.

To access financial markets, borrowers typically seek a rating from either one of the major international NRSROs (Moody's Investors Service, Standard & Poor's, Fitch Group, DBRS) or from a regional CRA. Examples of regional or local CRAs include Malaysian Rating Corporation Berhad, Rus-Rating in Russia, and Dagong Global Credit in China. RusRating and Dagong have also formed a joint venture with Egan-Jones of the United States called Universal Credit Rating Group.

Most CRAs are paid a fee by the rated borrower; this is known as the issuer-pays model. Of the NRSROs only two—Egan-Jones and Kroll—operate the investor-pays model. Both models are controversial and are subject to ongoing scrutiny, particularly the issuer-pays model due to the inherent conflict of interest it presents.

- A.M. Best Company, Inc.
- Egan-Jones Ratings Co.
- HR Ratings de Mexico, SA de CV
- Kroll Bond Rating Agency, Ltd
- Morningstar Credit Ratings, LLC

- DBRS, Inc.
- Fitch, Inc.
- Japan Credit Rating Agency, Ltd
- Moody's Investors Service, Inc.
- Standard & Poor's Ratings Services

FIGURE 5.4 NRSROs as of August 2014

In addition to credit ratings, CRAs also assign recovery ratings to individual instruments issued by low-rated firms (i.e., firms with high probability to default on their debt). This is an attempt by the CRAs to quantify recovery risk: the value a lender to these low-rated firms might expect to recoup on an obligation in the event of default. This approach effectively separates default risk from recovery risk.

5.6   Alternative Credit Risk Assessment Tools

Also referred to as market-derived ratings, these tools typically take market information such as bond prices or spreads, CDS prices, and equity perform-ance and translate them into market-implied ratings. Both Moody's Investors Service and S&P offer products that provide this (Moody's Market Implied Ratings and S&P's Market Derived Signals).

One of the objectives of these market-derived ratings is to identify where market sentiment may differ from an internal or external credit rating and may therefore be useful as an early warning signal to the portfolio manager. While these tools may be valuable for analyzing the market's perception of credit risk, the signals are often very volatile, reverse frequently, and cannot be relied on as predictors of an issuer's credit rating change. In addition, it is important to note that while a credit rating is based on a longer-term view of creditworthiness, market-derived signals are calculated based on daily trading data, and therefore the results may be skewed during periods lacking sufficient market activity.

5.7   Early Warning Signals

The purpose of early warning signals is to alert a bank of deteriorating credit risk or, in other words, of increasing default risk. A robust credit monitoring process should capture signals such as reporting of past-due loans. Early warning signals may come from macroeconomic stress, company-specific issues, or industry-wide characteristics. A checklist covering these and other issues provides a useful starting point in setting a standard of vigilance throughout the credit process. A well-crafted loan policy will set out what actions should follow upon the recognition of an early warning signal. It is important to remember that early protection actions provide the best chance to improve a bank's position, to reduce exposures to risk, and to exit deteri-orating relationships.

5.7.1   Accounting Issues

Accounting standards are reasonably prescriptive on many topics, but they allow some flexibility on topics such as revenue or cost recognition, one-off items, and the use of off-balance-sheet financing such as operating leases. The use of more aggressive structures by a company is not necessarily an early warning signal in itself, but it may well reflect a more risky business profile than what might have been originally expected. Early recognition of revenues—for example, booking the revenues from a five-year contract up front rather than over the life of the contract—will make the sales figure for that year higher than it would have been. If a company capitalizes operating costs (i.e., recognizing them as a capital expense rather than an expense in the income statement), profits from operations and capital assets will all be higher that year than they otherwise would have been.

EXAMPLE

In September 2014, Tesco, one of the world's largest retailers, issued a profits warning as a result of the overstatement of profits by GBP 250 million. As a result, its market value fell by GBP 2 million. The cause of the overstatement had been an accounting irregularity whereby revenue from promotional payments from suppliers was booked before being earned. It is an accepted accounting principle that revenues and costs should be recognized in the same accounting period.

5.7.2   Company Issues

Generally speaking, there are certain behaviors or characteristics that, like the accounting choices above, tend to reflect riskier companies. The strong growth trends of highly acquisitive companies may mask lackluster or even stagnating sales in the core business. Above-market returns—whether in earnings per share or in profit margins—may point to more aggressive business strategies or an unsustainable position. Complex organizational structures may be the product of geographically diverse operations or industries such as shipping where complicated funding structures are common. However, as noted in Section 4.7.5, it is important that structural risks are fully understood.

5.7.3   Management Issues

"Lending is not based primarily on money or property. No sir, the first thing is character." This quotation, attributed to J. P. Morgan, is relevant here in considering characteristics of company owners or managers that may alert a bank to potential problems. Allegations of unethical behavior, weak corporate governance, evidence of a lavish lifestyle, and lack of transparency with respect to financial or operational disclosure are all examples of possible early warning signals that a bank may encounter difficulties with a company.

5.7.4   Liquidity Issues

The one overriding objective in assessing credit risk is to evaluate whether a loan will be serviced and repaid in cash on schedule. Both liquidity (does the company have the internal sources of cash to service and repay the debt when due?) and solvency (does the company have access to alternative sources of cash flow, e.g., through asset sales or capital contributions to meet its interest and repayment schedules?) are fundamental issues that must be addressed early in the credit process. Through the credit monitoring process, careful attention should be paid to a company's liquidity position. Increased use of overdrafts, lateness in paying trade creditors, and decreasing cash balances may all signal a weakening liquidity position and a potentially increased probability of default.

5.7.5   Industry/Peers

Certain industries or sectors develop reputations for corruption or unethical practices. When uncovered, such actions may result in large fines, tarnished reputations, and loss of public confidence. This in turn may lead to a ratings downgrade and or a widening of a company's credit spreads, the difference between the yield on (risk-free) government bonds and the company's bonds of similar structure, both of which will have implications for the risk profile of the portfolio.

EXAMPLE

In September 2014, a Chinese court found a local subsidiary of UK pharmaceutical company GlaxoSmithKline plc (GSK) guilty of bribery, and fined the company RMB 3 billion (approximately USD 492 million)—at that time, the largest fine imposed by a Chinese court. The Chinese authorities accused GSK of bribing doctors and hospital officials to use GSK products. The case highlights the potential dangers to a company negotiating in countries where what is acceptable with regard to local practices may be unclear, and where a change in government may result in local laws being enforced more rigorously than had been the case in the past.

5.8   Remedial Management

Workout units are specialist teams that manage a bank's problem assets. Executed well, their efforts can avoid painful losses to a bank or even generate substantial profits, depending on the situation. Their remit is to ensure that the bank maintains a security interest in the assets and collateral and to actively pursue various legal options for recovery. However, there may be a trade-off between the actual cost of executing recovery and the ultimate value of the expected recovery.

One of the first analyses that the workout team needs to undertake is a root cause analysis (RCA) to determine the cause of the corporate distress. The output from the RCA should inform next steps: For example, a fast-growing company facing a liquidity crisis may need to factor receivables to alleviate its working capital problems, whereas a bank may need to accelerate a loan review process where fraud has been identified.

The earlier a bank identifies a weakening credit situation, the better its chances of reducing its exposure and limiting potential losses. Furthermore, once a problem has been identified, a bank needs a set of standard operating procedures to follow. One simple but effective framework is to consider the three Rs—namely:

- *Repayment.* Focus on the ability of the borrower to meet its interest and debt repayment schedule. Is there adequate liquidity from either internal or external sources?
- *Restructure.* Can the business be turned around to improve its position (e.g., a change of management or focus on core operations)?
- *Reschedule.* If the problem is the debt structure (e.g., unrealistic covenants or an overly burdensome repayment schedule), rather than a fundamental business problem, a bank should consider options to reschedule the loan. By taking proactive steps, a bank avoids potential loan losses and retains and protects a customer relationship.

5.9   Managing Default

If however, the situation cannot be remedied and the borrower does indeed default or is expected to default, there are a number of steps that need to be followed.

5.9.1   Documentation and Perfection

The first step is to check documentation regarding the collateral and confirm the bank's position.

- Check that no tax or judgment **liens** are in place—such liens will be the result of nonpayment of taxes or a lawsuit by another creditor for an unpaid debt.
- Ensure that liens on any special collateral such as patents or intellectual property rights have been perfected. Perfecting a lien is the legal process that establishes a lender's priority vis-à-vis other creditors. Typically it requires filing a record with the appropriate legal authority (e.g., the land records office). (This should have been done as a matter of course when the loan was originated.)
- Confirm the lender's rights under the appropriate legal jurisdiction. This will obviously require consultation with local legal counsel.

5.9.2 Review Collateral

It may be necessary to undertake site inspections, view equipment, and conduct a review of accounts receivable to ascertain the condition of the collateral and to estimate the value of the business as a going concern.

5.9.3 Review the Borrower's Plans

Consider the borrower's financial and business plans. In light of the current situation, are the plans reasonable or achievable? Is the incumbent management team staying or being replaced? What is the time frame for any expected turnaround?

5.9.4 Exercise Prudence

Consider forbearance if possible. Forbearance is a legal agreement between a borrower and a lender whereby the lender agrees to delay enforcement in order to allow the borrower additional time to meet a new repayment plan or schedule. The lender should make all commercially reasonable efforts to ensure that the borrower fully understands and acknowledges the implications of default.

5.9.5 Additional Credit Support

Revisit avenues of potential support that may previously have been denied (e.g., parent guarantees, letters of credit, equity injections, etc.).

5.9.6   Intercreditor Agreements

If an intercreditor agreement exists, review for any protections that may be afforded to the bank such as the ability to block payments or to enforce a standstill period, where the parties agree to take no action for a defined period of time; this may enable senior lenders to exercise remedies.

5.10   Practical Implications of the Default Process

Enforcement is usually the action of last resort and is to be avoided if at all possible due to:

- *Legal issues.* The high cost of legal actions may outweigh the actual possible recovery amount, and there could be an issue of lender liability. Lender liability refers to the possibility that the lender may legally be construed as having made improper use of acceleration or demand notices, failed to provide adequate notice to exercise remedies, or stalled the process with unwarranted requirements.
- *Loan loss reserves.* The bank will need to take a provision for the expected loss and will need to allocate additional capital as a result.
- *Reputation risks.* Even where a bank's credit analysis processes are extremely thorough, the reality is that some loans will go bad. However, the risk to a bank of losing its good name with customers, counterparties, its own shareholders or bondholders, and the regulators is another factor to consider when deciding whether to pursue a creditor.

5.11   Credit Risk and the Basel Accords

A key purpose of the Basel I Accord was to determine the regulatory capital for credit risk using a simple credit rating approach (see Section 3.3.3). Basel II expanded on Basel I and, under Pillar 1, required banks to calculate bank regulatory capital requirements for market and operational risk as well as for credit risk.

To calculate regulatory capital for credit risk, Basel II recommended that banks select one of three approaches (described below) that would determine their credit risk capital requirements or regulatory capital for credit risk. The three approaches—the Standardized Approach, the Foundation Internal Ratings-Based Approach, and the Advanced Internal Ratings-Based Approach—

differ not only in their methodology but also in the level of sophistication required of the bank's credit risk processes that support the calculations.

Basel III makes a number of changes to the rules and guidelines imposed by Basel II.

5.11.1 The Standardized Approach

The **Standardized Approach** evolved from the Basel I credit risk guidelines. In contrast to simple, fixed-risk weightings (a percentage that reflects the risk of a certain asset) assigned to asset types by Basel I, Basel II recognized that risk weightings for certain asset types, specifically loans to sovereigns (countries), corporations, and banks needed to be more flexible. Basel II therefore recommended that risk ratings be determined by the external credit ratings assigned to the borrower.

Basel II allowed available public credit ratings from some credit rating agencies to be incorporated into the Standardized Approach. It also allowed risk weights to reflect public credit ratings issued by rating agencies meeting certain standards. In many countries, the usefulness of public credit ratings is limited, because these countries have a relatively small number of public credit ratings available. This effectively limits the application of public credit ratings to government and large corporate credits (mainly bonds and other publicly traded debt), some banks, and certain government agencies that are large borrowers.

Under Basel III, the Standardized Approach has been updated to include risks associated with correlation trading and market risks associated with securitization, resecuritization, and credit derivative exposures. Correlation trading is a strategy in which the investor gets exposure to the average correlation of an index, rather than just individual shares.

5.11.2 Internal Ratings-Based Approaches

The Basel II Accord's two other approaches for calculating minimum credit risks permit banks to use internally generated credit ratings, provided the ratings are developed on sound financial logic and assigned appropriately. **Internal Ratings-Based** (IRB) approaches share several features but are implemented differently. They are referred to as:

- Foundation IRB Approach
- Advanced IRB Approach

5.11.3 Common Features to IRB Approaches

Both IRB approaches differ from the Standardized Approach by relying on a bank's own information to determine the regulatory minimum capital requirement. The bank's internal processes to assess the creditworthiness of borrowers generate the information to create credit models. Credit models build on common risk factors such as PD, LGD, EAD (see full definitions in Section 5.1.1), as well as the effective maturity (M).

The difference between the Foundation IRB Approach and the Advanced IRB Approach lies in how the bank's internal models forecast the different risk factors:

- Under the **Foundation IRB Approach,** a bank is required to estimate only the borrower's probability of default. To verify the PD, the bank must use at least five years of relevant loan performance data from various borrowers. The other risk factors of the credit model (listed above) are provided and determined by the bank's supervisor.
- Under the **Advanced IRB Approach,** a bank estimates all components of the model. At least seven years of historical data must be used for verification purposes. For all but large corporate exposures, a standard two and a half years may be assumed for maturity, subject to supervisor agreement.

With the Advanced IRB Approach, the bank must estimate all credit risk model components, including data collection, data management, and modeling techniques. The process demands a more sophisticated, and more costly, commitment by the bank.

5.11.4 Minimum Requirements for IRB Approaches

The core requirement is that the bank's complex credit risk measurement, management, and monitoring system should be a ratings-based system. A ratings-based system should accurately capture the inherent riskiness of each loan in the bank's loan portfolio and differentiate between individual loan exposures by correctly assessing the inherent riskiness of each loan relative to all the other loans. All ratings systems build on complex mathematical and statistical models that predict the PD, LGD, and EAD of each loan. Due to the complexity of these models, the sophisticated mathematical methodologies, and the detailed inputs and processes, the model must be well documented so that the regulators can easily validate the model by replicating its results.

For a ratings-based system to differentiate risk meaningfully, provide reasonably accurate and consistent estimates of risk, and support lending decisions, the Basel Accord requires banks to develop a ratings system with a minimum of eight probability of default rating grades. These should range from very low probability of default (such as the AAA or Aaa ratings or similar ratings by rating agencies) to very high probability of default (such as the C ratings or similar ratings by rating agencies). The criteria for rating definitions should be both plausible and intuitive and result in a meaningful differentiation of risk that is clear both to the employees of the bank and to auditors, regulators, and supervisors. Eight grades are the minimum. Within these eight grades, the system should be able to differentiate even further and become more granular to capture the different shades of credit risk.

The Basel Accord also requires the ratings-based system to be dynamic. A dynamic rating system should immediately reflect up-to-date and relevant borrower information and reassess the credit rating of the loan based on the new information. The rating system should also provide information that allows for continuous reassessment and performance evaluation. Both the bank and the supervisors should be able to evaluate how well the system performs by comparing realized PDs, LGDs, and EADs against those predicted by the model and comparing how well the credit ratings predict defaults and potential changes, such as credit migration over time (e.g., a highly rated credit weakens and drops to a lower rung on the credit ladder—perhaps from a AAA to an A rating—or a weak credit strengthens and becomes more highly rated). Evaluating the performance of the system should lead the bank's risk control unit to modify and improve the system continually. Ongoing monitoring by management and internal auditors is also required.

Ultimately, the ratings should help the bank evaluate each credit exposure (loan), assign each an appropriate rating, and allow for an evaluation of the performance of each exposure relative to all the others the bank has underwritten or is underwriting. They also help to more easily manage the credit risk of the banking book, provide an avenue to quantify exposure, and accurately assess the bank's regulatory minimum capital for credit risk. Moreover, to determine the regulatory capital that the bank should hold against its credit risks, the bank's internally developed ratings-based system should also be used for stress testing. The system must be able to capture not only the deterioration of credit quality of one specific borrower or a group of similar borrowers, but also the effects of economic and industry downturns, market risk events, and weak liquidity conditions. For a bank to adopt either of the IRB approaches, it must first demonstrate to its banking supervisory agency that it has been using a broad IRB-compliant system for at least three years.

A bank complying with the Foundation IRB Approach must have been estimating the probability of default for at least three years, while banks using the Advanced IRB Approach must also have been estimating their loss given default and exposure at default for at least three years.

5.11.5 Basel III Rules Regarding Securitization

During the global financial crisis of 2007–2009, it became apparent that banks did not always understand the risks involved in a securitization, nor were the quality and content of the underlying assets always clear. In addition, there was an overreliance on the rating agencies. This resulted in investors failing to perform their own due diligence and ask questions about the riskiness of the securities they were purchasing. To ensure that banks carry out their own due diligence, Basel III standards require them to meet specific operational criteria. Banks must, on an ongoing basis:

- Have a comprehensive understanding of the risk characteristics of their individual securitization exposures.
- Be able to access performance information on the underlying pools in a timely manner.
- Have a thorough understanding of all structural features of a securitization transaction that would materially impact the performance of the bank's exposures to the transaction.

If these criteria are met by a bank, it may use the risk weights specified in the Basel II securitization framework. Regulators have also been introducing rules to require banks to hold a proportion of the securities that they have sold to investors on their own balance sheets. This is known as having "skin in the game"—if the securities that the bank has structured and sold perform badly, then the bank will suffer along with the investors, providing the bank with an increased, and practical incentive to take extra care in offering these types of transactions to customers.

CHAPTER 6

Market Risk

T his chapter introduces market risk: the risk of losses on a bank's positions in financial assets or instruments due to adverse movements in market prices. Banks assume market risk because they trade as principals, risking their own capital, and hold positions in financial instruments. Failure to manage market risk can have significant direct effects on a bank's profitability and reputation. After exploring the sources of market risk and the trading instruments banks use in their trading operations, this chapter covers various market risk measurement and management considerations, including the approaches outlined in the Market Risk Amendment to the Basel I Accord.

Chapter Outline
6.1 Introduction to Market Risk
6.2 Basics of Financial Instruments
6.3 Trading
6.4 Market Risk Measurement and Management
6.5 Market Risk Regulation

Key Learning Points
- Market risk arises from the trading activities of banks and is a consequence of movements in market prices.
- Market risk affects all financial instruments and can be general market risk, which reflects the market movements of all comparable financial instruments, or a specific risk, which reflects the risk that an individual financial instrument moves in day-to-day trading.
- The basic financial instruments are currencies, equities, bonds, loans, commodities, and derivatives. Banks can take either a **long** or a **short position** in financial instruments.
- The four different types of market risks are equity risk (equities), interest rate risk (bonds and loans), commodities risk (commodities), and exchange rate risk (currencies). A fifth type of market risk is credit price risk (credit). This risk should not be confused with outright credit/default risk, as discussed in the previous chapter. Credit price risk is the risk that the price or value of a **credit position** will change on a day-to-day basis. To reduce market risk and the impact of market risk, banks can hedge their risk exposures.
- **Value-at-risk** is a methodology that yields an estimate of potential losses over a certain time period at a specific confidence interval. The estimate this process creates quantifies some of the risk the bank takes.
- The Basel II Accord provides two alternative processes for market risk measurement: the Standardized Approach and the **Internal Models Approach**.

MARKET RISK

6.1   Introduction to Market Risk

Market risk has two components: a general market risk that affects similar financial assets or financial markets and a specific risk that affects only individual financial assets. **General market risk or systematic risk** is the risk of an adverse movement in market prices that is applied across a range of assets.[1] Specific risk is the risk of an adverse movement in the price of an individual asset due to factors that apply only to that security or issuer and is not related to the general movement of the markets.

---

1. Systematic risk should not be confused with systemic risk (see Section 3.1.3), the risk that the financial system may collapse due to a catastrophe event.

EXAMPLE

When the price of shares issued by Andromeda Corporation declines, the cause of the decline can be due to either an event specific to Andromeda Corporation or an event that impacts the entire market. If the share price declines due to a general worsening of the economic outlook, which significantly depresses a wide range of different share prices in the stock markets, the cause of the decline is attributed to general market risk. However, if the share price declines because of a decline in the business of Andromeda Corporation, then the decline is a result of a specific risk that impacts only the company and its shares.

6.2   Basics of Financial Instruments

Basic financial assets are also called financial products or financial instruments. Banks use financial instruments for trading purposes and to hedge their financial activities. These financial instruments are considered "plain-vanilla" products because they are relatively simple and do not have complex features.

For instance, common stocks and corporate bonds are both considered plain-vanilla financial instruments.

Banks trade both plain-vanilla and complex products, with many complex products that can be broken down into two or more simpler products. New financial instruments usually remix already existing, plain-vanilla instruments into more complex structures, requiring sophisticated pricing and legal structures.

6.2.1   Currencies

Most countries (or groups of countries) have their own currency (i.e., money). They control its supply through their central bank or a similar institution. For example, the dollar is the currency of the United States, the renminbi is the currency of China, and the euro is the currency of the countries of the Economic and Monetary Union of the European Union, or Eurozone.

In foreign exchange transactions, one currency is exchanged for another currency. Banking institutions engage in foreign exchange transactions for a wide variety of reasons. For example, they may be conducting operations outside their home country, requiring them to have cash on hand in a foreign currency to fulfill their obligations in that country.

Exchange rates reflect the relative value of one currency in relation to another currency. For instance, if the exchange rate between the GBP (British pound) and the USD (United States dollar) is 1.50, this means that for each GBP you receive, you must pay USD 1.50. It also means that for each USD you receive, you must pay GBP 0.67 (= 1.5/1.0).

EXAMPLE

On January 10, Bank G purchases GBP 1,000,000 for USD—it sells USD to buy GBP. The exchange rate between the GBP and the USD is 1.50; for each GBP, the bank has to pay USD 1.50. To purchase GBP 1,000,000, Bank G must sell USD 1,500,000.

It is common to refer to the different exchange rates of one currency against other currencies in terms of spot exchange rates or spot cross rates. Spot exchange rates are so-called when a currency is quoted against the home currency (e.g., USD in the United States), whereas spot cross rates denote any currency quoted against any other where the home currency is not involved. Figure 6.1 shows the major exchange rates from September 2014. The table expresses the value of six major currencies against each other and is interpreted as follows: For one unit of the column currency, you must pay the amount shown in the appropriate row. So, on that date, one GBP was worth USD 1.6388, CAD 1.7931, EUR 1.2683, and so on. This implies that one USD was worth GBP 0.6102 (= 1.0/1.6388), CAD was worth GBP 0.5576 (= 1.0/1.7931), and one EUR was worth GBP 0.7884 (= 1.0/1.2683).

	USD	GBP	CAD	EUR	JPY	HKD
USD		1.6388	0.9139	1.2921	0.0092	0.129
GBP	0.6102		0.5576	0.7884	0.0056	0.0787
CAD	1.0942	1.7931		1.4138	0.01	0.1411
EUR	0.7739	1.2683	0.7072		0.0071	0.0998
JPY	108.64	178.03	99.28	140.37		14.01
HKD	7.7514	12.703	7.084	10.016	0.0713	

FIGURE 6.1 Foreign Exchange Rates from September 2014

There are multiple factors that influence exchange rates. Key factors include inflation rates, political changes and instability, and currency regimes. Currency regimes determine to what extent a country or its government manages its currency relative to other currencies. Governments may fix their exchange rates, whereby they attempt to keep the relative value of their currency fixed versus another currency or a basket of representative currencies, or float their exchange rates, whereby the relative value of the currency is determined by general market forces.

When banks trade currencies with each other, they sometimes act as a broker on behalf of their clients who need to secure foreign currency to pay their bills. Many large multinational banks also actively trade currencies as principals with other banks with the hope of profiting from exchange rate movements.

6.2.2   Fixed Income Instruments

Two of the most commonly referred to and traded fixed income instruments are loans and bonds. **Loans** and **bonds** are legally binding contracts through which the borrower (also referred to as the issuer of the bond or loan) borrows the principal amount specified in the bond or loan from an investor and in exchange pays a specified amount of interest, usually at regular intervals. The interest rate referenced in the contract is usually referred to as the **coupon rate** or **nominal rate**. This rate may be fixed or floating. For both bonds and loans, the fixed and floating interest rates behave as explained in Section 4.4.

At maturity (i.e., expiration), the borrower repays the principal amount to the investor. The repayment structure of fixed income instruments is similar to the structure discussed for loans in Section 4.4.7. Maturities can range from one day up to 40 years or more. There are bonds that have maturities exceeding 100 years, as well as "perpetual" bonds, where the principal amount is never repaid. For a plain-vanilla fixed income instrument, the amount of money the borrower receives is set on the day of the bond's issuance and will remain the same and not be affected by changes in the inflation or exchange rates that can happen over the life of the bond or loan. There are complex fixed income instruments that adjust the interest payments, and, in some cases, even the principal payments, to inflation rates.

EXAMPLE

Acme Inc. issues a five-year bond to a group of investors. With the bond, the company borrows USD 100 million at a fixed interest rate of 3% per annum. Each year, the company will make one interest payment of 3% * USD 100 million, or USD 3 million, to those investors who purchased and hold the bonds in accordance with their ownership interest. Five years from now, the company will make the last interest payment and repay the principal, the borrowed amount, of USD 100 million. Figure 6.2 shows the direction and size of these flows.

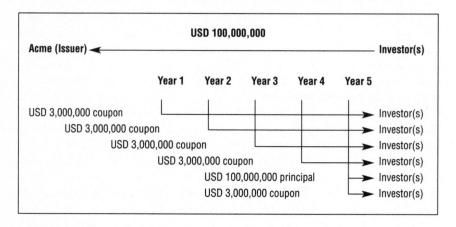

FIGURE 6.2 Direction and Size of Flows

One major difference between bonds and loans is that while there has been an active bond market for many decades, loans were typically not traded publicly and were usually kept on the bank's balance sheet in the bank's banking book until the loan was paid in full. Historically, banks bought and sold loans to other banks in a limited market to rebalance their respective banking books to achieve their desired portfolio composition. In recent years, however, the market for loans has grown into an active and sizable market, where large banks sell loans they have underwritten, without the intention of keeping these loans on their books, to nonbank investors. Occasionally banks may package groups of loans into what are termed off-balance-sheet vehicles or derivative products and then sell them to investors. These off-balance-sheet vehicles have formed the basis for many of the credit problems that banks have faced, starting in 2007. This process, termed securitization, was addressed in Section 5.2.3.

Once issued, most loans and bonds have fixed terms. That is, the coupon rate and the maturity date will not change, and so the size and timing of the loan payments are fixed.

The value of loans and bonds is affected by the interest rate, and the interest rate is driven primarily by three factors:

1. The interest rate of an equivalent risk-free fixed income instrument
2. The creditworthiness of the borrower or default risk
3. The time to maturity

If the interest rate increases, the value of the loan decreases, because for a fixed-rate bond, the fixed value of the future payments is worth less in present value terms. If the interest rate decreases, the value of the loan increases because the fixed value of the future payments is worth more in present value terms. Hence, loans and bonds are interest rate-sensitive instruments, and their value will fluctuate as interest rates change. There are also floating-rate bonds and loans where the interest rate and, consequently, the interest payments mirror an index that reflects the level of interest rates. When rates increase, the interest rate on the bond increases as well, and the value of the bond may remain unchanged. Investors should be careful to understand all the characteristics of the bond they may be considering investing in before actually buying the bond.

EXAMPLE

When the interest rate is 5%, then the value of USD 100 one year from now is not worth USD 100, but only USD 95.24, because investing USD 95.24 at 5% interest will grow the amount to USD 100. Similarly, when the interest rate increases to 10%, the same USD 100 one year from now is worth only USD 90.91, because investing USD 90.91 at 10% interest will grow the amount to USD 100.

In practice, a risk-free fixed income product would typically be a government bond, which may be considered to have no credit or default risk. If there is any risk of default, the interest rate must be adjusted with a premium that reflects the risk of default. Currently, U.S. Treasury securities are considered to be one of the safest government bond instruments. It should be noted that the concept of government issued securities being risk-free is now being questioned by regulators and investors around the world. With countries experiencing extreme stress as a result of the financial crisis (e.g., the

Greek debt crisis), and countries such as Italy, Portugal, Ireland and others requiring international attention to resolve increasing debt, sovereign issued debt instruments are no longer thought to be without risk.

EXAMPLE

Suppose a five-year government bond pays an annual coupon rate of 2%. In order to get investors to accept the default risk associated with the five-year corporate bond discussed previously, Acme Inc. must provide a premium above 2%, with the size of the premium being a function of the creditworthiness of the company (previously described as the credit spread). The more likely investors believe a company is to default, the higher the (interest) premium they will require from the company to invest in its bonds.

The chart in Figure 6.3 is a very simple way of remembering the relationship between interest rates and bond prices.

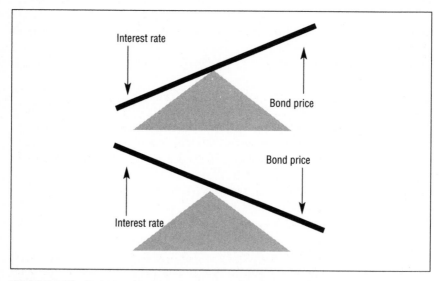

FIGURE 6.3 The Relationship Between Interest Rates and Bond Prices

The interest rate depends on several factors, including inflation, the general level of economic activity, the political and economic stability of the country where the issuer is located, and time to maturity. In general, the longer the maturity of the loans or bonds, the higher the interest rate. The explanation is simple: To lend money for a longer time, the lender needs more compensation for the risk of holding the instrument longer, which increases the level of uncertainty. Linking interest rates with maturity creates a **yield curve,** as shown in Figure 6.4.

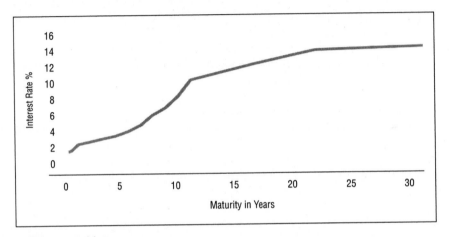

FIGURE 6.4 Yield Curve

Banks trade *bonds* with each other to manage their liquidity, to profit from price appreciation due to changes in interest rates, or to manage their earning assets. Banks trade *loans* with each other primarily when they realign their credit portfolio. Usually, the trading of loans is related to credit portfolio management, particularly as it relates to concentration risk (see Section 5.1.2).

6.2.3   Interbank Loans

Banks also make loans to each other. Some banks have excess deposits either from unexpected inflows of deposits or because they cannot find suitable loan or investment alternatives for their deposits. These banks sell their excess funds to banks that need them to finance the loans they underwrite or investments they make. **Interbank loans** can have very short maturities— as short as one day (or overnight). Banks also consider interbank loans to make funds available to their depositors and to manage their liquidity requirements. In many countries, these markets are very active. Like loans and bonds, interbank loans are interest rate-sensitive instruments.

Interbank loans are often priced off an index, such as the **London Interbank Offered Rate,** or LIBOR. LIBOR is a daily reference rate average based on the interest rates that London banks charge when lending funds to other banks. LIBOR is quoted for numerous currencies and across different maturities ranging from overnight (one day) to one year. LIBOR rates, irrespective of their maturity, are quoted on an annual basis. LIBOR rates can influence the pricing of various types of financial instruments, including loans that banks make.

EXAMPLE

A USD 10 million floating-rate bond issued by Acme Inc. is priced at a 250 bp (2.50%) premium over three-month LIBOR. The interest rate on the floating-rate bond is determined at the beginning of each quarter.

- On January 1, LIBOR is 3.45%; the interest rate on this floating-rate bond for the next three months would be 3.45% + 2.50%, or 5.95%. The interest payment that Acme Inc. will make for the coming three-month period would then be USD 1,487,500, or USD 10 million * 5.95%/4, as interest rates are quoted on an annual basis.
- On April 1, LIBOR is 2.95%. The interest rate on the floating-rate bond for the next three months would be 2.95% + 2.50% or 5.45%. The interest payment that Acme Inc. will make for the three-month period would then be USD 1,362,500, or USD 10 million * 5.45%/4.

6.2.4   Equities

Equities, also called **shares** or **stock,** represent a stake in the ownership of a company. The owners of the company are the shareholders, and they participate in the business of the company by voting their shares for or against proposals presented to them by the company's board of directors, who the shareholders elect. Shareholders, in most cases, receive dividends from the company's profits. However, some companies do not pay dividends. Instead, they rely on the company's rapidly growing business prospects to entice new stock investors to drive the stock value higher. Examples of these types of companies are early-stage technology firms that rarely pay dividends.

Shareholders also gain from an appreciation in the value of the shares: The more successful the company, the better the return earned by the holder and the better the opportunity for the company to grow and earn additional revenues to increase its dividend payments. The price of a share represents the market's perception of a company's current value and the value of its projected earnings. The price of shares will fluctuate as the market adjusts its valuation of the company in response to new information about the company.

6.2.5   Commodities

Commodities are generally homogeneous products irrespective of the geographical or physical market where they are being sold. For example, agricultural products such as corn, soybeans, and wheat, and energy products such as crude oil, natural gas, and gasoline, are considered commodities, as are precious metals such as gold and silver.

The price of a commodity is chiefly determined by the supply of and demand for the commodity. The rate of change to the supply and demand conditions for a commodity varies widely. For example, a drought in a country's farming region over several months leads to a decrease in corn growth, resulting in a decrease in the number of bushels of corn that would come to market for a prolonged period of time. As long as the demand for corn stays the same or increases, the price of corn due to its limited supply would increase until the supply and demand imbalance disappears. By contrast, within days, a hurricane can close down oil production in the Gulf of Mexico off the coast of the United States, resulting in a decrease in the number of barrels of oil that would come to market over the next week. As supplies are limited and demand is not expected to change due to these events, the price of oil would also increase until the demand and supply are balanced. These and other factors make commodity pricing inherently complex.

Example

Through distillation, crude oil is refined into products such as kerosene and butane. Each of these products is referred to as a specific commodity, and each one of them has its own market and price. Price differences may be determined by factors such as where they were refined and the cost of moving the final product to the user. But each underlying market price is determined by supply and demand factors affecting the global market for each product.

Banks, through their brokerage units, may trade commodities on behalf of their customers and also as principals. Commodity trading by banks is neither as common nor as important as foreign exchange, fixed income, or equity trading. In fact, many banks are now exiting commodity trading because of increasing capital requirements associated with those types of transactions.

6.2.6   Derivatives

Over the past 20 years, derivatives have emerged as an integral part of the financial markets. Derivatives are financial instruments whose value changes in response to changes in the value of related underlying assets that can also be bought, sold, and traded. Examples of derivative contracts include futures, options, and forward agreements, among others. There are derivatives on currencies, interest rates, equities, commodities, and the price of credit. The main types of derivatives are the following:

- A **forward** is a nontransferable contract that defines the delivery of assets such as commodities, currencies, bonds or stocks at a specified price, at a specified quantity, on a specified future date. An example of a forward is discussed in Section 6.4.5. Forwards are traded in the **over-the-counter (OTC) market**.
- A **futures** contract is a standardized and transferable contract that defines the delivery of assets such as commodities, currencies, bonds, or stocks at a specified price, at a specified quantity, on a specified future date. Futures are traded on recognized exchanges.

EXAMPLE

On June 1, Acme Inc., based in Europe, knows that six months later, on December 1, it will have to pay JPY 150 million for goods from a Japanese supplier. On June 1, the exchange rate is 150 JPY/EUR. Foreign exchange futures with a maturity around December 1 also trade at 150 JPY/EUR. To lock in the 150 JPY/EUR exchange rate and to ensure that it will pay EUR 1 million for the goods (JPY 150 million/150 JPY/EUR = EUR 1 million), it purchases—goes long—futures contracts equivalent to JPY 150 million.

- **Options** convey certain rights to the buyer of an option. The two main types of options are a call option and a put option:[2]
  - A **call option** gives the buyer the right, but not the obligation, to buy a financial instrument from the seller of the option on or before a specified time (expiration date) for a specified price, called the strike price.

2. Other alternative approaches may be used to distinguish between the different types of options.

EXAMPLE

On the exchange, Bank D buys a call option to buy 40,000 shares in Acme Inc. at EUR 35 per share on the expiration date of March 31. The option is sold to Bank D by Bank G. This gives Bank D the right the buy the shares in Acme Inc. at a known price of EUR 35 per share from Bank G. Bank G must sell the shares to Bank D at that price; in return, Bank G receives a premium of EUR 1 from Bank D. As long as the price of shares is less than EUR 35 per share, Bank D will not exercise the option to buy the shares at the strike price because it will be able purchase the shares in the open market at the lower price. As soon as the share price is greater than EUR 35, it makes sense for Bank D to exercise the option and buy the shares from Bank G for EUR 35. If the price of the shares at expiration is EUR 40, Bank D makes a profit of EUR 5 per share, or EUR 200,000 in total, less the premium paid. This profit also represents the amount lost by Bank G, which sold the option to Bank D. In other words, what the buyer of the call option gains, the seller loses, and gains and losses cancel each other out.

The payoff of a **long position** in a call option is depicted in Figure 6.5. As the price of Acme Inc. shares increases, so does the value of the call option.

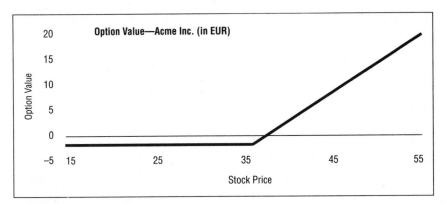

FIGURE 6.5 Payoff Call Option

- A **put option** gives the buyer the right, but not the obligation, to sell a financial instrument to the seller of the option at a specified time (expiration date) for a specified price, called the strike price.

EXAMPLE

On the exchange, Bank G buys a put option to sell 10,000 shares in Acme Inc. at EUR 35 per share on the expiration date of March 31. The put option is sold to Bank G by Bank V. This gives Bank G the right to sell the shares in Acme Inc. at a known price of EUR 35 per share to Bank V, which is obligated to buy the shares at that price. In return, Bank V receives a premium of EUR 1 from Bank G. As long as the price of shares is higher than EUR 35 per share, Bank G will not exercise the option to sell the shares at the strike price, since it can sell the shares at a higher price. As soon as the share price is below EUR 35, it makes sense for Bank G to exercise the option and sell the shares to Bank V for EUR 35. If the price of the shares at expiration is EUR 25, exercising the option is profitable for Bank G. The profit is EUR 10 per share, or EUR 100,000, less the premium paid by Bank G to Bank V. This profit also represents the amount lost by Bank V, which was obliged to buy the 10,000 Acme Inc. shares at EUR 35 per share though they are currently worth EUR 25. In other words, what the buyer of the put option gains, the seller loses, and the gains and losses cancel each other out.

The payoff of this transaction is depicted in Figure 6.6. As the price of Acme Inc. shares decreases, the value of the put option increases.

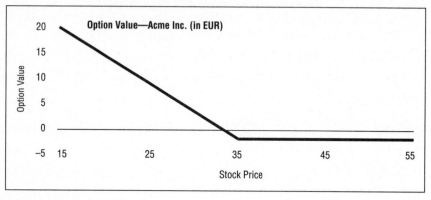

FIGURE 6.6 Payoff Put Option

- **Swaps** allow two parties to exchange cash flows with each other at a future date.

EXAMPLE

Acme Inc. obtains a EUR 10 million loan from Bank G for two years, agreeing to pay a floating interest rate set every three months based on LIBOR + 250 bp. Soon thereafter, the company comes to the belief that interest rates will rise over the two-year period and decides it would be best to lock in a fixed rate. Bank G, however, does not wish to convert the floating-rate loan into a fixed-rate loan. Acme Inc. can work around this by entering into an interest rate swap with Bank A. Acme Inc. agrees to pay to Bank A a fixed rate of 5% annualized every three months, calculated on the same principal amount as its loan with Bank G, or EUR 10 million. In return, Bank A agrees to pay a floating interest rate set every three months at LIBOR to Acme Inc. Figure 6.7 shows the direction of the flows among the three entities involved in the transaction:

1. Acme Inc. pays LIBOR + 250 bp to Bank G.
2. Acme Inc. pays fixed 5% to Bank A.
3. Bank A pays LIBOR to Acme Inc.

The payment that changes hands between Bank A and Acme Inc. reflects the relative differential between LIBOR and the 5% fixed interest rate on the loan. Acme is now paying Bank G a floating interest rate set at LIBOR + 250 bp every three months on the loan, but receiving the same LIBOR-determined interest flow from its swap with Bank A. As a result of these transactions, Acme Inc. locked in an annual interest rate of 7.50%.

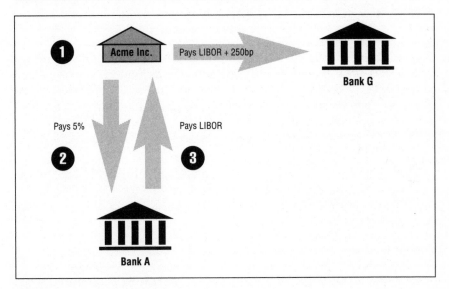

FIGURE 6.7 Payment Flows in a Swap

On January 1, LIBOR is 3.45%; the interest rate on this floating rate loan for the next three months would be 3.45% + 2.50% or 5.95%.

1. The interest payment that Acme Inc. will make to Bank G for the coming three-month period would then be EUR 148,750, or EUR 10 million * 5.95%/4, as interest rates are quoted on an annual basis.

2. The interest payment that Acme Inc. will make to Bank A for the coming three-month period would then be EUR 125,000, or EUR 10 million * 5.00%/4, as interest rates are quoted on an annual basis.

3. The interest payment that Acme Inc. will receive from Bank A for the coming three-month period would then be EUR 86,250, or EUR 10 million * 3.45%/4, as interest rates are quoted on an annual basis.

The net effect of these three payment streams is
− EUR 148,750 − EUR 125,000 + EUR 86,250 = − EUR 187,500

This net EUR 187,500 payment for every three months equals EUR 750,000 per year, or 7.5% of the EUR 10 million loan. Acme Inc. was able to transform a floating-rate loan through the swap into a fixed-rate loan, and the company was able to reduce the uncertainty surrounding its interest expenses. Even if LIBOR were to exceed 5%, the interest rate that Acme would be paying would be capped at 7.50%.

Financial derivatives can be used to hedge, or, in other words, to reduce or cancel, the risk of an unwanted exposure. For example, if a bank wanted to protect itself against an increase in interest rates because it holds a large quantity of bonds in its trading portfolio, it could sell futures contracts equivalent to the portfolio's value, to set up a hedge against a decrease in bond prices. A further example of a hedge will be set out in Section 6.4.5.

- **Index swaps** are OTC instruments used to manage portfolio risk, as opposed to single-name risk. Index swaps are used to hedge both equity risk and credit price risk.

Example

An equity investor has assembled an investment portfolio consisting of shares in the 100 largest capitalized companies on the London Stock Exchange in the same proportions as contained in the FTSE 100 stock index. The investor can hedge the portfolio in one of two ways. The investor can sell off shares from the portfolio, but will have to be careful not to change the relative balance among the stocks in the portfolio, and then deposit the funds generated from the sale. Alternatively, the investor can sell via an equity index-linked swap and convert their equity return into an interest-related return.

Fixed-income investors can hedge bond portfolios in similar ways by taking positions in **CDS index swaps**. The two main index series are CDX and iTraxx. CDX covers North American and emerging markets, while iTraxx covers the rest of the world.

6.3 Trading

Banks engage in trading operations and buy or sell financial instruments. In some cases, the trading is conducted on behalf of the bank's customers—where the bank acts as an intermediary—and does not directly risk the bank's capital. In other cases, the trading is done to benefit the bank itself by seeking short-term profits from favorable moves in the market prices. This type of trading, known as proprietary trading, puts the bank's capital directly at risk. Currently, U.S. banks are being discouraged from conducting proprietary trading as a result of the Volcker Rule under the 2010 Dodd-Frank Act.

Trading is risky: Prices may not move in the direction the bank expects, and the value of the financial instruments may change adversely and hurt the bank. The bank must decide how much risk it is willing to assume to make a profit, usually referred to as a bank's **risk appetite**. Generally, higher risk implies higher expected return. But higher risk also means that the likelihood of loss increases as well. The trade-off between risk and return is fundamental to any institution. This relationship is shown in Figure 6.8.

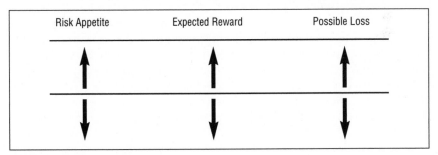

FIGURE 6.8 The Relationship Between Risk and Reward

6.3.1 Fundamental Trading Positions

In financial markets, a **position** refers to the ownership status of a particular financial instrument. There are two fundamental trading positions: the long and the short position. The holder of a long position bought, or owns, the financial instrument and will profit if the price of the instrument goes up or will incur a loss if the price of the instrument goes down.

EXAMPLE

The trading desk of Bank G expected the price of crude oil to increase in the future from its current level of USD 75 per barrel. To capitalize on this positive price view (increase in price), it purchased 500 crude oil futures contracts at USD 75 per barrel. Several weeks later, the price of crude oil increased to USD 95 per barrel. If Bank G were to exit from the trade (sell its position) now, it would sell the contracts for USD 95 per barrel and realize a profit of USD 20 per barrel. The bank had a long position in the crude oil contracts and would benefit from the price increase in crude oil. However, had the price decreased to USD 65 per barrel, the bank would have lost USD 10 per contract.

The opposite position is a short position. The term *short position* has two different meanings, depending on whether the investor/trader is dealing in futures contracts or in stock, bonds, or other financial instruments.

The holder of a short position in a commodities futures contract has the obligation to deliver a commodity when the contract expires. Usually, producers of commodities sell short their future production to lock in the price of the commodity in advance. The holder of a short position will profit if the price of the commodity goes down or incur a loss if the price goes up.

In equity markets, if an investor believes that shares of a company are overvalued (i.e., too high) and thinks the price will go down in the near term, the investor can establish a short position by borrowing shares from a broker and then selling the shares. At some time in the future, the investor can buy the shares back and return them to the broker. If the investor sold the shares for more than the cost to purchase the shares, it profits; otherwise, it incurs a loss. This applies to bonds, stocks, or any other financial instruments.

EXAMPLE

The trading desk of Bank G expected the price of gold to decrease in the future from its current level of EUR 800 per ounce. To capitalize on this negative price view, it sold short several hundred gold futures contracts at EUR 800 per ounce. If Bank G held onto these futures contracts until they expired, it would be required to deliver the amount of gold that represented the several hundred contracts it sold. Several months later, the price of gold fell to EUR 750 per ounce. To exit from the trade and close out its position, the bank had to buy the same number of contracts for EUR 750 per ounce. Because Bank G purchased the gold futures contracts for less than it sold them, it realized a profit of EUR 50 per ounce. The bank had a short position in the gold contracts and benefited from the price decline in gold. However, had the price of gold increased to EUR 850 per ounce, Bank G would have lost EUR 50 per ounce on the deal if it sold its contracts at that time to limit its loss. Figure 6.9 gives an overview of the relationship between the value of the position and the price change of a long or a short position.

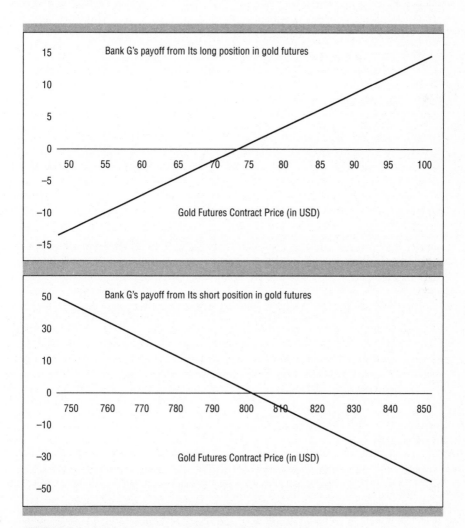

FIGURE 6.9 Risks and Rewards of Long and Short Positions

Speculation involves buying (long position), holding, selling, and short-selling (short position) financial instruments such as stocks, bonds, loans, commodities, foreign exchange, derivatives, or any financial product in the expectation that price fluctuations will generate a profit. Specifically, a bank is not seeking to hedge or protect itself from a price change in a position it already owns; it is simply buying or selling with the hope of earning a profit. The two previous examples using Bank G also show how speculation in the marketplace works. The bank did not own the actual crude oil or physical gold commodities; it simply bet on the prices of those commodities going up or down. However, if for some reason the bank held either the oil or gold futures contracts to expiration, it would have had to purchase the physical oil and gold in the marketplace in order to fulfill its futures contracts obligations.

6.3.2   Bid-Ask Spreads

In buying and selling financial instruments, traders will quote prices at which they are willing to buy or sell the financial instrument. The difference between the buy price (bid) and sell price (ask) is called the **bid-ask spread.**

EXAMPLE

A trader at Bank G offers to buy stock of Acme Inc. at EUR 10.15 per share, and another trader offers to sell the same stock at EUR 10.25 per share. The bid-ask spread is EUR 0.10.

The size of the bid-ask spread is an indicator of **market liquidity**: The narrower the bid-ask spread, the closer the buyers and sellers are to placing a true market value on the financial instrument and the more transactional volume or liquidity the market has. This liquidity, referred to as market liquidity, is a very important component of any marketplace, and liquidity is a highly desirable market characteristic that market participants actively seek.

EXAMPLE

Expanding on the above example, unforeseen market events have negatively affected Acme Inc. Virtually all buyers have exited the market for Acme Inc., and interest in its stock has disappeared, resulting in diminished liquidity of, or demand for, its stock. Low liquidity and few buyers contribute to a drop in the bid price from EUR 10.15 to EUR 9.75. The ask price remains the same, EUR 10.25; the bid-ask spread has widened to EUR 0.50.

Note that **market** or **asset liquidity** refers to the ability to trade in and out of a position without significant price effects. This type of liquidity is fundamentally different from the liquidity that banks must manage on a daily basis: the ability to repay depositors on demand (see Chapter 2), also called funding liquidity.

6.3.3 Exchange and Over-the-Counter Markets

Financial instruments such as foreign exchange contracts, bonds, equities, commodities, and derivatives are traded on either regulated financial markets, called exchanges, or the over-the-counter markets.

An **exchange** is a centralized marketplace where brokers and traders meet and, on behalf of their customers or on their own account, buy and sell standardized financial instruments such as equities, bonds, commodities, options, and futures. For any financial instrument to be traded on an exchange, it must meet both regulatory requirements imposed by the exchange's regulator and listing requirements imposed by the exchange itself. For instance, many stock exchanges impose listing requirements on the listed company regarding the number of shareholders, the stability of earnings, and the size of the company's assets. Futures exchanges list standard contracts that first must be approved by a regulatory body. Any changes to the contract's terms must also be approved.

Historically, exchanges possessed a central physical location where trades took place called "trading floors." However, trading floors are being replaced in many markets by purely electronic trading platforms: there is no physical meeting place and brokers execute all transactions electronically, through purpose-built computer systems (trading platforms) supporting the exchanges. On these trading floors or in these electronic trading platforms, brokers interact with each other, buying and selling (trading) instruments on behalf of their clients—buyers or sellers—or for their own account. The transactions that the brokers execute, either as agents on behalf of their clients or for their own account, contractually and legally bind the parties to complete the trade as agreed. Moreover, all the trades between the brokers are logged, recorded, and displayed by the exchange. Because both the price and the volume of trades are available and often prominently displayed on the trading floor or in the electronic marketplaces and are disseminated through price reporting services electronically, exchanges create price transparency that allows market participants to continually price their own holdings of financial instruments.

Whether the transaction takes place on the trading floor of an exchange or in an electronic marketplace owned by an exchange, the parties to the transaction operate according to an agreed set of exchange rules, which in many cases requires clearing their trades and transactions through a **clearinghouse** that is typically affiliated with the exchange. A clearinghouse, often referred to as the central counterparty (CCP), becomes the buyer to each seller and the seller to each buyer, effectively standing in the middle of the transaction to guarantee the financial performance of the trade as agreed by the parties to the transaction. Each clearinghouse or central counterparty has its own rules, regulations, and conventions, which may differ across the different types of financial instruments that are traded on the same exchange that the clearinghouse or central counterparty clears. However, a clearinghouse typically offers credit support mechanisms, which are supported by the clearinghouse's members and are transparent to the market participants to ensure that the parties to the trade will receive financial compensation if the counterparty to the trade is not able to deliver on the trade as agreed. The different sources of credit support include insurance and collateral, or margin that the clearinghouse members post with the clearinghouse.

Clearinghouses require members clearing through the clearinghouse to post collateral or **margin**. (It should be noted that not all brokers are clearinghouse members. Those who are not would trade through a clearing member using what is called an omnibus account.) When the broker posts the margin, it provides and transfers to the clearinghouse a high-quality instrument that is both liquid and exhibits low price variability; generally government bonds, such as U.S. Treasuries, or cash deposits serve as an acceptable form of margin. The amount of the required margin (**margin requirement**) that the brokers are obligated to post is determined by various material considerations, including the different types of instruments the broker trades on the exchange, the risk of the instrument, and the overall trading volume. The amount of the margin is recalculated at least daily to reflect the trades or other exposures that the broker has, and the broker is required to maintain a margin requirement with the clearinghouse. Were the clearinghouse to deem that the margin posted by the broker is insufficient—due to an adverse price movement in the instruments that the broker trades in or holds, or a sudden, unexpected, and material decline in the value of the collateral provided by the broker—the broker must post additional margin so that the collateral provided reflects the broker's exposure and meets the clearinghouse's minimum aggregate margin requirements. When a broker is required to post additional collateral to fulfill the margin requirements, the notification is termed a **margin call**.

In case the broker fails to deliver on a trade that it has executed at the exchange, for whatever reason, the clearinghouse liquidates the collateral posted by the broker and uses the proceeds from its sale to compensate the broker's counterparty. The availability of and access to collateral significantly mitigate the counterparty credit risk inherent in buying and selling financial instruments. How this compensation is paid depends on the specific financial instrument that was traded between the parties and on clearinghouse rules, regulations, and commercial conventions. It can include some form of financial compensation paid directly to the party that was adversely impacted from the default.

Buyers and sellers who transact as customers through a broker are required to post collateral with their brokers. The amount of the initial margin required to be posted by the broker's customers is determined by the type of financial instrument traded. The margin posted in the customer's account with the broker must meet the minimum margin requirements, as determined by the exchange or clearinghouse. There are brokerages that may insist on higher margin requirements to protect themselves from the risk that a customer may become unable or unwilling to settle the transaction as agreed. It is the margin posted by the brokers' customers that is often used to support the margin that the broker, in turn, posts with the clearinghouse. Additionally, the customers must also meet the required minimum margin requirements imposed by the clearinghouse; the broker has the obligation to maintain the customers' margin or issue its own margin call, requiring the customer to replenish the account by providing securities or cash.

In the case of futures markets, the daily profits and losses are added or subtracted from the customer's account (marked-to-market). This adjustment made to the customer's margin requirement based on daily mark-to-market value of the account is called **variation margin**.

While exchanges offer standardized products, price transparency, clear rules that govern the transactions between the buyers and sellers, and collateral support through the clearinghouse, they do not offer the flexibility many sophisticated investors need, as such investors must individually structure the trades that they want for **hedging** or other purposes. These transactions are executed in the over-the-counter markets instead, where both the flexibility and the ability to customize trades and transactions exist.

The over-the-counter or OTC market does not have a physical location for its marketplace. However, there has been a major drive toward requiring the trading of OTC transactions through a centralized electronic marketplace to allow for greater transparency around the OTC marketplace, and a perceived increase in safety as it would relate to counterparty default. For example, the electronic trading of swap transactions, one form of derivative, would be conducted through Swap Execution Facilities (SEF). SEFs allow multiple parties to execute trades by accepting bids and offers from those pre-approved to participate in the SEF. As OTC contracts become more standardized, they will be required to be cleared through a central clearing facility. However, there will remain OTC contracts that will not be standardized. Those instruments will still be traded in the over-the-counter market and not through a centralized trading facility.

In the OTC market, the buying and selling of financial instruments takes place directly between the two parties to the transaction through the use of phones or computer networks, with each party directly assessing and taking on the risk of the creditworthiness of the other party to the transaction. Most notably, foreign exchange, derivatives, bond, and commodity trading, and some equity trading activities are conducted in the OTC markets. Due to the general need and/or desire in the market to customize instruments and to match as closely as possible the needs and desires of the two parties to the transaction, the OTC market is significantly bigger than the exchange marketplace.

The use of collateral in the OTC market is not regulated or standardized, as it is in the exchange-traded markets. When parties to an OTC transaction demand collateral from each other, they negotiate to determine the size and quality of the specific type of collateral they would be willing to accept to ensure that performance will occur as agreed. In some limited instances, standardized OTC transactions will move to an exchange marketplace for the primary reason of using a clearinghouse to guarantee the transaction. The movement of these transactions to an exchange for this purpose of ensuring counterparty credit is developing rapidly, reflecting the interest from market participants to extend the protection offered by central clearinghouses to OTC transactions. Figure 6.10 is a general comparison.

According to data from the Bank for International Settlements,[3] the daily OTC turnover in April 2013 on the foreign exchange markets, including spot, forward, and swap transactions, averaged USD 5.3 trillion (USD 1,300 trillion annualized), and the daily turnover of various OTC interest rate derivatives averaged USD 2.3 trillion (USD 575 trillion annualized) in notional principal amount (NPA).

---

3. Source: http://www.bis.org/publ/rpfx13.htm.

	Over-the-Counter Market	Exchange-Traded Market
Contract terms	Separately negotiated	Standardized
Size of a trade	Parties to the transaction agree on the size.	Set by the exchange, depends on the product and standardized specifications. May need to purchase multiple contracts, depending on how much of the product is required.
Price	Parties determined price through negotiation.	Generally reflects the value market participants trade at. Price is disseminated by price-reporting services.
Legal requirements	Separately agreed and documented between the parties, although form "master agreements" are usually set forth in general terms with annexes used to customize the agreement.	Parties agree to abide by the rules of the exchange, which are legally binding.
Transparency	Little if any transparency	Highly transparent
Counterparty risk	Each party determines the risk of its counterparty and limits its transactions according to its own risk appetite for that counterparty.	Exchange clearinghouses guarantee the transaction, eliminating the need to consider the counterparty's risk profile. However, should look at exchange guarantee system to ensure comfort with exchange clearinghouse guarantee system and risk.
Collateral	Individually negotiated and held by the party demanding the collateral.	Broker requires collateral from its customer, which is calculated on the exchange's margin requirements, although the broker may ask for more from the customer than the exchange may require. The broker transfers the margin to the exchange to cover all its customer positions at that exchange. The broker's margin requirement is tied directly to the exchange's margin requirements.

FIGURE 6.10 A General Comparison between OTC and Exchange Markets

Many issues are currently being dealt with by global regulators in their attempt to bring more OTC trades to a centralized electronic marketplace. Issues such as cross-border recovery in the event of a default, collateral requirements, and risk assessments of the central clearing facility, among others, will understandably take time to resolve given this relatively new requirement and the need to provide for global coordination in what has become a very highly interconnected global marketplace for financial services.

6.4   Market Risk Measurement and Management

There are five general **market risk** categories: foreign exchange, interest rate, equity, commodity, and credit price risk. Market risk can be either general or specific. General market risk refers to adverse change in a market that affects market participants broadly. Specific risk refers to change in conditions that affect only one submarket (e.g., the oil market, instead of commodity markets generally).

6.4.1   Types of Market Risk: The Five Risk Classes

To better understand the five different types of **market risk**, this section describes each risk type.

1. **Foreign exchange risk** is the potential for loss due to an adverse change in foreign exchange rates, and applies to all exchange rate–related products whose positions are valued in a currency that differs from the bank's reporting currency.

EXAMPLE

In August 1998, it was reported that Telekomunikasi Indonesia had incurred a loss of USD 101 million as a result of movements in foreign exchange rates. The losses were due to borrowings of USD 306 million, JPY 11 billion, and FRF 130 million, each of which had been converted into IDR, Indonesia's local currency. The Indonesian government devalued the IDR against major currencies, including the U.S. dollar, Japanese yen, and the French franc. The devaluation meant that the bank had to pay more IDR to repay the loans it took out in USD, JPY, and FRF.

2. **Interest rate risk** is the potential loss due to adverse changes in interest rates. (As discussed above, the value of a bond will increase if interest rates decrease and decrease if interest rates increase.) Note that the value of fixed income instruments will change if either the creditworthiness of the borrower changes or the risk-free interest rate changes. The potential change to the creditworthiness of the borrower is the credit risk associated with the loan. The potential change to the interest rate is the market risk associated with the loan.

EXAMPLE

In the early 1990s, the treasurer of the Orange County Retirement Fund in the state of California was responsible for managing a portfolio of USD 7.5 billion belonging to current and former employees of Orange County schools, cities, and the county itself. The treasurer's investment strategy assumed that interest rates would either fall or remain low. This approach worked well until 1994 when interest rates increased. The increases in interest rates drove the value of the county's bond investments so low that in December 1994, the government of Orange County announced that its investment pool had suffered a USD 1.6 billion loss. Subsequently, the county declared bankruptcy. This was stunning news to the markets, as it represented the largest loss ever recorded by a local government authority in the United States.

---

3. **Equity risk** is the potential loss due to an adverse change in the price of stocks and applies to all instruments that use equity prices as part of their valuation—for example, derivative products such as futures contracts.

EXAMPLE

Enron, a company in the United States, filed for bankruptcy following an unprecedented accounting scandal that was uncovered in late 2001. Over several years, Enron had accumulated a wide range of energy-related holdings and businesses in the United States and abroad, and had become a dominant player in the energy business. Throughout these expansive years, the company provided financial information to the shareholders that indicated Enron's growth was robust and that management had successfully created a financially stable, strong, and highly profitable company. In reality, however, the company's management used complex, materially misleading, and fraudulent accounting transactions that effectively hid the true financial position of the firm: its substantial and accelerating losses and sizable liabilities. The deceptive accounting practices involved highly complex and opaque legal transactions that moved Enron's losses to corporations that were affiliated and controlled by Enron. However, due to the structuring of Enron's accounting transactions, their total impact on the company's financial health was not transparent. Enron did not have to disclose this information. Moreover, as Enron's affiliated corporations were not publicly traded, their true financial condition was not disclosed to the public. Only the top executives of Enron were aware of the extent of the deceptive accounting practices.

Since very few individuals outside the top management of Enron were aware of the systematic deceptive accounting practices, the financial markets perceived Enron as a very successful company. Its stock was considered to be a good and safe investment, and appreciated considerably over time. By August 2000, Enron's shares were trading at USD 90. Slowly, over the following 14 months, the price of the company's shares started to decline, mainly due to a material weakening in the financial markets.

While the company's management publicly encouraged investment in Enron, as Enron's share prices softened, many executives, who were either directly involved or able to recognize the severity of the misleading accounting statements, began to sell their shares aggressively. By August 2001, the shares had dropped to around USD 40. At that time, more and more—previously undisclosed—information came to the market that showed the company's accounting information and accounting practices were systemically fraudulent and misleading. As the true financial situation of Enron emerged, the price of the shares dropped from USD 40 to mere pennies by the time Enron was forced into bankruptcy in December 2001.

4. **Commodity risk** is the potential loss from an adverse change in commodity prices. This applies to all commodity positions and any derivative commodity positions such as futures contracts.

EXAMPLE

Between July 2008 and October 2008, the price of crude oil fell significantly. During July 2008, the price of one barrel of crude oil was roughly USD 135 to USD 140. These prices were the highest oil prices ever recorded, and many believed that oil prices would continue to climb during 2008 and could reach USD 160 per barrel or more by the end of the year.

High oil prices are a threat to companies whose business is very sensitive to the price of crude oil. To reduce the price they expected to pay for crude oil later in the year, many energy price–sensitive companies entered into agreements where they purchased crude oil for delivery in October 2008 at the price prevailing in July 2008, or roughly USD 140 per barrel. For example, if a company in June 2008 purchased 1,000 barrels of crude oil for delivery in October 2008, it paid about USD 140,000. The significant and unprecedented price appreciation abruptly stopped, however, and by December 2008, the price of crude oil had dropped below USD 50 per barrel. Companies that had entered these contracts with the expectation that the price of oil would stay roughly the same or increase started to receive crude oil worth USD 50 per barrel, yet were paying USD 140 per barrel. The loss of USD 90,000 was entirely due to commodity risk—an adverse change in commodity prices.

The loss to these companies was pure gain to the sellers of crude oil, who held contracts to sell crude oil for USD 140 when the price was USD 50.

5. **Credit price risk** is the risk that a long or a short position in a credit-risky instrument can lead to a loss due to adverse market prices for that credit risk. This risk type applies to cash instruments, such as loans and bonds, as well as to derivatives instruments, such as credit default swaps (CDs), in both single-name and index form.

EXAMPLE

On October 8, 2013, the cost to insure default risk on Time Warner Cable Inc. (TWC) bonds was 217 bp per annum for five years. On the same day, buyers of default protection on Republic of Italy bonds were required to pay 237 bp for the same five-year protection. The currency of protection is USD in both cases.

Suppose an investor is long USD 10 million in TWC bonds with remaining maturity of five years and that the bonds yield a return of 4.20% to the investor. This yield in part reflects the investor's exposure to interest rate risk—the yield on credit-risk-free U.S. Treasury bonds—and in part exposure to credit risk—the credit spread on the TWC bonds.

If the investor now wishes to neutralize the entire credit risk in the bond position, the investor can buy USD 10 million **notional principal amount** of TWC five-year CDS at a cost of 2.17% per year. The investor's effective risk is now interest rate risk on U.S. Treasuries and counterparty risk on the seller of the CDS. The net income is in this case 4.20% – 2.17% = 2.03% per annum.

6.4.2 Value-at-Risk

To measure market risk in their portfolios, banks commonly use a concept termed Value-at-risk (VaR). VaR provides a qualified answer to the question, "How much could we lose in the next day (or week, month, year)?" Formally, VaR is defined as the predicted loss at a specific confidence level (e.g., 95%) over a given period of time (e.g., 1 day). Note that VaR does not provide the worst-case loss, but instead uses a confidence level, generally 95% or higher. With a 99% confidence level, for example, VaR estimates the loss level such that 99% of the time (e.g., in 99 trading days out of 100), the actual loss level will be less than that number. VaR makes no prediction about what the loss could be on the worst day. If a 95% confidence level were used, then VaR is estimating the 6th worst daily loss in a 100-day horizon, but does not provide any additional information about how much worse the five worst daily losses will be.

EXAMPLE

Bank G's risk management team calculates a 1-day, 99% VaR for market risk to be EUR 3 million. This means that there is a 1% chance markets could turn against it and it could lose more than EUR 3 million. That also means that there is a 99% chance that losses will be less than EUR 3 million the next day.

VaR calculations make assumptions about the likely movements of market values in the future. One way to do this is to look at how market values moved in the past, and to assume that they will move that way in the future. If a company's stock price has moved up and down by significant amounts in the past, one might assume that it will continue to do so in the future. Similarly, if a company's stock price rarely moves above USD 100, although sometimes it falls as low as USD 70, again one could assume that its price will remain in that range in the future.

Clearly, if historical data is to be used as a guide to future price movements, then the time period that is used when collecting data on price movements is important. If the period used is too short, the data may not capture a wide range of possible price movements. Similarly, if data is used from a time when economic conditions were stable and benign, they may not be much use in predicting how prices will move under more difficult economic conditions.

Calculating VaR involves closely examining current positions and estimating the distribution of possible return values the portfolio could see during the next time period (typically one day for market risk). The graph in Figure 6.11 shows an example of a return distribution for a portfolio and can be interpreted as follows. The horizontal x-axis represents possible gains and losses. Losses would be points to the left of zero and profits to the right. For any return value x, the area beneath the curve for all return values less than or equal to x represents the probability that return value is less than or equal to x, and so, the area under the entire curve is equal to one. At any particular gain or loss value, the height of the curve represents the relative likelihood of that gain or loss. Very low return values (far left points on the curve) and very high return values (far right points on the curve) have values close to 0, since these return values are highly unlikely. The peak of the curve occurs for return values close to 0 (middle of the curve) since these return values have the highest likelihood of occurring.

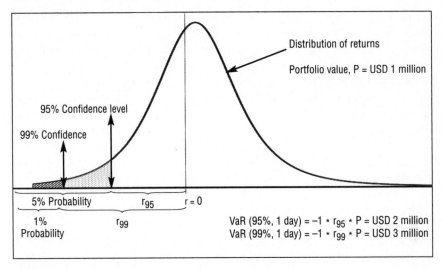

FIGURE 6.11 Graphical Interpretation of Value-at-Risk

For Bank G, the figure above offers graphical interpretation of its VaR. The line labeled 95% confidence level is at USD –2 million. The shaded area under the curve to the left of the line is 5%, indicating that there is a 5% chance losses could be greater than USD 2 million, and so, the 1-day 95% VaR is USD 2 million. Further to the left, at USD –3 million, there is a line labeled 99% confidence level. The area under the curve left of that line is 1% and indicates that there is a 1% chance that losses could exceed USD 3 million. Therefore, the 1-day 99% VaR is USD 3 million.

Most of the effort in calculating VaR involves estimating the return distribution (the gain or loss values that the current portfolio might return and the probability of each value); there are three common approaches. One approach is to assume that the return values follow a known probability distribution, such as the Normal distribution, also known as a bell curve (e.g., the return distribution shown in Figure 6.11) and to use the properties of the distribution to determine the required confidence level. Another approach is to simulate possible returns and losses, which allows for a wider variety of return distributions and financial products to be considered. Finally, one approach is to use historical daily returns over a defined look-back horizon and to consider the gains and losses that would have been realized for the current portfolio; this approach has the advantage of not requiring any assumptions about the underlying distribution. When implementing a VaR system, risk managers must be cognizant of the different strengths and weaknesses, relative to accuracy and computational effort, of the various approaches.

Given an estimated return distribution for the current portfolio, the VaR value corresponds to the loss level x such that the probability that losses are less than x equals the given confidence level. In Figure 6.11, the rightmost bar on the horizontal axis corresponds to the 1-day 99% VaR.

EXAMPLE

A bank calculates that its 1-day 95% VaR is USD 100 million. The head of market risk tells the chief risk officer that the bank stands to lose no more than USD 100 million 95 days out of every 100. The chief risk officer decides that is too much risk for the bank to be taking so she tells the head of market risk to sell volatile positions and buy bonds and stocks that have shown price stability in the past. After the head of market risk has done this, the bank's VaR is reduced to USD 60 million.

Summary

VaR is a very general concept that attempts to provide a concise snapshot of the current market risk profile of the bank's portfolio. VaR has broad applications in risk management, including market, credit, and operational risk. VaR as a concept has some shortcomings that are important to emphasize:

- *VaR is measured with estimation error.* That is, the estimated return distribution is derived from a quantitative model that typically makes simplifying assumptions and is therefore not a precise statement of the range of possible outcomes.
- *VaR does not give any information about the severity of loss by which it is exceeded.* That is, if the loss amount does exceed the VaR value, VaR does not provide any information about how much greater the loss might be. Risk managers will typically consider a range of confidence levels to understand better the range of possible losses and alternative risk measures such as expected shortfall.
- *Most importantly, VaR does not describe the worst-case loss but the worst case for a specified confidence level.* This is a point to be emphasized and remembered.

6.4.3 Expected Shortfall

Given the limitations of VaR, regulators and financial organizations are putting more emphasis on another risk measure, expected shortfall (ES), to more fully estimate risk in the tail of the return distribution. ES is also referred to as conditional VaR (CVaR) or Expected Tail Loss (ETL). For a given time period and confidence level, ES is the average loss that could occur in excess of the loss calculated by VaR over the same time period and using the same confidence level. By construction, ES will always be a larger number than its corresponding VaR because it is estimating the average loss in the extreme tail of the distribution beyond the VaR loss value. Like VaR, ES is NOT the worst case loss, which for many portfolios cannot be estimated. Because it requires even greater information about the extreme tail of the return distribution, ES is more difficult than VaR to calculate and has greater estimation error.

6.4.4 Stress Testing and Scenario Analysis

Although a 99% VaR measure may capture a wide range of all possible outcomes, risk managers must pay particular attention to the remaining 1% of outcomes since these events could cause banks serious financial problems. Stress testing and scenario analysis are important tools of any risk management system that seeks to understand how a portfolio will perform in extreme cases. Given the reliance on modeling, risk measures need to be closely examined and tested against extreme events.

Stress testing considers instances for particular value changes, such as a rapid change in interest rates or equity indices. Scenario analysis evaluates portfolio performance in severe states of the world, either hypothetical or historical.

For example, scenarios that a risk manager may consider for an equity portfolio would be to model and use the U.S. stock market crash of 1987 or the 1997 Asian financial crisis. Other scenarios might be based on natural disasters, wars, changes in political situations—virtually anything that would have a dramatic effect on market prices.

Stress tests are an essential part of risk management and involve a number of supporting activities, such as ensuring that the assumptions underlying each stress test are reasonable. Stress testing has become more important over the years and is now a major part of a bank's, and regulator's, risk management activities.

6.4.5   Market Risk Reporting

Communication is a key part of effective risk management, and once risks have been measured, risk reports must be shared with traders, risk managers, senior management, and members of the board of directors. Contents of the risk report typically vary according to the business line and seniority of the users, but most reports include information about trading and balance sheet positions being held by the bank, the reason for the position, where it is being held, the date of its maturity, current profit/loss status, the volatility of the position, and many other factors. Risk reports will also typically provide current risk metrics, including value-at-risk (VaR) values for several confidence levels, stress test results, and analysis of risk by sector, geography, and other factors. Risk reports should allow users to quickly assess the current risk level of the portfolio and identify possible areas of overexposure where risk mitigation may be needed.

The frequency of risk reports may vary according to the user of the information. For example, the most demanding users of market risk information, in addition to a bank's risk managers, are the bank's traders, who will need real-time risk reports in order to function properly.

6.4.6   Hedging and Basis Risk

Hedging

Banks and individuals hedge in order to reduce or cancel out a risk. When a bank **hedges** a position it currently holds in a financial instrument, the position is matched as closely as possible with an equal and opposite offsetting position in a financial instrument that tracks or mirrors the value changes in the position being hedged. Usually, hedging involves a position in a derivative that mirrors as closely as possible the value changes of the underlying asset.

Hedging is the opposite of speculation. In a speculative trade, the bank chooses to take a calculated risk in the expectation of a positive future return. In a hedging trade, the bank chooses to limit some of the risk exposures it has by sacrificing some, if not all, possible future returns.

While hedging sounds complicated, in fact it is not. In our everyday lives, we all hedge. The simple act of buying car insurance is a hedge against the financial impact of an accident. In exchange for our payment to the insurance company, the company provides insurance. The insurance company promises to pay expenses associated with an accident that we are involved in. What the insurance achieves is simply to reduce the effects of risks that we are exposed to. It is important to remember that the risks still exist; the insurance does not reduce the likelihood that an accident will occur, but, rather, offers financial compensation to us when things go wrong—that is, when there is an undesirable outcome.

Similarly, checking the weather before embarking on a lengthy journey is a hedge against bad weather. We cannot control the weather, but we can, in fact, adjust what we pack for the journey and when we take off on the trip. By adjusting our behavior, we are hedging against the impact of bad weather—the undesirable outcome.

Hedging financial exposures is akin to buying car insurance or checking the weather report. The intended effects are the same—reduce the impact of the undesirable outcome. But the ways financial hedges are created are significantly more complex. The following equity example is a straightforward illustration of hedging in the financial sense. It involves an exposure—the stock or equity—we want to hedge and the "insurance" that we use to hedge our exposure—the put option. For financial hedges, the insurance often involves a derivative. Options are derivatives. The reason we use derivatives to hedge financial exposure is because they derive their value from another asset, usually from the asset that we hedge or an asset that has similar characteristics to the one that we hedge.

For instance, if an investor owns equity in a company, an option would replicate the value of that asset. If the value of the asset increases, the value of the option changes as well; the direction of the change depends on the type of option. As the value of the asset increases, the value of a call option (see Section 6.2.6) increases, and the value of the put option decreases. Conversely, as the value of the asset decreases, the value of a call option decreases, and the value of the put option increases.

To summarize:

- In a long equity position, the undesirable outcome is that the value of the equity decreases; to hedge, a put option should be purchased (long position in a put option) because the value of the put option increases as the value of the stock decreases.
- In a short equity position, the undesirable outcome is that the value of the equity increases; to hedge, a call option should be purchased (long position in a call option) because the value of the call option increases as the value of the stock increases.

The equity example can be extended to more complex situations, but the principles remain the same. The approach can also be extended to interest rate risk—the risk that interest rate changes adversely impact the bank. In most cases, this means that the cost of borrowing is greater than the income the bank earns on its loans. This is an undesirable outcome, and the banks use derivatives that reduce this risk.

EXAMPLE

Bank G has purchased 2,000 shares of Acme Inc. at EUR 30 per share, paying EUR 60,000. The bank would like to hedge this equity risk and buys put options (see Section 6.2.6). The put options on Acme Inc. with three months to expiration and a strike price of EUR 30 has a EUR 3.50 premium. By purchasing 2,000 put options (with three months to expiration and a strike price of EUR 30) for EUR 7,000, the bank has hedged the equity risk for this position over the next three months. To see this more clearly demonstrated, consider the possible prices of Acme Inc. after three months in Figure 6.12.

Price of Acme Inc. in 3 Months (P_{ACME})	Value of Put Option at Expiration	Value of Combined Positions (shares + put options)
< EUR 30	EUR 30 − (P_{ACME})	$2{,}000 * (\text{EUR } 30 - (P_{ACME}) + (P_{ACME}))$ = EUR 60,000
≥ EUR 30	EUR 0	$2{,}000 * (\text{EUR } 0 + (P_{ACME})) =$ EUR 2,000 $* (P_{ACME})$

FIGURE 6.12 Value of Positions

If the price of Acme Inc. in three months is greater than or equal to EUR 30, the put options would be worthless—the bank would not want to sell the shares for EUR 30 because the current price is greater than that. However, the shares would be worth EUR 2,000 * P_{ACME}, which is greater than or equal to the EUR 60,000 Bank G paid. If the price of Acme Inc. in three months is less than EUR 30, the bank would exercise the put options and sell the 2,000 shares to the seller of the put options for EUR 30 each for a total value of EUR 60,000. The effect of these changes on the value of the position is depicted in Figure 6.13.

By purchasing the put options, Bank G has eliminated the possibility of loss from this equity position, assuming that the counterparty does not collapse and expose the bank to counterparty default risk. The value of the equity position, no matter how low the equity price drops, will be offset by the increase in the value of the long position in the put options, less the premium paid for the options. Note that for this insurance, the bank paid a EUR 7,000 premium, the cost to hedge this risk. This cost does not change and is not at risk (it cannot increase); it has been incurred by Bank G and will not be returned to it. This is the out-of-pocket cost of entering into the hedge.

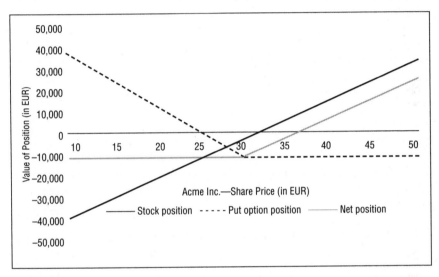

FIGURE 6.13 Payoff Position in Acme Stock and Put Option

In a similar manner, banks can use derivative products to hedge interest rate risk, commodity risk, and foreign exchange risk. An example of derivatives that reduce interest rate risk is forward contracts.

Derivatives have a wide use in banking and allow a bank to lend/borrow funds at a fixed rate for a specified period starting in the future, thereby reducing the effect that changing interest rates have on the interest rate margin. Derivatives, such as the swap described in Section 6.2.6, help borrowers to modify the interest rate on loans they pay.

EXAMPLE

When a bank needs to borrow funds from another bank, its concern is that interest rates will increase, making borrowing more expensive. Conversely, when a bank needs to lend funds to another bank, the concern is that rates will decrease, making lending less profitable. In both of these cases, the undesirable outcome is caused by changing interest rates. Through hedging, the interest rate each party may earn is set in advance, so the effects of changing interest rates can be calculated by the bank into its returns.

In a transaction involving forwards, there is no exchange of principal. When the forward contract matures, a cash payment is made for the difference between the rate of the contract and the reference rate, usually LIBOR.

EXAMPLE

On February 1, when one-year LIBOR is 3%, Bank A forward contracts to lend Bank D USD 1,000,000 on April 30 for one year at an interest rate of 3%. No exchange of money takes place on February 1. On April 30, the amount of money exchanged depends on the interest rate that day.

- If one-year LIBOR rates are 2.5% on April 30, Bank A stands to profit because Bank D is obliged to borrow the USD 1 million at the pre-agreed 3% rate. Bank A's profit on the transaction will be (3% − 2.5%) * USD 1,000,000, or USD 5,000.
- If one-year LIBOR rates are 4.0% on April 30, then Bank A will lend the money at 3%. This means Bank A will lose (4% − 3%) * USD 1,000,000, or USD 10,000. Bank D reduces its borrowing expenses, paying 3% for the loan instead of having to pay 4%.

The gains and losses cancel each other out. In the first example, Bank A gains USD 5,000; that gain equals Bank D's loss. In the second example, Bank D gains USD 10,000; the loss to Bank A is the same. This is the result of using the forward contract and other financial derivatives: transferring risks between the two banks. The objective of the above transactions is to reduce or share risks. In return for bearing certain risks, the companies involved are willing to accept a reduction in their profits.

Reducing the impact of undesirable outcomes is the same as reducing risks. This is the essential objective of hedging.

Basis Risk

Basis risk is the result of imperfect hedging and can also be referred to as hedging risk. For example, 90-day U.S. Treasury bills have neither currency nor maturity mismatch risk. The residual risk is basis risk.

To achieve perfect hedging, a trader will need to trade an equal and opposite position to the one at risk. A trader who is long a particular type of instrument will therefore have to sell it again in order to neutralize the risky position completely. This may not always be desirable for a trader, who would rather try to hedge with a proxy to the risk taken.

Thus, a trader with a long position in 10-year U.S. Treasury bonds may hedge most of this exposure by selling the necessary number of 10-year U.S. Treasury bond futures. The trader's remaining—or basis—risk is an exposure to the basis between the 10-year yield on the underlying bond for the futures contract and the 10-year U.S. Treasury yield on the actual bond held.

This illustration denotes a composite portfolio consisting of a long position and a short position with approximately the same underlying risk. The trader is short the basis in this instance. If the basis increases in the near future, the trader will have a loss overall. If, however, the basis decreases, the trader will make a profit.

6.4.7   Market Risk Measurement of Credit Risk (CS01, DTS, RR05)

As credit risk has become increasingly tradable, risk managers have been looking for ways of expressing this credit price risk in quantitative ways that can be easily understood. This has especially been the case with the relationship between risk-free yields and credit spreads. During the bond boom of the 1980s, risk-free yields were high and credit spreads low (mostly because the appetite for speculative-grade investments was small by comparison to that for investment grade securities). As a result, the proportion between the two components was large for risk-free yields and small for credit spreads. Risk managers, in the interest of expediency, mostly focused on the larger of these risks and developed the PV01 (present value of one basis point) concept. It is essentially the same as a bond's **effective duration** and describes quantitatively how much the bond's price changes if the smallest imaginable yield change, 1 bp, should occur.

CS01

Times change, and markets are now much more open to risky fixed income investments than before, meaning many credit spreads are high to very high. At the same time, global monetary policies of the 2000s have kept risk-free interest rates very low. The combined result for risk managers is that they now have to focus on the price risk of credit (i.e., the credit spread) much more than the rate risk associated with government yields. To this end, they have adopted the same principle used in PV01 and moved that to the credit spread with a new risk parameter, the CS01 (credit price sensitivity to one basis point change in the spread). The calculation is identical to that of PV01.

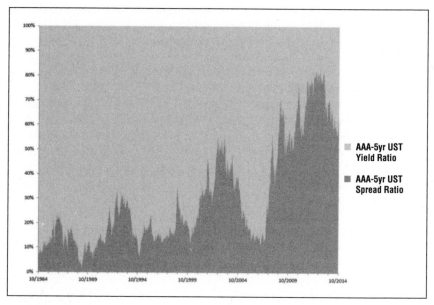

FIGURE 6.14 Yield-Spread Ratio

The yield-spread ratio graphic (Figure 6.14) illustrates how much of an AAA bond yield is due to the risk-free rate and how much to the credit spread. The data have been normalized and cover a period of 30 years.

The chart shows how the risk-free rate accounted for the majority of AAA yields in the 1980s and early 1990s. During this time traders and investors focused on the risk metric PV01, which calculates the bond profit or loss (P/L) for small changes in the risk-free yield.

This changed in the 2000s as the credit spread for AAA bond yields covered an increasingly large proportion of the total yield for these instruments. This renders the PV01 metric less significant, while changes in the credit spread become simultaneously more significant. Price sensitivity to a one-basis-point change in the credit spread on a bond, or CS01, has therefore taken over as a key risk metric in credit-bond market risk management.

Duration Times Spread

Duration times spread (DTS) is an evolution on CS01 that takes into account a weakness of that model: a tendency to overestimate CS01 for stronger credits and underestimate it for poorer credits. This is done by adjusting for/multiplying by the effective duration of the underlying position to arrive at a more intuitive outcome: bonds with large spreads are riskier than bonds with small spreads, given identical duration. Some models use the **spread duration** instead of the effective/price duration.

RR05

Almost every bank today has to compute its own loss given default (LGD), if not for regulatory reporting, at least for internal risk management purposes. This risk parameter is calculated as one minus the recovery rate $(1 - RR)$. The recovery rate is often assumed to be of a certain level, say 40% for senior unsecured credit exposures. What happens to credit exposure if this measure is incorrect? The RR05 (impact of a 5% change in recovery rate) provides an easy way to measure this type of risk.

These are some of the more frequently used measures for the market riskiness of the credit risk in a portfolio. Many banks have internal limits for CS01, and some even have regulatory limits for this variable.

6.5 Market Risk Regulation

6.5.1 The Market Risk Amendment

The Basel I Accord considered only credit risks. In 1996, after consultations with the financial community, the Basel Committee issued the Market Risk Amendment, which was implemented at the end of 1997. The objective of the amendment was to create a capital cushion to balance the negative effects of price movements. Bank trading activities were the primary focus. The bank's trading book refers to the portfolio of financial instruments held by a bank to facilitate trading for its customers, to profit from speculative positions, or to hedge against various types of risk. The Market Risk Amendment created a capital requirement for market risk for:

- Interest rate–related instruments and equities in the trading book
- Foreign exchange and commodities positions throughout the bank

The Market Risk Amendment introduced two methods for banks to use in calculating market risk capital requirements: the Standardized Approach and the Internal Models Approach.

- The Standardized Approach is similar to the standardized credit risk approach and consists of instrument-specific risk weights. These weights are applied to all the bank's holdings that are exposed to market risk. The bank's total market risk regulatory capital is the summation of its risk capital requirement across the risk categories of equities, commodities, and currencies.

  This approach uses an arbitrary risk classification: an 8% capital charge is uniformly applied to equities, currencies, and commodities without regard to their actual risk and volatility. Since the risk charges are systematically added up across the different sources of risk, this approach does not account for any offsetting of risks by looking at a bank's entire portfolio or by looking at how well the bank is diversified. This approach tends to lead to a higher regulatory capital requirement, or less risk-based capital requirement.

- The Internal Models Approach relies on the bank's own internal risk management models and improves on the Standardized Approach. This approach determines the regulatory capital requirement based on the bank's VaR calculations. The bank calculates its 10-day, 99% VaR for adverse changes in interest and exchange rates, and commodities, equity, and option prices. Since the VaR is based on the portfolio of the bank's positions, it considers both correlations and portfolio effects across instruments and markets, and rewards risk diversification. Thus, banks using this approach to determine their regulatory capital requirements would generally have lower regulatory minimum capital than those using the Standardized Approach. It would also generally be more costly to set up and manage the Internal Models Approach, and this is a trade-off that banks have to consider.

  In using the Internal Models Approach, the bank's internal risk management models must meet certain regulatory requirements. These regulations also provide banks with incentives to improve the accuracy of their internal estimates of their market risk exposure.

6.5.2   Basel II

The Basel II Accord's rules on market risk were largely unchanged from the 1996 Market Risk Amendment. Under Pillar 1 banks were still required to use either the Standardized Approach or the Internal Models Approach. The framework did refine the definition of a bank's trading book and under Pillar 3 introduced disclosure requirements for market risk.

6.5.3   Basel III

Basel III changes both the Standardized Approach and the Internal Models Approach.

The Standardized Approach has been updated to include risks associated with correlation trading and market risks associated with securitization, resecuritization, and credit derivative exposures. As noted earlier, correlation trading is a strategy in which the investor gets exposure to the average correlation of an index, rather than just individual shares.

The Internal Models Approach has been refined to improve risk measurement and ensure that banks hold sufficient capital against market risk during times of stress. In addition to calculating standard VaR (using data from the most recent one-year period), banks must also calculate the stressed market VaR for the same portfolio of trades. The stressed VaR must be calculated using data from a one-year period of significant stress.

An Incremental Risk Capital (IRC) charge is introduced to the new VaR framework. The IRC captures default and migration risk within the trading book. Default risk is the potential for direct loss due to an obligor's default as well as the potential for indirect losses that may arise from a default event. Migration risk is the potential for direct loss due to an internal or external ratings downgrade or upgrade as well as the potential for indirect losses that may arise from a credit migration event.

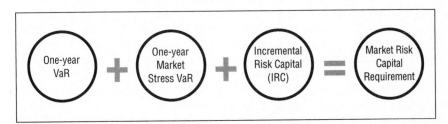

FIGURE 6.15 Market Risk Capital Requirements under Basel III

An important innovation is to penalize banks applying the Internal Models Approach if they experience exceptions exceeding those permitted by the confidence level used in their internal models. Should this happen, a bank is relegated to using the Standardized Approach until the number of exceptions is brought back into line with expectations. Banks facing this threat will find their capital charge increasing. This regulatory tool provides a strong incentive for banks to fine-tune their model design and use.[4]

Figure 6.15 shows the components of the new capital requirements for market risk under Basel III.

To provide further stability to the financial system, Basel III enhances counterparty credit risk practices, including higher Pillar 1 capital requirements determined by stress tests. A bank must add a capital charge to cover the risk of mark-to-market losses on the expected counterparty risk to over-the-counter (OTC) derivatives. This capital charge is called a credit value adjustment (CVA) and is essentially an adjustment made to the value of OTC-derivative contracts to better reflect the credit risk of the counterparty. Broadly speaking, the fair value of a derivatives position should be equal to its risk-free value plus CVA. In other words, CVA is the market price of derivatives counterparty risk.

To improve market discipline through increased transparency, the Basel Committee has implemented deeper and broader disclosure standards. The objective of these changes is to ensure that market participants have an increased ability to better assess the risks other banks may pose.

---

4. BIS, "Fundamental Review of the Trading Book," October 2013, http://www.bis.org/publ/bcbs265.pdf.

CHAPTER 7

Operational Risk

O perational risks are present in virtually all bank transactions and activities and are a major concern of bank supervisors, regulators, and bank management. Failing to understand operational risk increases the likelihood that risks will go unrecognized and uncontrolled, resulting in potentially devastating losses for the bank.

Chapter Outline
  7.1 What Is Operational Risk?
  7.2 Operational Risk Events
  7.3 Operational Loss Events
  7.4 Operational Risk Management
  7.5 Basel II and Operational Risk

Key Learning Points
  ▪ Operational risks are inherent in business and reflect losses from inadequate or failed internal processes, systems, human error, or external events.
  ▪ The Basel II Accord identifies five different operational risk events: internal process risk, **people risk**, legal risk, **external risk**, and **systems risk**. These risks are interrelated.

- Operational risk events are characterized by their frequency and impact on the operations of the bank. Banks focus their operational risk management on **high-frequency/low-impact** risks and **low-frequency/high-impact risks.**
- Operational risk inventory that collects information on operational risk events can be either top-down or bottom-up.
- The Basel II Accord provides three different approaches to calculate **operational risk capital:** the **Basic Indicator Approach,** the Standardized Approach, and the Advanced Measurement Approach.

OPERATIONAL RISK

7.1   What Is Operational Risk?

Operational risk relates both to problems in the bank's internal processes and to external events affecting the operations of the bank. In recent years, banks have started to address their operational risks, such as fraud and theft, in the same formal manner as they manage credit and market risks.

Operational risk is the potential loss resulting from inadequate or failed internal processes or systems, human error, or external events. This definition, from the Basel II Accord, includes legal risk but excludes strategic and reputational risk.

The last 20 years have seen an increase in the number of operational risk events that have severely impacted both business prospects and profitability. Many events were severe enough to cause catastrophic losses for a bank, far in excess of their capital, such as the collapse of Barings Bank and the demise of Kidder Peabody, once a highly regarded U.S. securities firm. The following is a description of an operational risk event at Barings Bank that erased the venerable bank's capital and ultimately resulted in its collapse.

EXAMPLE

In 1995, Baring Brothers and Co. Ltd. (Barings), headquartered in London, collapsed after incurring losses of GBP 827 million following the failure of its internal control processes and procedures. One of the company's traders dealing on both the Singapore Futures Exchange and the Osaka Securities Exchange had been able to hide losses from his ever-increasing trading activities for more than two years by manipulating trading and accounting records. The trader anticipated an increase in the Japanese stock market and acquired a significant position in Japanese stock index futures. When a devastating earthquake hit the Japanese city of Kobe in January 1995, the Japanese stock market dropped precipitously. This led to considerable losses on the trading positions.

Initial assessments considered this a "rogue trader" incident. However, subsequent analysis revealed that better internal controls could have minimized or prevented the loss. The trader had the authority not only to approve his own trading activities, but also to handle the operational aspects of the very same trades he made. The bank's senior management failed to ensure a segregation of duties between the trader and the operational activities that supported his trading. This fundamental shortcoming resulted in the loss of GBP 827 million, twice the bank's available trading capital. Barings was unable to cover that loss. By March 1995, Barings, including all of its liabilities, was acquired for a nominal GBP 1 by the Dutch bank ING.

7.2 Operational Risk Events

Operational risk events are inherent in running any type of business, not only banks. Banks fully expect that operational risk events will happen, and the more complex the operations of a bank are, the more likely it is that there will be significant operational risk events that can affect the bank's profitability. Banks often make provisions in their financial plans for operational losses.

The accepted definition of operational risk considers five broad categories of events:

1. Internal process risk
2. People risk
3. Systems risk
4. External risk
5. Legal risk

These operational risk events are interrelated. Figure 7.1 provides examples for various operational risk events.

Operational Risk Category	Example
External risk	• Events having negative impact that are beyond the bank's control, such as terrorist attacks or natural disasters
Internal process risk	• Failure of the bank's processes and procedures • Inadequate control environment
Legal risk	• Uncertainty of legal action • Uncertainty of rule and regulation applicability
People risk	• Management errors • Inadequate staff training
Systems risk	• Computer, technology, and systems failure • Cyber crime

FIGURE 7.1 Operational Risk Events

Additional operational hazards include business risk, strategic risk, and reputational or headline risk.

- *Business risk* is the potential loss due to a weakening in the competitive position of the bank.
- *Strategic risk* is the potential loss due to poor business decisions or incorrect execution of business decisions.
- *Reputational or headline risk* is the potential loss due to a decrease in a bank's standing in public opinion.

Although excluded from the Basel II regulatory definition of operational risk, many banks include the management of reputational risk within their operational risk function. Over the past decade, the risk to a bank's reputation has increased significantly in terms of both the severity of its impact as well as the speed with which losses can occur. This is because financial markets are global, are trading 24 hours a day, and are operating in a media-intensive world. Thus, damage to an international bank's reputation can happen at any time and in any part of the world, and be reported in real time across the globe. Consequently, reputational risk is one of the critical risks for a bank to manage because:

- The maintenance of reputation is crucial to the survival of an institution.
- Effective management is now a key source of competitive advantage.
- Reputational losses are systemic in nature.
- Reputational damage is difficult to manage and eradicate.

To fully manage reputational risks, many banks not only have policies and procedures detailing how the institution itself manages its reputation, but are extending these to cover how employees use social media both inside and outside the workplace.

Banks are increasingly concerned with managing conduct risk, because failure to do so has, in many cases, had a significant impact on the institution's reputation, leading to large financial loss. Conduct risk is the potential of loss to a bank's customers, clients, or counterparties because of the inappropriate execution of the bank's business activities.

EXAMPLE

UK banks mis-sold interest rate hedging swaps to small businesses that did not understand the complexity or riskiness of the products in which they were investing. In addition to the loss of reputation and trust experienced by the banks, the out-of-pocket cost to the UK banking industry could be in excess of GBP 3 billion once all fines have been paid and compensation payments to affected customers have been made.

7.2.1 Internal Process Risk

Internal process risk is the risk associated with the failure of a bank's processes or procedures. In carrying out a bank's day-to-day operations, the staff conducts business according to prescribed procedures and policies. Corporate policies and procedures include the checks and controls required to ensure that customers receive appropriate service and that the bank operates within the laws and regulations governing its activities. Examples of internal process risk include:

- *Lack of controls.* Failure to audit recorded transactions in and among bank and customer accounts.
- *Marketing errors.* The bank represents that a service includes a specific feature (e.g., a checking account that provides free checks for the life of the account) that in reality is not actually offered.

- *Money laundering.* Engaging in a transaction or transactions to conceal where money is coming from, whose money it is, and/or where the money is going.
- *Documentation or reporting failures.* Reports required by the bank's regulators are not accurate or correct; account opening documentation is incorrect or insufficient.
- *Transaction error.* A teller adds an extra zero to a deposit, making it GBP 3,000 instead of GBP 300.
- *Internal fraud.* Intentional behavior on the part of an employee to enrich himself or herself at the expense of the customers, clients, or the bank itself.

Errors often occur when a process is unnecessarily complicated, disorganized, or easily circumvented, all of which are signs of inefficient business practices. Reviewing and improving a bank's internal processes to improve operational risk management often enhance the bank's operating efficiency and overall profitability. Similarly, auditing processes and analyzing procedures can often reduce internal process risk.

EXAMPLE

At the end of November 2001, UBS Warburg, a Swiss bank, lost an estimated USD 50 million on its trading book due to a mistake by one of its employees. A UBS Warburg trader in Tokyo, Japan, incorrectly sold 610,000 Dentsu shares at 16 yen each, rather than 16 shares at 610,000 yen each. Though the order was questioned by the computerized trading system, an operational failure allowed the trade to go through with the incorrectly transposed amount and price. The computer notification system was not programmed to provide adequate controls..

7.2.2 People Risk

People risk, the risk associated with an employee of a bank, is a common source of operational risk. People risk can occur in every part of a bank, even in the bank's risk management function. People risk is most likely to occur due to:

- *High staff turnover.* Frequent changes in staffing mean new people do not have the required background, experience, or training; may not fully understand the processes; and are more apt to commit errors frequently.

- *Poor management practices.* An unclear oversight structure where employees report different risk events to several separate risk functions, and each separate risk function follows conflicting practices, procedures, and policies.
- *Poor staff training.* During the training of new staff, errors are likely to occur, particularly when the trainers themselves are relatively recent hires.
- *Overreliance on key staff.* This gives rise to burnout of overworked staff.

EXAMPLE

In May 2009 Morgan Stanley was fined USD 2.4 million after the management of its credit derivatives desk allowed a trader to overvalue his position for six months. Management failed to prevent the mispricing by the trader of complex credit derivative products. The problem came to light in 2008 when Morgan Stanley began a review of its valuations. The trader initially tried to hide his mismarking by creating new wrongly priced positions, but eventually confessed to his managers. During a subsequent investigation it was discovered that serious weaknesses in how management oversaw the trader's activities allowed him to circumvent internal valuation checks. Morgan Stanley then had to write down the trader's position by USD 120 million.

7.2.3　Systems Risk

Systems risk is associated with the use of computer technology and computer systems. All banks rely heavily on computers to support their day-to-day activities. In fact, banks today cannot operate without computer systems. Technology-related systems risk events can be caused by the following:

- *Data corruption.* An electrical surge alters data as they are being processed.
- *Inadequate project control.* A failure to properly plan could affect the quality of a risk report produced by the computer system.
- *Programming errors.* Computer models can be inadvertently programmed to generate inaccurate results.
- *Overreliance on "black box" technology.* This is a problem when users believe that the computer systems' internal mathematical models are correct without considering the problem and its solution from a conceptual or qualitative perspective, and without stress-testing the system adequately.

- *Service interruption(s).* An electrical failure results in staff not being able to access reports.
- *System security problems.* Computer viruses and computer hacking are increasingly problematic.
- *System insuitability.* System hardware might not be sufficient to handle high traffic volumes and crashes, or it provides inaccurate results.

In theory, the failure of a bank's technology could lead to a catastrophic event, even the bank's collapse. Heavy reliance on technology makes technology failure an important consideration for senior management—banks have invested heavily to ensure that their operations can continue despite technology failure events. This process is called continuity planning or business resumption planning.

EXAMPLE

Events at Royal Bank of Scotland (RBS) in June 2012 and again in December 2013 are excellent examples of how technology failure can lead to serious problems. In 2012, the Royal Bank of Scotland Group, including Natwest and Ulster Bank, faced computer system problems when a corrupted software update, which controls the payment processing system, was applied on June 19. Customers' transactions were disrupted; many were locked out and could not access their bank account details or utilize ATMs. This had major effects on the bank's operations and reputation. Even weeks later some transactions were still affected. Customers experienced problems, such as delays in completing property purchases; bills could not be paid; one customer faced prison, while another was threatened with having his life support withdrawn as medical payments had not been cleared.

Just over a year later on Cyber Monday, December 2, 2013, one of the busiest shopping days of the year, the Royal Bank of Scotland Group faced another technical glitch. During the hours of 6.30 to 9.30 P.M. the bank's information technology (IT) systems went down. An estimated 750,000 customers were unable to pay for purchases; cash machines were not working, which created long queues; and shops saw hundreds of thousands of customers abandoning their shopping. The RBS Group, over decades, had failed to invest in its technological systems and in adequate business continuity or business resumption planning. It has faced the consequences of two major, systemwide technological failures that have meant it was unable to serve as a bank, to provide customers with basic services (at times for weeks on end), and to compete effectively in the marketplace. These technology failures, so close together, have also impacted RBS' Group reputation.

One system risk of significant concern to the banking industry is cyber crime. **Cyber crime** is any crime with some sort of computer or cyber aspect. Cyber crime is a global problem for the banking industry and has surpassed illegal drug trafficking as a way for criminals to make money. It is estimated that the global cost of cyber crime is at least USD 375 billion.[1] Examples of cyber crime include:

- Hacking
- Denial of service
- Computer viruses
- Identity theft
- Information theft
- Industrial espionage/theft of intellectual property rights
- E-mail fraud
- ATM fraud
- Cyber money laundering
- Theft, for example, using key logging and remote access devices

EXAMPLE

In May 2013, it was announced that a global cyber crime organization had stolen USD 45 million from two Middle Eastern banks by hacking into credit card computer systems and withdrawing money from ATMs located around the world. The criminals broke into the computers of two credit card processing companies, one in India and the other in the United States. The hackers increased the available balance and withdrawal limits on prepaid debit cards issued by the two Middle Eastern banks. They then distributed counterfeit debit cards to "cashers" in 27 countries, who used them to withdraw millions of dollars from ATMs in a matter of hours. In one attack, USD 40 million was stolen from ATMs in 24 of the 27 countries in just over 10 hours.

In 2009, a similar cyber crime targeted prepaid debit cards of Royal Bank of Scotland (RBS). In this case RBS lost more than USD 9 million in less than 12 hours.

There are government initiatives to benchmark banks on the ability of their IT systems to defend themselves against concerted attempts to steal customer information and/or funds. These "cyber stress tests" are becoming as

---

1. "Net Losses: Estimating the Global Cost of Cybercrime—Economic Impact of Cybercrime II," Center for Strategic and International Studies, June 2014.

important as the more high-profile capital strength exercises regularly conducted by regulators. Banks considered to have weak defenses are being ordered to strengthen their security.

7.2.4   External Risk

External risk is the risk associated with events occurring beyond the direct control of the bank. External risk events are generally rare, but when they occur, they can have significant impact on a bank's operations, substantial enough to merit extensive media coverage. Examples of such external events are large-scale robberies, fire, natural disasters, riots, and civil protests. Such events can be caused by:

- Events at other banks that impact banks industry-wide (widespread bank closures, or a bank run)
- External fraud and theft
- Terrorist attacks
- Transport system interruption, which can prevent bank staff from getting to work

EXAMPLE

On September 11, 2001, the 110-floor World Trade Center twin towers in New York City were destroyed by two airplanes that were deliberately flown into them; another airplane destroyed parts of the Pentagon outside of Washington, D.C.; a fourth plane crashed in the state of Pennsylvania. These acts of terror significantly impacted the financial markets, as the World Trade Center was located near Wall Street, the financial heart of New York City, and many financial institutions had offices either in the destroyed buildings or in buildings nearby that had to be evacuated, because of the debris or precaution.

Because the attacks occurred before trading on the major exchanges had opened in New York, the stock exchanges did not open for business that day and reopened for trading only on September 17, 2001. When stock market trading started again on Wall Street, equity values declined significantly. The trading floor of the New York Board of Trade, a commodities exchange, was located in the World Trade Center complex and was destroyed in the attacks. That exchange was able to resume trading on September 17 from a backup facility that it opened after the 1993 terrorist attack on the World Trade Center.

Trading in government bonds halted after the attacks and resumed on September 13, but trading was low as several major government bond dealers had had offices in the World Trade Center. One of them, Cantor Fitzgerald, the market-leading government bond dealer, lost all its employees who were working that day. In the immediate aftermath of these attacks, many banks and other financial institutions evacuated their personnel working in New York and elsewhere, causing further disruption in the financial world.

7.2.5 Legal Risk

Legal risk is the risk associated with the uncertainty of legal actions or the application or interpretation of contracts, laws, or regulations. Legal risk varies greatly from country to country. In some cases, legal risk results from unclearly stated laws, which can lead to murky legal interpretation.

Laws passed in the European Union or the United States often reach across borders and may restrict a bank's international banking activities. With the passing of complex anti-money-laundering, antiterrorism, and customer data protection legislation all around the world, legal risk has evolved as a prominent risk.

EXAMPLE

In early 2012, Wegelin & Co., Switzerland's oldest private bank, announced it would close after paying USD 75 million in fines and penalties to U.S. regulators. Wegelin was prosecuted by the U.S. authorities for helping its American clients hide more than USD 1.2 billion from the U.S. tax authorities. Wegelin had believed that Swiss banking secrecy laws and the fact it had no offices in the United States shielded it from prosecution. Wegelin stated that "it didn't know it would be punished for what it was legally entitled to do under Swiss law." It had acted in accordance with, and not in violation of, Swiss law and considered such conduct common in the Swiss banking industry. The U.S. authorities, however, argued that by allowing U.S. citizens to hide funds, Wegelin was guilty of aiding and abetting tax fraud.

7.3 Operational Loss Events

Operational loss events are commonly classified by the frequency with which they occur, as well as the severity of the potential loss. As shown in Figure 7.2, operational risk management practices focus on two general loss types: loss events that occur often, but with low impact or severity (high-frequency/low-impact events), and loss events that occur infrequently, but with high impact (**low-frequency/high-impact events**). Banks generally are not concerned with the other extremes: low-frequency/low-impact events that would cost more to manage and monitor than the losses from these events would merit, and high-frequency/high-impact events, which would imply a very poorly managed bank that was destined to fail. As shown in Figure 7.2, operational risk management should strive to ensure that high-frequency operational risk events are very low-severity events, and that high-severity events are very low-frequency events.

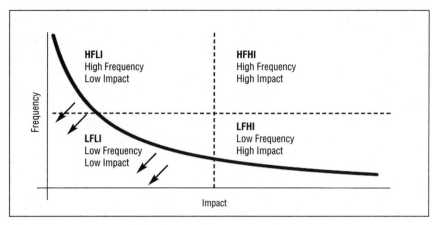

FIGURE 7.2 Loss Impact and Frequency Chart of Operational Risk Events

7.3.1   High-Frequency/Low-Impact Risks (HFLI)

At an individual incident level, losses from **high-frequency/low-impact (HFLI) operational risks** may be minor, but collectively, HFLI events are considered important enough to include in the bank's business decision-making processes. Many financial services providers will factor in these kinds of losses within their product pricing structures. For example, petty fraud and process failures can occur relatively frequently (high frequency), but with relatively low cost, and so are viewed as a cost of doing business. HFLI risk is generally managed by improving business efficiencies.

EXAMPLE

Credit card fraud in the form of unauthorized purchases is common. Identifying potentially unauthorized charges on credit cards is integral to any bank's operational risk management function. To identify and prevent unauthorized charges, complex computer programs analyze every single transaction for each credit card. Based on the location, the frequency, the type, and the amount of the transactions, these programs establish a spending pattern unique to each card.

When a credit card that is primarily used to pay for groceries in rural Germany is suddenly charged with the purchase of expensive jewelry in a different part of the world, the bank's software identifies the jewelry transaction as a pertinent deviation from the card's spending pattern. The risk management function usually suspends any further transactions for that particular card and immediately contacts the owner to inquire whether the transactions were in fact made or authorized by the owner.

If the credit card transactions were made without the consent of the credit card owner, the bank has successfully identified a compromised credit card and will invalidate or cancel the transactions. Then, the bank will replace the compromised card with a new credit card.

This process is costly. When banks adjust their credit card pricing structure, fees, annual interest rates, and membership fees, it is often to provide for the costs of fraud detection and deterrence. Credit card fraud is HFLI—high frequency, low impact. Though costly, it would be of much higher impact if banks did not aggressively monitor cardholders' usage.

7.3.2   Low-Frequency/High-Impact Risks (LFHI)

Low-frequency/high-impact operational risks represent a challenging dimension for risk managers. Because losses from this category of operational risk rarely occur, these events are difficult to model and predict. But because losses from these events can be extremely large, LFHI risks must be considered and managed. Rogue traders, terrorist attacks, and fires are examples of LFHI risks. LFHI events can result in the collapse of a bank.

EXAMPLE

In 2013, HSBC paid USD 1.9 billion to U.S. regulators after it was found to have permitted Latin American drug cartels to launder billions of dollars through its Mexican subsidiary. HSBC Mexico was accused of failing to monitor more than USD 670 billion worth of wire transfers and more than USD 9 billion of U.S. currency purchases. It was alleged that a lack of proper controls allowed the Sinaloa drug cartel in Mexico and the Nortedel Valle cartel in Colombia to move more than USD 881 million through HSBC's U.S. unit from 2006 to 2010. The bank also violated U.S. economic sanctions against Iran, Libya, Sudan, Myanmar (Burma), and Cuba. It also hid transactions with Iran through the practice of "wire stripping": the process of altering details in a wire transfer to hide the origin of a transaction. HSBC agreed to pay a USD 1.25 billion forfeiture and a USD 665 million fine as part of a settlement agreement with the U.S. regulator.

7.3.3   Near Miss and Gain Events

Unlike some other risk types, not all operational risk events lead to banks incurring losses. Operational failures can result in no loss to a bank, a **near miss**, or even lead to a bank making a profit, a **gain event**.

EXAMPLE

Near miss: An ATM located at a bank's branch malfunctions, giving a customer more cash than is debited from the customer's account. Instead of keeping the extra cash, the customer informs staff of the error, allowing the bank to recover funds dispensed by mistake and to stop other customers from using the ATM until it is repaired.

Gain event: A trader exceeds his trading limit, but earns a profit for the bank. Although the bank made money, the operational deficiency that allowed the trader to exceed his trading limit could just have easily resulted in a loss to the bank. (See below.)

When controls fail, an operational risk event occurs irrespective of the financial outcome. Even though such events may result in a profit, they should not be ignored, because they have the potential to result in a loss if they occur again. Recording and understanding such events is important because they:

- Are events with the potential to cause damage.
- Are opportunities to improve processes, systems, and controls.
- Can be early warning signs.
- Help to build as complete a data set as possible.
- Are useful for scenario analysis.

It is helpful to understand that operational risk management can be considered a learning process. When an event occurs, irrespective of the financial consequences, it is important that the event is recorded and steps are taken to prevent its recurring.

7.4   Operational Risk Management

The **operational risk management** process aims to reduce the bank's overall risk level to one that is acceptable to both the bank's senior management and its regulatory supervisor. The typical operational risk management process can be split into five fundamental steps illustrated in Figure 7.3:

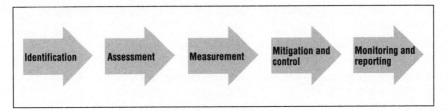

FIGURE 7.3 Steps in the Operational Risk Management Process

- *Identification.* The first step is to consider all the bank's services, processes, and procedures and to identify the potential risks and controls in place relating to each service, process, or procedure. Process mapping and self-assessment questionnaires are common methods used in identifying operational risks.
- *Assessment.* The next step is to consider each identified risk and assess the effectiveness of existing controls in mitigating the risk's potential impact. The risk assessment process provides a good indication of the bank's risk profile at both aggregate and individual business unit levels, and highlights those areas that require improved controls.
- *Measurement.* Operational risk measurement involves quantifying the potential losses from each identified risk. Operational risk can be approximated using simple measures based on the size of the organization or particular business units or modeled based on frequency and severity, as discussed in the previous section.
- *Mitigation and control.* Once operational risks have been identified, assessed, and measured, additional controls and process improvements can be developed and implemented to further mitigate identified risks to levels that are consistent with the risk level of the organization. Process design enhancement and segregation of duties are examples of methods for reducing operational risk.
- *Monitoring and reporting.* Operational risk management (like all risk management) requires ongoing monitoring of risks and concise, timely communication to bank managers, employees, and regulators. Regular risk reports on operational risk events allow bank management to better understand and assess the operational risk profile of the institution and to allocate required resources effectively to guard against unexpected increases in risk events.

7.4.1   Functional Structure of Operational Risk Management Activities

Banks can choose from several organizational structures to manage operational risk. These designs differ in implementation and location in the bank's internal organization. Usually, the bank's operational risk management function is a part of the following business structures:

- A *centralized risk function* is responsible for risk management across the entire bank.
- A *business line risk function* is responsible for evaluation of an individual business line.
- An *individual business unit risk function* is responsible for operational risk management for a business unit and is supported by a central risk management group or function.

To achieve efficiencies, banks commonly adopt a mixed approach. Many banks locate the **risk analysis** function centrally at the headquarters, or main office, level. The **risk monitoring** functions are located as close to business units as possible. Defining clear roles and responsibilities for the operational risk management functions strengthens the operational risk management system. Independent of how a bank structures its risk analysis, monitoring, measuring, and management functions, there are two main approaches to building a companywide operational risk profile:

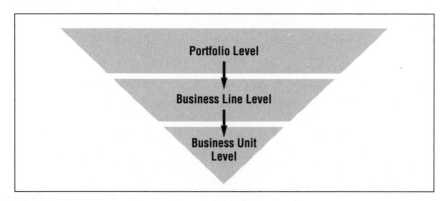

FIGURE 7.4 Operational Risk—Top-Down Approach

- The **top-down approach** first establishes a general assessment of risk from the highest or broadest levels within the organization; see Figure 7.4. It then refines this portfolio-level assessment by breaking the risks down into their individual components, carefully reviewing the individual processes and their attendant risks. This analysis always moves from a broad-based approach to an increasingly specific approach—from a portfolio level to a business line level to the business unit level—to better gauge the risk's potential effects. The results of this analysis are then used to assess the gravity of both the individual risks and their financial effects, and to provide inputs for the firm's operational risk capital calculations.

EXAMPLE

Bankers Trust initiated a top-down approach to assess its operational risks. One of the first steps in this process was to ask the bank's key business line managers about potential loss scenarios within their business that "kept them awake at night." For each of these businesses, the desk managers were then asked to assess the operational risks they encounter. Then, the bank quantified past losses for each business and assessed the likelihood that these risks could occur again. Managers were also asked about effective risk response approaches to mitigate the impact of these operational risks. This review led to the creation of an extensive inventory of risk classes. The inventory was then used to quantify the bank's overall exposure to each type of operational risk.

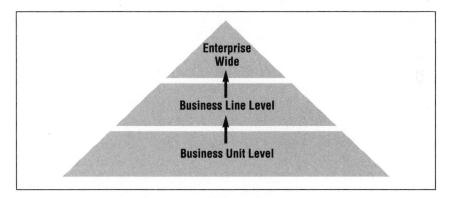

FIGURE 7.5 Operational Risk—Bottom-Up Approach

- In the **bottom-up approach,** first the risk management function assesses all processes within each business unit separately and benchmarks each unit's risk profile; it then aggregates identified risks at a corporate level. The information is presented to a risk management committee or other oversight risk control function to generate a companywide risk profile. This risk profile is the aggregate of risk profiles of each individual business process; see Figure 7.5. Based on these results, the bank's operational risk capital is assessed.

EXAMPLE

Bank of Tokyo-Mitsubishi UFJ created a complex risk self-assessment database in which each risk event was analyzed. The system contained 103 different types of risks. For each risk event, the appropriate risk types had to be identified, and managers had to assess what the potential losses could be, predict how frequently these events would likely occur each year, define factors that could predict the occurrence of the risk event, list procedures that could reduce these operational risks, and assess how effective the procedures could be.

Although the operational risk assessment approaches of Bankers Trust and Bank of Tokyo-Mitsubishi UFJ seem similar, there is one fundamental difference between the two. Bankers Trust, based on its historical experience, created a companywide operational risk inventory, which then helped it to quantify its aggregate operational risk exposure. Bank of Tokyo-Mitsubishi UFJ looked at each of its business processes and, based on this self-assessment, developed operational risk management and measurement approaches. It then based its calculations of the bank's aggregate operational risk exposure on these results.

Whichever of these approaches—top-down or bottom-up—a bank adopts, it must be consistently maintained and appropriate to the overall risk profile of the bank. Factors that influence this decision include the size, sophistication, nature, and complexity of the bank's activities.

7.4.2   Three Lines of Defense

A commonly adopted model for the governance of operational risk management is the "three lines of defense" model. All staff within a bank have a role in ensuring that operational risk is managed effectively, and this model helps to clarify responsibilities. Defining clear responsibilities enables all those involved in the management of operational risk to understand their role and how they fit into the overall risk and control structure. Within operational risk management, the three lines of defense are defined as:

1. Business lines management
2. Independent operational risk management function
3. Independent review and challenge (audit)

Irrespective of the size, complexity, and risk profile of a bank, the "three lines of defense" model provides a simple and effective way of communicating operational risk management responsibilities and clarifies essential roles and duties.

7.4.3 Operational Risk Identification, Assessment, and Measurement

Operational risk management begins with the identification and assessment of the risks inherent in the bank's services, policies, and procedures. The contemporary best practices used to study, assess, and analyze operational risks include:

- *Audit oversight.* The focus is on a review of individual business processes by external auditors. This practice is usually used to supplement the bottom-up approach.
- *Critical self-assessment.* Each business unit analyzes the nature of the operational risks it faces. This subjective method leads to an inventory of various risks, including an evaluation of the frequency and severity of past losses. Often this approach would include the development of risk control processes, such as checklists and questionnaires. This is a bottom-up approach.
- *Risk mapping.* This relates process flows, organizational units, and business units to various operational risk types to help management understand the location of operational weaknesses within the bank. This is considered a bottom-up approach.
- *Causal networks.* A map of the factors that directly or indirectly cause an operational risk event is created. Using complex models, these causal networks are used to measure the magnitude and distribution of operational risk losses and improve the understanding of them. This bottom-up approach is widely used because it captures the causes of risks.
- *Key risk indicators.* These measure the change in risks over time, indicating how risky an activity is by applying objective statistical methods. This approach builds on the assumption that as activities with key risk indicators of an activity increase, so will the likelihood and magnitude of an operational risk event from such an activity. Using early warning signs (increased staff turnover, trade volumes, number of failed trades, the frequency and severity of errors within one business unit, etc.), potential losses can be estimated. This approach can be both top-down and bottom-up.
- *Actuarial models.* The focus is on the frequency and magnitude of operational risk losses and is based on internally collected or externally sourced information. This approach uses mathematical modeling meth-

ods from the insurance industry and can be used from either a bottom-up or a top-down modeling approach.

- *Earnings volatility.* The earnings of various operational units within the bank are analyzed, and the historical changes in the earnings are calculated. This approach assumes that variations in earnings reflect operational risk events and not changes in the business environment. It relies heavily on historical data and thus is a backward-looking measure of risk. A shortcoming of using earnings volatility as a measure is that changes in operational risk management approaches within a business due to improved processes or better understandings of risk events are not quickly recognized in this top-down approach.

7.4.4   Example of Operational Risk Measurement and Management

To better understand the operational risk management process, consider the following simple example in which a bank reviews the process mapping of a check deposited in an account. The process of depositing a check at a bank usually consists of the steps shown in Figure 7.6.

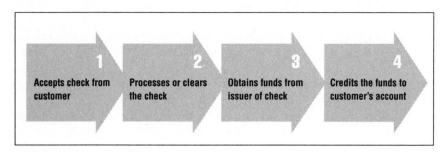

FIGURE 7.6 The Process of Depositing a Check at a Bank

In identifying the potential operational risks, the bank considers employees' responsibilities at each step of the process and the possible operational risks that present themselves along the way. Suppose that during this process, the bank notices a number of problems that occurred, for example, with clearing international checks deposited in customer accounts from certain countries.

In assessing the problems with international check deposits, the bank finds that for the 50,000 transactions with a total value with EUR 6 billion it processed last year involving foreign checks from three countries, 950, or about 2%, experienced problems and processing errors, resulting in a loss to the bank of EUR 100,000. The bank concludes that international check processing for these three countries is a high-frequency, low-impact event: Correcting each of the 950 events costs the bank EUR 105 in personnel and other related expenses. The bank now has sufficient historical information to estimate both the distribution of frequency and the severity of future losses from international check deposits.

To mitigate these losses, the bank decides to implement a control that causes checks from these three countries to be flagged for special attention to ensure they are properly cleared.

Finally, the bank monitors and reports the frequency and severity of losses from all international check deposits so that managers can identify patterns, trends, and clusters of errors, providing valuable objective and other analytical information that will assist in preventing problems and/or determining the root cause of an event (failure). Bank supervisors also have access to these reports through their oversight function, and will review them and make recommendations to bank management if they uncover issues of importance.

7.5   Basel II and Operational Risk

The Basel II Capital Accord made operational risk management a new priority. Under Pillar 1 of the Accord, banks are required to quantify operational risk, measure it, and allocate capital as they do for credit risks and market risks. Basel II defines operational risk as the risk of loss resulting from inadequate or failed internal processes, people or systems errors, or external events. Basel II outlines principles for developing and operating an operational risk framework that addresses the following:

- Development of an appropriate internal risk management environment
- Risk identification, assessment, monitoring, and mitigation/control
- The role of bank supervisors
- The role of disclosure

Basel II expects banks to manage operational risk to reduce the probability of adverse risk events. Properly managing operational risk should directly improve the bank's calculation of its operational risk capital.

Operational risk capital is capital allocated against possible operational losses. In drafting Basel II, the Basel Committee was aware that introducing an operational risk capital requirement could significantly impact the amount of regulatory capital that banks need to hold. The committee also recognized that requiring banks to value their operational risk and calculate risk capital (for many banks, for the first time) could present onerous challenges and expenses, particularly for smaller banks with simple risk profiles. For some banks, the cost of implementing highly complex methodologies for calculating operational risk capital could very well be greater than the potential benefits. So the Basel Committee allowed flexibility, suggesting banks could use any one of three different approaches to calculate operational risk capital, or any combination of the three approaches:

1. Basic Indicator Approach
2. Standardized Approach
3. Advanced Measurement Approach

By allowing banks to choose from the three approaches, the Basel II framework encourages banks to become more precise in their approach to assessing the operational risks and calculating operational risk capital. Each approach is increasingly sophisticated and more costly to implement than the previous one, but each is also believed to target a bank's operational risk capital requirement more accurately. The more accurate the analysis and assessment, the more certain a bank can be that it is not overestimating its actual operational risk capital needs, which would reduce its potential profitability.

7.5.1   Basic Indicator Approach

The Basic Indicator Approach uses the bank's total annual gross income as a risk indicator for the bank. This approach assumes that the more income the bank earns, the larger it is and the greater its operational risk. The bank's required level of operational risk capital is computed as a fixed percentage of the bank's annual gross income averaged over the previous three years (excluding negative and zero annual gross income years and averaging over the remaining positive years). The fixed percentage as set by the Basel Committee is currently 15%.

Given its simplicity, the Basic Indicator Approach is certainly the least costly in terms of internal systems and support. However, it is a generally inferior alternative for measuring the magnitude of operational risk—the bank may be setting aside more capital to cover operational risks than it needs to. Most banks engage in a wide variety of different types of businesses, each with an inherently distinctive risk profile, specific internal operational risk monitoring requirements, and earnings potential. That all business activities represent the same level of risk is a potentially hazardous oversimplification, and therefore the fixed percentage set by the Basel Committee attempts to overestimate the risk potential, resulting in a higher operational risk capital requirement. In practice, the Basic Indicator Approach is limited because it is not a true indicator of risk and does not require a methodical review of the bank's services, policies, and procedures. However, it is simple and requires little in the way of direct expense.

EXAMPLE

Bank A makes loans only to corporate entities with assets in excess of EUR 200 million and high-net-worth individuals with assets in excess of EUR 10 million. It also focuses its business to deal with only a select number of these corporations and high-net-worth clients. Bank B specializes in home mortgages and equity lines of credit to a wide, rapidly expanding, and predominantly retail customer base. Both banks have the same positive gross annual income for each of the past three years. Bank A's business is likely to present less operational risk. Yet, under the Basic Indicator Approach, both banks would calculate their operational risk capital allocation as the same proportion of their gross income.

7.5.2   Standardized Approach

The **Standardized Approach** to calculating a bank's operational risk capital requirement attempts to address some of the concerns related to the lack of risk sensitivity in the Basic Indicator Approach. The Standardized Approach divides the activities of a bank into eight business lines and then applies a fixed percentage, or **beta factor**, against the average positive annual gross income (over three years) of each. The beta factor varies, depending on the business line, as seen in Figure 7.7.

Business Unit	Fixed Percentage (Beta Factor)
Corporate finance	18%
Payment and settlement	18%
Trading and sales	18%
Agency services	15%
Commercial banking	15%
Asset management	12%
Retail banking	12%
Retail brokerage	12%

FIGURE 7.7 Beta Factors to Calculate Operational Risk Capital in Standardized Approach

The Standardized Approach refines the Basic Indicator Approach by recognizing that operational risk can vary by business unit. For example, a bank's trading and sales business unit is considered to carry a higher overall operational risk than its asset management business unit. The beta factor used in the calculation can be specified by the bank's regulator and can be adjusted to reflect the relative riskiness of diverse banking operations.

By splitting the bank into separate business lines and assigning a different risk calculation percentage to each, the Standardized Approach attempts to link a bank's operational risks more closely to its capital requirement. While this may be a better approach for many banks, the Standardized Approach is limited—it does not capture the bank's actual operational risk, as it does not involve detailed risk assessment.

Under the Standardized Approach, an aggregate amount of capital is calculated for each of the previous three years. These aggregated amounts are then simply averaged to give the operational risk regulatory capital amount required under the Standardized Approach. The aggregate regulatory capital for a single year is calculated by adding up the results of gross income, multiplied by the beta for each business line. It is not important if the gross income for any business line is negative, as it can simply be included within the calculation. If the aggregate for any given year is negative, then it is replaced with a zero in the average calculation, and the average is still calculated over three years.

EXAMPLE

GammaBank operates several different business lines and is evaluating the operational risk capital estimates that the Basic Indicator Approach and the Standardized Approach provide. The relevant annual gross income for the various business lines for the past three years is in Figure 7.8.

These two approaches offer two different minimum capital calculations; using the Standardized Approach, the operational risk capital estimate is CHF 0.90 million less (CHF 20.25 million − CHF 19.35 million = CHF 0.90 million).

	Annual Gross Income in CHF Millions			Basic Indicator Approach	Standardized Approach
	2006	**2007**	**2008**	**Beta Factor**	**Beta Factor**
Corporate finance	20	30	25	15%	18%
Retail banking	35	55	30	15%	12%
Commercial banking	55	60	20	15%	15%
Agency services	15	10	5	15%	15%
Retail brokerage	10	25	10	15%	12%
Total	**135**	**180**	**90**		

Basic Indicator Approach:
Operational risk capital charge = (135 * 15% + 180 * 15% + 90 * 15%) / 3 = 20.25

Standardized Approach:
2006 component = (20 * 18% + 35 * 12% + 55 * 15% + 15 * 15% + 10 * 12%) = 19.5
2007 component = (30 * 18% + 55 * 12% + 60 * 15% + 10 * 15% + 25 * 12%) = 25.5
2008 component = (25 * 18% + 30 * 12% + 20 * 15% + 5 * 15% + 10 * 12%) = 13.05
Operational risk capital charge = (19.5 + 25.5 + 13.05) / 3 = 19.35

FIGURE 7.8 Comparison of Risk Capital Charge under the Basic Indicator Approach and Standardized Approaches for GammaBank

7.5.3   Advanced Measurement Approach

The **Advanced Measurement Approach (AMA)** is the most sophisticated approach to calculate operational risk capital and allows the bank to use internally generated models to calculate its operational risk capital requirements. Use of the AMA is subject to stringent regulatory requirements and rigorous bank supervisory oversight. The Basel Committee has not recommended any particular models for banks to use under the AMA, leaving it up to each bank to develop its own internal operational risk measurement systems.

In developing the bank's AMA, the bank may draw from its own risk experiences, including its loss history. The bank can complement this information with the pooled loss histories of other institutions. Moreover, the bank can consider, model, and measure its own business and internal control environment. Clearly, developing the methods and infrastructure to model and measure operational risk is significant and costly. The benefits are twofold. First, the Basel Committee presumes (and regularly monitors the validity) that the bank's AMA provides a more accurate assessment of its operational risk, thereby allowing banks to move away from the simple, overly conservative weights used in the Basic Indicator Approach and the Standardized Approach. Second, banks using the AMA benefit from the careful consideration of their business practices that must occur in assessing and measuring operational risk.

7.5.4   Criteria for Using Different Approaches

Banks must meet a "credibility" test in order to use the two more sophisticated approaches. Credibility is determined by the bank's regulatory supervisor, who compares the operational risk capital requirement the bank calculates against the requirements calculated by similar peer banks using the same approach. This comparison allows the bank supervisor to make an educated determination as to whether the bank's results are fairly stated and credible relative to those of its peers. If the results are not credible, the supervisor can direct that the bank use a simpler methodology to calculate its operational risk charge.

The Basic Indicator Approach, being the simplest, sets no criteria for adoption. Banks must meet certain stipulations in order to use the Standardized Approach or Advanced Measurement Approach:

Standardized Approach
To use the Standardized Approach, the bank must have a dedicated operational risk function and systems in place to support it. Internationally active banks must also have systems and procedures to collect, store, maintain, and report internal operational risk data. The operational risk management function of an international bank must have clear lines of responsibility, and the bank must provide incentives for improving the management of operational risk throughout the firm. As a practical matter, the bank's supervisors can insist on a testing and monitoring period before allowing the Standardized Approach to be used for regulatory purposes.

Advanced Measurement Approach
Banks using the AMA are subject to strict qualitative and quantitative criteria. The bank must fulfill the Standardized Approach criteria regarding

international banks and must augment its internal processes with external operational risk data. It must also develop and properly implement a dedicated and appropriate operational risk framework. The bank must also actively involve major business lines, control areas, audit areas, and the bank's board of directors and senior management in its operational risk oversight.

- **Qualitative Criteria**
  The bank must adhere to a minimum set of quality standards, including those focusing on the independence and design of the operational risk measurement, management, and monitoring structure.
- **Quantitative Criteria**
  To ensure that an internal model meets required standards, the Basel Accord specifies that the bank must be able to demonstrate that its approach captures potentially severe loss events, and the bank must maintain rigorous procedures for operational risk model development and independent model validation.

Lastly, as determined by its supervisor, a bank wanting to deploy the Advanced Measurement Approach is subject to a compulsory period of supervisory monitoring.

A bank does not have to start with the Basic Indicator Approach. Provided the bank meets the criteria outlined by Basel II and its regulators, it can implement either the Standardized Approach or the Advanced Measurement Approach. A bank can also migrate down from a more advanced methodology to a simpler one. Such a move requires the approval of the bank's supervisor. If the bank's regulator is not satisfied with the bank's advanced approach calculations, or if the bank subsequently fails to meet certain regulatory and/or Basel standards, the regulator can require the bank to revert to a simpler approach.

The Basel II Accord also allows a bank to use a mix of approaches for calculating operational risk capital. For example, if the bank meets preset criteria, its supervisor could allow it to use the Basic Indicator Approach or the Standardized Approach for some parts of its operations and the Advanced Measurement Approach for others.

7.5.5 Basel II and Operational Risk Management

As mentioned, Basel II requires, for the first time, that banks hold regulatory capital against their operational risks. It is expected that approximately 12% of a bank's capital will be held against these types of risk. The Basel Committee has adopted both a quantitative and a qualitative approach to determine comprehensively a bank's operational risk capital. Inherent in these requirements is the fact that banks need to understand their own operational risks, be able to collect operational risk loss data, and create functions that focus on managing, monitoring, and mitigating operational risks. Banks, regulators, and supervisors understand that the processes relating to and associated with operational risk analysis, operational risk event measurement and management, and risk capital calculations are dynamic and not just one-time or yearly reoccurring events.

7.5.6 Basel III and Operational Risk Management

Although the Basel III Accord makes no specific changes to operational risk regulation, the introduction of the new regulations has led to a period of change within banks. This may impact the operational risk profile of banks and increase the potential for operational risk failures.

The new accord recognizes that reputational risk events may give rise to credit, liquidity, market, and legal risk. Under Basel III, a bank should identify potential sources of reputational risk, incorporate these into its risk management processes, and make appropriate liquidity contingency plans. Once a bank identifies its potential reputational risks, it should measure the amount of support it might have to provide or losses it might experience.

CHAPTER 8

Regulatory Capital and Supervision

T he Basel Accords aim to maintain the stability of the international banking industry by setting international standards for capital adequacy and, in the case of the most recent accord, for liquidity.

The first Basel Accord set a minimum standard for risk-weighted capital adequacy and provided a simple methodology for calculating it. The Basel II Accord introduced a three-pillar framework for assessing capital adequacy. Under Pillar 1 of Basel II, Basel I's measurement of risk-weighted capital was increased in scope and made more sensitive (and more complicated). Basel II increased the minimum capital requirements by including operational and market risk alongside credit risk within the scope of Pillar 1.

Pillar 2 introduced the concept of **supervisory review**, under which bank supervisors would review how a bank was calculating its capital ratios and assess the adequacy of that process. Under Pillar 2, the supervisor can require a bank to hold more capital than the regulatory minimum specified under Pillar 1.

Pillar 3 introduced the concept of market discipline. Under Pillar 3, banks are required to disclose significant amounts of information about the risks they face and the capital they hold, on the assumption that with that information available, market participants will form an opinion on a bank's capital adequacy.

Basel III retains the three pillars introduced by Basel II and also the requirement to hold capital against credit, market, and operational risks. As a result, many features of Basel II remain the guiding standards on bank capital calculation, even after publication of Basel III.

Basel III also introduced standards on liquidity for the first time, as neither Basel I or Basel II addressed this issue.

It is important to recognize that the Basel Accords are standards on capital and liquidity and are not in themselves regulations. The Basel Committee has no power to enforce the standards that it sets. Only national regulators (or, in the case of the European Union, a regional regulator) have the power to do that.

Beyond the mandates of regulatory capital, bank management has a responsibility to address the long-term well-being of the organization. Economic capital is the capital level a bank must maintain to withstand large but unlikely losses so that it can survive over the long term.

Chapter Outline
8.1   Pillar 1—Bank Regulatory Capital
8.2   Types of Bank Regulatory Capital under Basel II
8.3   Bank Capital under Basel III
8.4   Pillar 2—Supervisory Review
8.5   Pillar 3—Market Discipline
8.6   International Cooperation
8.7   Beyond Regulatory Capital

Key Learning Points
- The Basel II Accord provides a general framework for how a bank's overall capital should be structured, defines "tiers" of eligible capital, and provides specific rules on the relationships between different tiers.
- Under Basel II, the eligible capital for regulatory purposes must be greater than or equal to 8% of the risk-weighted asset value.
- Basel III addresses the shortcomings of the Basel II Accord. It strengthens the quality of capital held by banks to ensure that they have capital that will retain its value when needed, and it also increases the quantity of capital that banks must hold.
- Pillar 2, supervisory review, ensures compliance with minimum capital requirements and encourages banks to use the best risk management techniques and to address risks beyond the scope of Pillar 1.

- Pillar 3 focuses on disclosure requirements to provide transparency with respect to a bank's capital structure, risk exposures, and capital adequacy.
- Economic capital establishes the capital level a bank must maintain to withstand large but unlikely losses so that it can survive over the long term.
- Banks use economic capital models to decide the level and structure of capital. The development and implementation of a well-designed economic capital model can help a bank identify, understand, mitigate, and manage its risks more effectively, leading ultimately to a more effective and stable bank.

REGULATORY CAPITAL AND SUPERVISION

8.1 Pillar 1—Bank Regulatory Capital

The Basel II Accord defines a three-pillar framework to ensure that banks adopt a consistent approach to their capital adequacy requirements. The three pillars are:

- Pillar 1: Minimum Capital Standards
- Pillar 2: Supervisory Review Process
- Pillar 3: Market Discipline

The objective of Pillar 1 is to set minimum capital standards for a bank's credit, market, and operational risk exposures. Pillar 1 details the approaches for measuring a bank's credit, market, and operational risk and the amount of capital that a bank should hold in respect of those risks. It therefore links risk and capital. As discussed in the previous three chapters, Basel II defines, for each risk type, several approaches to estimate the riskiness of the bank's exposures, from basic to more sophisticated, as shown in Figure 8.1.

	Credit Risk	**Market Risk**	**Operational Risk**
Approaches (ordered from least to most sophisticated)	1. Standardized Approach 2. Foundation Internal Ratings-Based (IRB) Approach 3. Advanced IRB Approach	4. Standardized Approach 5. Internal Models Approach	6. Basic Indicator Approach 7. Standardized Approach 8. Advanced Measurement Approach
Result	Risk-weighted asset value for credit risk	Market risk capital charge	Operational risk capital charge

FIGURE 8.1 Methods for Calculating Capital According to Basel II

Pillar 2 of Basel II describes how bank supervisory review is to be used both to determine that banks meet the minimum capital standards and to encourage best practices in risk management. Pillar 3 defines disclosure standards that allow market participants to readily assess a bank's capital structure and adequacy, thereby allowing market discipline to further compel banks toward sound capital practices.

8.1.1 Basel II Minimum Capital Standard

As discussed in previous chapters, the Basel II Accord requires banks to measure their credit, market, and operational risks. For each, the Basel framework defines a set of approaches, varying in complexity, for quantifying the amount of risk. Basel also defines a minimum level of eligible regulatory capital, which is determined as a function of the risk-weighted asset values.

The Basel I formula used a simple ratio for computing the required regulatory capital. This ratio, termed the capital ratio, was set at a minimum of 8%, but national supervisors were given the discretion to impose a higher capital ratio. The formula for determining whether a bank meets the capital ratio is:

$$\frac{\text{Eligible Regulatory Capital}}{\text{Risk-Weighted Assets}} \times 100 \geq \text{Capital Ratio (minimum 8\%)}$$

In words, the eligible capital for regulatory purposes must be greater than or equal to 8% of the risk-weighted asset value. Under Basel I, the calculation was simple, as the regulation required banks to consider credit risk only; however, Basel II extended the risk coverage to include a capital charge for market risk and operational risk. Basel II multiplies the market risk capital charge and operational risk capital charge each by 12.5 (which is equal to 1/8%) to convert those requirements into market risk risk-weighted assets and operational risk risk-weighted assets, respectively. Basel II retained the minimum capital requirement of 8% of the bank's total risk-weighted assets.

Using one of the approved approaches for quantifying and calculating the riskiness of its credit, market, and operational risk, a bank will have derived the following values:

- Risk-weighted assets for credit risk, denoted by RWA_C
- Market risk capital requirement, denoted by MR_C
- Operational risk capital requirement, denoted by OR_C

The total risk-weighted assets (RWA_T) value for the bank is:

$$RWA_T = RWA_C + 12.5 * (OR_C + MR_C)$$

The **Basel II minimum capital standard** states that:

$$\frac{\text{Eligible Regulatory Capital (RC)}}{\text{Total Risk-Weighted Assets (}RWA_T\text{)}} \times 100 \geq \text{Capital Ratio (minimum 8\%)}$$

In words, the eligible capital for regulatory purposes must be greater than or equal to 8% of the total risk-weighted asset value. The required regulatory capital (R_C) can be determined by:

$$RC = RWA_T * \text{Capital Ratio} = RWA_T * 8\% \text{ (minimum)}$$

The Basel Committee retains the ability to adjust the 8% minimum parameter according to historical results over time.

EXAMPLE

Bank A seeks to comply with Basel II standards and has determined that it has the following credit, market, and operational risks:

Credit risk-weighted assets (RWA_C):   USD 1,200 million
Market risk charge (MR_C):   USD 60 million
Operational risk charge (OR_C):   USD 40 million

Its total risk-weighted assets (RWA_T) are calculated as follows:

$$RWA_T = RWA_C + 12.5 * (OR_C + MR_C)$$

$$RWA_T = 1,200m + 12.5 * (60m + 40m) = 1,200m + 1,250m = 2,450 \text{ million}$$

Assuming an 8% capital ratio, the minimum amount of regulatory capital that Bank A will need to hold is $RC = RWA_T * 8\% = 2,450m * 8\% = USD$ 196 million.

Examples of regulatory capital can be seen by viewing sample historical interim quarterly reports of international banks. As most large international banks are transitioning form Basel II to Basel III, for the sake of clarity, Basel II figures are used for this example of four banks.

In all of the cases for the four banks:
- Tier 1 capital is greater than or equal to Tier 2 capital, in line with Basel II standards.
- Credit risk is the dominant contributor to risk-weighted assets, as credit risk is generally the biggest risk for banks.
- Capital ratios comfortably exceed 8%, the minimum standard of Basel II. Basel II defines the minimum standard, but bank management may set higher thresholds to maintain a target credit rating and/or to avoid potential increases to regulatory charges if the bank were to fall below the regulatory minimum.

	Bank A (million CHF)	Bank B (million USD)	Bank C (million euros)	Bank D (million euros)
Shareholders' Equity and Other Deductions	56,203 (18,703)	154,787 (46,936)	37,069 (9,369)	30,270 (9,556)
Tier 1 Capital	**37,500**	**107,851**	**27,700**	**20,714**
Subordinated Debt and Other Deductions	14,181 (1,012)	53,781 (14,682)	18,775 (1,306)	13,355 (490)
Tier 2 Capital	**13,170**	**39,099**	**17,469**	**12,865**
Other Deductions	0	0	(717)	0
Total Capital	**50,670**	**146,950**	**44,452**	**33,579**
Credit Risk: RWA_C	260,578	1,071,482	283,746	Not provided
Market Risk: MR_C	1,535	4,202	3,237	Not provided
Operational Risk: OR_C	3,472	8,597	2,282	Not provided
Total Risk-Weighted Assets	**323,166**	**1,231,470**	**352,734**	**268,357**
Capital Ratio (Total Capital/Total RWA)	**15.7%**	**11.9%**	**12.6%**	**12.5%**
Min. Capital Requirement	**25,853**	**98,518**	**28,219**	**21,469**
(8%) Capital Surplus	**24,817**	**48,432**	**16,233**	**12,110**

FIGURE 8.2 Sample Regulatory Capital Reports

8.2   Types of Bank Regulatory Capital under Basel II

A bank's **regulatory capital** is the minimum capital that regulators require the bank to hold against the risks it is running. Equity capital is usually the primary asset that makes up the bank's regulatory capital. The Basel II

Accord provides a general framework for how a bank's overall capital should be structured, and defines guidelines for eligible capital. In particular, Basel II defines tiers of capital and provides specific rules on the relationships between different tiers that must be followed to meet mandated minimum capital requirements.

8.2.1   Tier 1 Capital

The amount of **Tier 1 capital** held by a bank is considered a core measure of its financial strength. The primary element of Tier 1 capital is **shareholders' equity** (the amount of capital left over after subtracting the bank's liabilities from its assets). To this core Tier 1 capital, a bank can add **innovative capital** such as complex financial instruments that have both equity and debt features. Bank supervisors place strict rules on this innovative Tier 1 capital. The complex financial instruments that would be considered innovative capital for Tier 1 consideration are beyond the scope of this book.

8.2.2   Tier 2 Capital

Tier 2 capital is the second most important type of capital that can be used to meet a bank's regulatory minimum capital requirements. Tier 2 capital may consist of items such as **subordinated term debt** and reserves. Subordinated debt is debt issued by the bank that ranks lower on the repayment scale than depositors in the event of a bank default. One type of reserves is revaluation reserves, where the new value which reflects the difference between the original value and the new higher value can be recorded on the company's books.

EXAMPLE

Bank B owns government bonds that have increased in value by USD 20 million. The bank is considering selling the majority of these bonds in the near future. However, the bank cannot actually realize this profit until it sells the bonds. As such this price appreciation is considered "unrealized" profit. If these bonds can be revalued according to regulatory guidelines and with the consent of the bank's supervisor to reflect their unrealized profit, this unrealized profit of USD 20 million can be added to a reserve account and used for Tier 2 capital calculations.

8.2.3 Tier 3 Capital

Tier 3 capital includes a wider variety of subordinated debt than that allowed for Tier 2 capital and may include profits from the bank's trading activities. *Tier 3 capital can only be used to support the market risk the bank takes in its trading book.* Instruments that can be counted as Tier 3 capital are generally too risky to be used for material portions of a bank's capital calculation. For example, using trading profits in the capital calculation is obviously risky, as the trading profits could disappear at any time.

8.2.4 The Ratio of the Capital Tiers

The Basel Committee also defines rules governing the ratios that banks must maintain between different classes of capital. One primary restriction is that Tier 2 capital cannot be greater than Tier 1 capital.

There are additional capital calculations for credit and market risk.

- *For credit risk:* Eligible Tier 1 and Tier 2 capital for credit risk must be greater than $8\% * RWA_C$.
- *For market risk:* Eligible Tier 1, Tier 2, and Tier 3 capital for market risk must be greater than the market risk capital requirement.

In addition, banks will calculate their eligible regulatory capital (RC) as follows:

$$RC = \text{Tier 1 Capital} + \text{Tier 2 Capital} - \text{Deductions}$$

8.2.5 Deductions and Adjustments from Regulatory Capital

Certain capital items cannot be included in a bank's regulatory capital calculation. These include:

- Goodwill, which arises when the purchase price of a business is greater than the book value of the capital of the acquired company. Goodwill is a subjective assessment by the market and so is not included in the capital calculation.
- Investments in subsidiaries engaged in banking and similar activities under certain conditions.
- Shares held by the bank in another bank.

EXAMPLE

Bank A seeks to comply with Basel standards and has determined that it has the following credit, market, and operational risks:

Credit risk-weighted assets (RWA_C):   USD 1,200 million
Market risk charge (MR_C):   USD 60 million
Operational risk charge (OR_C):   USD 40 million

Bank A has determined that its total risk-weighted assets (RWA_T) are USD 2,450 million.

Bank A has the following eligible capital:

- Tier 1 capital: USD 150 million
- Tier 2 capital: USD 110 million
- Tier 3 capital: USD 0 million
- Deductions from capital: USD 10 million

The total amount of regulatory capital (RC) held by Bank A is:

RC = Tier 1 capital + Tier 2 capital + Tier 3 capital – Deductions
RC = 150 + 110 – 10 = USD 250 million
Capital ratio = $RC/RWA_T \geq 8\%$

Regulatory capital ratio = USD 250/USD 2,450 million = 10.2%, which exceeds the minimum standard of 8% under the Basel II Accord.

Any eligible capital level in excess of USD 196 million (8% * USD 2,450 million) will satisfy the minimum regulatory capital requirement for Basel II.

8.2.6   New Capital

Usually, growing banks retain some of their profits to add to their Tier 1 capital base. Retained capital allows the bank to support new business without raising new capital from activities such as issuing new shares, issuing debt, or seeking private investors. Raising new capital can be a time-consuming and expensive process.

The Basel Committee allows interim annual profits, adjusted for some items, to be added to Tier 1 capital as long as the bank's auditors also allow it. This is particularly useful for banks with rapidly growing balance sheets. If these banks were forced to wait until the end of their fiscal year before profits could be counted as regulatory capital, they might need interim injections of capital from shareholders to maintain their business growth.

8.3   Bank Capital under Basel III

Basel III's main focus is increasing the quantity and quality of capital held by banks. These changes are being implemented incrementally to:

- Allow regulators, banks, and the financial industry adequate time to assess the efficacy of these newly introduced regulatory tools.
- Ensure that the various supervisory approaches are correctly and consistently calibrated, implemented, and applied.

8.3.1   The Quality and Quantity of Capital

The new framework simplifies the regulatory capital definition and harmonizes the various types of financial instruments that are eligible for inclusion when computing regulatory capital requirements. Basel III introduces a stricter definition of capital that banks can use to meet their regulatory capital requirement. Essentially, the new regulation means that capital must have a greater ability to absorb losses, which allows banks to withstand extended periods of more severe stresses.

Tier 1 capital remains the predominant form of capital, and consists mainly of common shares and retained earnings, known as Common Equity Tier 1 (CET1) capital, although limited use of equity-like instruments is permitted. The types of instruments that can be used as Tier 2 capital are simplified and can become loss-absorbing capital under certain circumstances. Tier 3 capital is eliminated.

Under the new framework, the quantity of capital a bank must hold is increased by emphasizing the crucial role that common equity capital plays in absorbing losses and providing banks with an essential capital base. The Tier 1 capital requirement was raised from 4% to 6% of total risk-weighted assets. The regulatory requirement for CET1 was raised to 4.5% of total risk-weighted assets. Basel II effectively required 2%. As the minimum capital ratio remains at 8%, the maximum amount of Tier 2 capital required under Basel III is now 2% of a bank's total RWA. Tier 3 capital was eliminated to ensure the same quality of capital across credit, market, and operational risks.

8.3.2 Capital Conservation Buffer

In addition to the minimum Tier 1 and Tier 2 capital, Basel III requires banks to hold an additional capital conservation buffer (CCB). This buffer is intended to absorb losses during periods of financial and economic stress and must be funded by Common Equity Tier 1 capital. The capital conservation buffer was set at 2.5% of a bank's total RWA.

Combining the CCB and the basic capital requirement means that Basel III stipulates a minimum Common Equity Tier 1 capital ratio of 7% and a total regulatory capital requirement of 10.5%, a significant increase over Basel II.

8.3.3 Countercyclical Capital Buffer

The global financial crisis of 2007–2009 emphasized the pro-cyclical nature of risk-based capital requirements. During good times, when underwriting practices are generous, credit volumes can easily become excessive. During bad times, when underwriting practices are stringent, credit is hard to secure. Credit losses reduce the amount of available capital, and the value of mark-to-market credit products is highly sensitive to the volatility patterns of the markets.

The new regulations introduce a framework for creating, implementing, and releasing a countercyclical capital buffer. The buffer is designed to protect the banking sector, at a national level, from periods of excessive credit growth. The size of the buffer is set by local regulators and ranges between 0% and 2.5% of total RWA. It must consist of Common Equity Tier 1 capital.

8.3.4 Systemically Important Financial Institutions

Basel III recognizes that given the interconnectedness of many large banks and other financial institutions, their failure could trigger a systemwide crisis. Those institutions that are considered systemically important are now required to hold additional loss-absorbing capital to strengthen their ability to survive periods of financial stress.

Using both quantitative and qualitative factors, the Financial Stability Board has identified a number of global systemically important banks (G-SIBs). These G-SIBs have to meet additional loss absorbency requirements by holding more Common Equity Tier 1 capital. This additional requirement ranges from 1% to 3.5% of a bank's total risk-weighted assets, depending on its systemic importance.

The additional capital requirements for the countercyclical capital buffer and the G-SIB surcharge could theoretically add an additional 6.5% common equity capital requirement. This is in addition to the standard Basel III 10.5% capital standard for banks.

EXAMPLE

Bank A has determined that its total risk-weighted assets (RWA_T) are USD 2,450 million.

Under the Basel II Accord, it would have to hold a minimum of USD 196 million in regulatory capital, of which a minimum of USD 98 million would need to be held as Tier 1 capital.

Under Basel III, Bank A will need to hold USD 196 million of core capital (8% of RWA_T), of which a minimum of USD 147 million will need to be held as Tier 1 capital.

Tier 1 capital = RWA_T * 6% = 2,450m * 6% = 147 million

In addition, Bank A will need to hold a capital conservation buffer of USD 61.25 million.

RAW_T * 2.5% = 2,450m * 2.5% = 61.25 million

Thus Bank A's minimum regulatory requirement will increase from a minimum of USD 196 million under Basel II to a minimum of USD 257.25 million under Basel III.

8.4 Pillar 2—Supervisory Review

Pillar 1 defines the calculations to determine the minimum regulatory capital required with respect to market, credit, and operational risk. Pillar 2 sets out the principles of the supervisory review process that national authorities should use (in addition to the Pillar 1 capital calculations) to evaluate a bank's capital adequacy.

In particular, Pillar 2 addresses three main areas that are either not covered or fall outside the scope of Pillar 1. These are:

- Risks not fully considered by Pillar 1, such as **credit concentration risk** where a bank would have too much of its risk concentrated in any one region or asset, for example, in home loans in a certain part of a country

- Risks not considered at all by Pillar 1, such as interest rate risk in the banking book
- Factors external to the bank (e.g., business cycle effects)

In addition, Pillar 2 defines the supervisory assessment of a bank's compliance with the minimum standards set for the use of the more advanced methods of capital calculation in Pillar 1. This review by bank supervisors ensures compliance with minimum capital requirements and encourages banks to develop and use the best risk management techniques. However, it is not a substitute for good management. The board of directors and senior management of a bank have the responsibility to ensure that they maintain adequate capital to support the bank's business activities, including those beyond the scope of Pillar 1.

Bank management is responsible for developing an internal capital adequacy assessment process (ICAAP) that evaluates the risk and control environment across all the bank's operations. Capital assessment is an ongoing process that is an integral part of managing a bank's business activities. The process not only evaluates current capital requirements, but also estimates future capital requirements. Bank management uses the estimates for each of its businesses to set capital targets that are aggregated to determine the bank's overall capital requirement. Bank management then monitors the bank's actual capital requirement, as determined by the business it conducts, against its previously estimated targets.

The quality of the internal capital adequacy assessment process is evaluated by the supervisory authorities. This evaluation, combined with other factors, determines the target capital ratio set for the bank. Any deficiencies in the process may result in the supervisor imposing an increased capital ratio requirement for the bank. Higher capital requirements imply that fewer funds are available to lend or invest, which may result in lower profits. Banks therefore have a commercial, as well as a prudential, incentive to develop and maintain a high-quality capital assessment process.

Although bank supervisors can raise the capital ratio in response to deficiencies identified during a review, they may also use other measures to address perceived deficiencies, such as:

- Setting targets for improvements in the risk management structure
- Requiring tighter internal procedures, or measures to improve the quality of staff through training or recruitment
- In extreme cases, curtailing the level of risk the bank can incur or business activity it can engage in until problems are resolved or controlled

The Basel Committee sees the supervisory review process as an active dialogue between a bank and its supervisor. The two should be working together to identify and, if necessary, take rapid action to restore the bank's capital position to a satisfactory level.

8.4.1 Four Key Principles of Supervisory Review

Pillar 2 identifies four key principles of supervisory review, described in detail.

Principle 1
Banks should have a process to assess their overall capital adequacy in relation to their risk profile as well as a strategy to maintain their capital levels.

Bank management bears primary responsibility for ensuring that the bank has adequate capital to meet its current and future requirements. Its capital targets must be set with integrity and be consistent with its risk profile and environment. The capital targets must be integral to the bank's strategic planning and should incorporate extensive stress testing.

In particular, Basel II describes five features of a rigorous capital assessment process:

- *Board and senior management oversight.* Bank management is responsible for understanding the nature and level of risk taken by the bank and monitoring the relationship between the level of risk and the bank's capital requirement. The board of directors or its equivalent must set the level of risk that the bank is willing to take (risk appetite) and establish an internal framework to assess risk, relate the level of risk to capital targets, and monitor compliance with internal limits and controls. The framework should also incorporate a capital planning process that is consistent with the bank's strategic business plan.
- *Sound capital assessment.* The target capital ratio should be related to the bank's strategic business plan, and there should be a transparent link between risk and capital.
- *Comprehensive assessment of risk.* All material risk exposures should be measured or estimated, including those risks identified by Pillar 1 and others, such as interest rate risk, liquidity risk, and credit concentration risk.
- *Monitoring and reporting.* The bank must establish a system for monitoring and reporting risk that allows management to assess how changes in risk affect its capital requirements. Bank management should receive

regular reports that show the bank's capital level and its capital requirements. The reports should allow management to evaluate the level and trends of material risks, evaluate the sensitivity and reasonableness of current risk measures, and determine that the bank holds sufficient capital against the various risks and that it is in compliance with established capital adequacy goals.

- *Internal control review.* The bank's internal control framework is a key element in the capital assessment process. An effective review of this framework should include an internal or external audit.

Principle 2
Supervisors should review and evaluate banks' internal capital adequacy assessments and strategies, as well as their ability to monitor and ensure their compliance with regulatory capital ratios. Supervisors should take appropriate supervisory action if they are not satisfied with the result of this process.

The supervisory review process may involve on-site visits, off-site reviews, meetings with bank management, reviewing relevant work carried out by external auditors, and monitoring periodic reports. The regular review process should:

- Closely examine the calculation of risk exposures and the translation of risk into a capital requirement
- Focus on the quality of the process and on the quality of internal controls around the process
- Ensure that the composition of the capital held is appropriate for the scale of the business activity it supports
- Evaluate how the capital assessment process is monitored and reviewed by bank management
- Ensure that targets are appropriate for the current operating environment
- Ensure that the bank takes into account the effects of extreme or unexpected events when setting capital targets
- Identify any deficiencies in the capital assessment framework

On completion of the review, supervisors should take action if they are not satisfied with all or part of a bank's risk assessment process.

Principle 3
Supervisors should expect banks to operate above the minimum regulatory capital ratios, and they should be able to require banks to hold capital in excess of the minimum.

The minimum capital requirements set in Pillar 1 provide a baseline for banks and supervisors to gauge capital levels. In practice, banks will maintain a buffer above the minimum capital requirement, due to:

- Risks/business activities not properly covered by Pillar 1
- Bank-specific conditions that warrant additional capital
- Local market conditions
- Need/desire of the bank to maintain or achieve a high credit rating
- The need to ensure that the bank will not be required to raise capital quickly if market conditions change

From the supervisory review process, supervisors may also require banks to hold additional capital if they are not convinced that current capital is sufficient for the risks faced by the assets of the bank.

Principle 4
Supervisors should seek to intervene at an early stage to prevent capital from falling below the minimum levels required to support the risk characteristics of a particular bank and should require rapid remedial action if capital is not maintained or restored.

If a bank is failing to maintain its capital requirement, supervisors can use their discretion in taking action to correct the situation. Bank supervisors can require a bank to suspend dividend payments and/or raise extra capital to restore its capital ratio. If the problem is likely to take some time to resolve, supervisors could increase monitoring of the bank and require the bank to submit a plan to restore the capital ratio to a level set by the supervisor.

Bank supervisors can increase a bank's capital requirement as a short-term measure while underlying problems are resolved. The increase in capital could be withdrawn when the supervisor is satisfied that the bank had overcome its operating difficulties.

8.4.2 Specific Issues to Address during Supervisory Review

The four principles in Pillar 2 describe a framework for supervisors to use in developing their own review procedures. The Basel Committee has also identified a number of other important issues that should be included in all supervisory reviews. These are issues that either form part of the standards set for the use of the advanced calculation methods, or cover areas not directly addressed in Pillar 1—for example, stress testing and scenario analysis in liquidity testing.

Interest Rate Risk in the Banking Book

As discussed in Section 2.2, interest rate risk in the banking book refers to the potential loss in a bank's lending and deposit activities due to changes in interest rates. The Basel Committee considers interest rate risk in the banking book a significant risk that needs capital support. However, the committee also accepts that the nature and management of this risk are very diverse across the international banking community and that this risk should be addressed under Pillar 2. Bank supervisors have discretion to implement a mandatory capital requirement if they feel it is appropriate for their own banking community. The committee recognizes that the reporting of this risk relies on the banks' own internal risk management systems. Supervisors also require reports based on a standard interest rate shift to allow for comparison across the banks under their jurisdiction. If a bank is deemed to be holding insufficient capital to cover its interest rate risk, supervisors must require the bank to reduce its risk, hold more capital, or implement a combination of both.

Stress Tests under the Internal Ratings-Based (IRB) Approach in Pillar 1

Banks using the IRB Approach must ensure that they have sufficient capital to cover the IRB Approach's requirement. They must also have sufficient capital to cover any deficiencies identified in the credit risk stress tests carried out as part of the IRB Approach.

Definition of Default

The Basel Committee defines the event of default to have occurred when either or both of the two following events have taken place:

1. The bank considers that the obligor is unlikely to pay its credit obligations to the banking group in full without recourse by the bank to actions such as taking formal possession of any collateral held.
2. The obligor is past due more than 90 days on any material credit obligation to the banking group. Overdrafts will be considered as being past due once the customer has breached an advised overdraft limit or been advised of a limit smaller than its current outstanding obligation to the bank.

Banks must use the Basel-referenced definition of default in their internal estimates for the probability of default (PD), loss given default (LGD), and exposure at default (EAD). However, bank supervisors will issue guidance on the interpretation of the default definition in their own jurisdiction.

Supervisors should evaluate the impact of how a bank interprets the definition on the calculation of its capital requirement.

Residual Risk

Pillar 1 allows banks to mitigate their credit exposures by using collateral, guarantees, or credit derivatives. The capital offset allowed against an exposure assumes that the risk-mitigating method (sometimes referred to as a hedge) has been perfectly executed. However, there may be residual, legal, or documentation risks that could result in the bank having a greater exposure than it had originally recorded. Banks should develop policies and procedures to minimize their exposure to such residual risks. Banks must evaluate the quality of their policies and procedures to determine whether their credit exposures should or can be fully offset by their mitigation methods. Supervisors will review the bank's evaluation and will take action if they feel the process has deficiencies.

Credit Concentration Risk

A risk concentration is any single exposure or group of exposures that has the potential to generate losses that could jeopardize a bank's ability to carry on its business. Credit risk concentration is the most common concentration risk because lending is often a bank's primary activity.

EXAMPLE

In January 1998, Hong Kong–based Peregrine Investment Holdings, one of Asia's biggest independent investment houses, went into liquidation with outstanding debts of some USD 400 million. Concentration risk was a principal cause of the collapse, as Peregrine had lent approximately 20% of its capital base to Steady Safe, an Indonesian taxi and bus operator that went bankrupt.

Risk concentration is a major cause of banking problems. Credit risk concentration can take different forms and may include:

- Significant exposures to a single counterparty or financially related group of counterparties
- Exposures to counterparties in the same economic region or geographical location
- Exposures to counterparties that are dependent on the same business activity or commodity

■ Indirect exposure to credit mitigation methods such as holding a single type of collateral

Banks must identify and manage credit risk concentrations as part of their risk management process. Credit risk concentrations should be defined in relation to the bank's operations and relevant risk limits and exposures set either in relation to regulatory capital requirements or in relation to total assets. Banks should ensure that their internal procedures are effective in identifying, measuring, monitoring, and controlling credit risk concentrations. Concentration risk is not covered by Pillar 1 requirements.

Operational Risk

The use of gross income as a proxy to reflect operational risk exposure under both the Basic Indicator Approach and the Standardized Approach may in some cases underestimate the risk. Supervisors should examine the nature of the bank's business and compare the risk calculations with similar banks in their jurisdiction.

Securitization

Through securitization, the bank removes (sells) and transfers its credit risk to the investors who are buying the securitized product. As a result, the bank needs less capital on its books—securitization brings capital relief. The bank supervisory review of the securitization process should examine how completely the securitization has transferred the bank's risks, determining whether the bank has retained any residual risk(s). If some risk remains, supervisors may decrease or remove the capital allowance calculated under Pillar 1. The aim is to determine a level of capital allowance that reflects the level of credit risk transferred by the securitization.

8.4.3   Supervision—Basel III Enhancements

The global financial crisis of 2007–2009 highlighted numerous issues such as whether bank management exercised proper oversight, whether bank leadership was competent and prudent in its managerial activities, and whether banks were properly valuing their positions. It was recognized that the governance, risk management, and supervision of banks needed to be reviewed and improved.

Updating Pillar 2, Basel III addresses a number of these deficiencies. It strengthens the regulation to:

- Capture the risk of off-balance-sheet exposures and securitization activities
- Provide incentives for banks to undertake long-term management of risks and returns
- Ensure compensation practices are in the long-term interest of the bank and not the short-term interest of the employee
- Improve stress testing
- Improve corporate governance

Basel III enhances the regulatory process to require banks to include in their stress tests economic scenarios that could cause them to fail. Banks must explain to the supervisory authority how the bank would be liquidated in the event of failure, referred to as resolution planning, and any additional capital requirements. Consequently, the role of the internal capital adequacy assessment process (ICAAP) is increased under Basel III. ICAAP emphasizes:

- The importance of stress testing
- The ability of a bank's regulatory capital to absorb losses during times of stress (will the capital retain its value when a bank actually needs it?)
- The long-term capital requirements of the bank (does the bank have appropriate capital levels throughout the economic and credit cycle?)

In October 2010 the Basel Committee published Principles for Enhancing Corporate Governance, which addressed the fundamental deficiencies in corporate governance seen in banks leading up to, during, and since the financial crisis. Areas of particular focus include:

- The role of the board and senior management
- The qualifications and composition of the board
- The importance of an independent risk management function, including a chief risk officer or equivalent
- The importance of monitoring risks on an ongoing firmwide and individual entity basis
- The board's oversight of the compensation systems
- The board and senior management's understanding of the bank's operational structure and risks
- The importance of supervisors regularly evaluating the bank's corporate governance policies and practices and their implementation

8.5   Pillar 3—Market Discipline

Disclosure is the dissemination of material information that allows a proper evaluation of a bank's business. This information guides investors and the market and gives bank customers a clearer view of the bank's operations and risk exposures. Disclosure requirements ensure that corporate entities share pertinent information about their financial performance with investors, with the information being presented according to generally accepted standards.

Both privately held and publicly traded companies are required to produce financial statements: profit and loss reports, balance sheets, and tax reports. These statements must be signed by the company's external auditors and reflect relevant, generally accepted accounting principles. To perform this task, auditors are required, among other things, to test and verify the quality of the company's internal controls as they relate to its financial reporting.

Publicly traded companies must also make additional disclosures required by the exchange their shares are traded on, often known as "filings." The filings reflect the shareholders' information needs and contain very detailed financial information. In some countries, the management of publicly traded companies must also certify, subject to incurring legal liability for falsely doing so, that the company's financial statements correctly and fully reflect the actual financial position of the company. In the United States, this is required under the Sarbanes-Oxley Act.

EXAMPLE

In the mid-1990s, Parmalat, an Italian dairy and food corporation, aggressively bought other dairy and food companies all around the world through the use of debt instruments. By 2001, many of the newly bought companies were losing money. Irrespective of the poor performance of its portfolio of companies, the company continued its aggressive expansion, but instead of financing it with debt, Parmalat issued complex financial products, including derivatives. Derivatives enabled the company to hide its losses and the significant debt it had accumulated. By the end of 2003, the fraudulent accounting practices at Parmalat were exposed, including the selling—to themselves—of credit-linked notes. Parmalat's bank, Bank of America, released a document attesting that EUR 4 billion reported to be in Parmalat's bank account was not there. The actual extent of the accounting fraud has been estimated to be about EUR 14 billion. The firm was declared insolvent, and eventually the CEO, Calisto Tanzi, was sentenced to 10 years in prison for financial fraud. While Parmalat was not a bank, many banks are publicly held companies and are just as accountable to their shareholders as was Parmalat. A bank's failure to meet disclosure requirements of an exchange, regulator, or supervisor can have equally disastrous effects.

Pillar 3 focuses on disclosure requirements to complement the minimum capital requirements (Pillar 1) and supervisory review process (Pillar 2). Pillar 3 disclosure focuses on capital information, not financial performance, and addresses the company's:

- Capital structure
- Risk exposures
- Capital adequacy

Pillar 3 requires that the information considered for disclosure be material to the company's operations and investors' evaluation of the company's operations. The Basel II Accord considers information material if "its omission or misstatement could change or influence the assessment or decision of a user relying on that information for the purpose of making economic decisions." But under Pillar 3, banks are not required to disclose proprietary or confidential information, including confidential customer information.

Under Pillar 3, most banks make their disclosures every six months. There are three exceptions to this standard:

1. Small banks with stable risk profiles are permitted to make yearly disclosures.
2. Large international banks must publish their Tier 1 and total capital adequacy ratios, as well as those ratios' components, quarterly.
3. Banks can make their qualitative disclosures of a general nature (information about the bank's principles and procedures that it uses to assess its risks) yearly.

8.5.1   Accounting Disclosures

Basel II recognizes that risk disclosures and financial disclosures are dissimilar, and reconciling these two different types of disclosures can be expensive and time-consuming, if not unfair, for banks with stable risk levels.

Given the different purposes of financial accounts (investor information) and regulatory risk reports (relationship between risks and capital), any detailed reconciliation between risk disclosures and financial disclosures would be costly and difficult. For many banks, such reconciliation would involve significant systems expenditures. Basel II therefore suggests that banks publish their annual report and other financial statements separately from the required supervisory regulatory reports.

8.5.2   General Disclosure Requirements

The Basel II Accord requires banks to develop formal disclosure policies and processes to validate their disclosure and to reevaluate what information should and should not be disclosed in the future. These policies and procedures should be approved by the bank's board of directors.

Pillar 3 requirements apply to both quantitative and qualitative disclosure with regard to the following:

- *Bank, group, and subsidiary structure.* Disclosure requirements generally apply to the consolidated banking group—the entire bank, with all its banking and nonbanking subsidiaries.
- *Capital structure.* Banks must disclose details of their capital structure. The qualitative disclosure focuses on the different types of capital the bank has, while the quantitative disclosures include the following:
  - Amount of Tier 1 capital, by capital source (shares, reserves, etc.), amount of Tier 2 capital, and amount of Tier 3 capital, if needed
  - Deductions from capital, if needed
  - Total regulatory capital
- *Capital adequacy.* The bank must discuss how it assesses its capital adequacy (a qualitative disclosure), and the bank's capital requirements for credit risk, market risk, and operational risk; its total capital; and its Tier 1 capital ratio (all quantitative disclosures).

8.5.3   Disclosing Risk Exposure and Risk Assessment

Pillar 3's risk disclosure requirements depend on the approach the bank uses to calculate its required risk capital. The complexity of the approaches used by the bank will dictate what information needs to be disclosed.

General qualitative disclosure would include information on:

- Risk management objectives and policies relating to each defined risk area.
- The structure and organization of the relevant risk management function.
- The use of hedging and risk-mitigating strategies.

Quantitative disclosure requirements are complex, and any detailed listing would be lengthy. Generally, **credit risk disclosures** include information on:

- Gross and average credit exposure by major products.
- Geographic, industry, and maturity distribution of exposures by major products.
- Loans, provisions, and write-offs by industry, by counterparty, and by geographic area.

Generally, **market risk disclosures** include information on:

- The capital requirements for the four main types of general market risk: interest rate risk, equity risk, foreign exchange risk, and commodity risk.
- High, average, and low value-at-risk (VaR) values over the reporting period and an evaluation of the reliability of these calculations.

There are no quantitative **operational risk disclosure** requirements other than those covered in the capital adequacy disclosures.

Finally, banks with interest rate risk in the banking book have to disclose information that allows a qualitative assessment of the models used to assess these risks. Model inputs include assumptions on prepayments and withdrawals of deposits. The quantitative disclosure concerning a bank's interest rate risk would reflect the effects that interest rate changes have on the earnings or value of the bank.

8.5.4 Pillar 3 Market Discipline—Basel III Enhancements

Prior to the financial crisis, the market of tradable collateralized debt obligations (CDOs) and other securitized obligations became huge. However, no one realized just how great the exposures were either for an individual bank or to other banks, or even how the financial system had become so interconnected, despite the majority of banks being Basel II compliant. Owing to limitations of the disclosure requirements of Pillar 3 for CDOs and securitizations,

- There was no detailed reporting of exposures, and market participants did not know much about the concentration of risk involved.
- There was a general lack of transparency, as it only became apparent how much the banks were holding when the crisis occurred.

In response, Basel III strengthened the regulatory framework by improving transparency through increased disclosure. Expanded disclosure requirements were particularly focused on improving disclosures relating to securitizations and regulatory capital.

The disclosure requirements for securitization and resecuritization exposures include information on:

- Valuation approaches.
- Sponsorship of off-balance-sheet vehicles, including qualitative disclosures of all securitization activities that the bank sponsors.
- Internal assessment approach and liquidity facilities, disclosing the approach taken by the bank in determining its capital requirements.
- The pipeline and warehousing risks of securitization exposures, detailing information about future securitization activities, valuation, and exposure levels.
- The types of risks assumed and retained with resecuritization.
- How the processes in place to monitor changes in the credit and market risk for resecuritization exposures differ from those in place for securitization exposures.
- The bank's policy governing the use of **credit risk mitigation** to mitigate the risks retained through securitization and resecuritization exposures.
- The aggregate amount of resecuritization exposures retained or purchased.

To strengthen the level of confidence in a bank's regulatory capital disclosures, the details of the components of regulatory capital and their reconciliation to reported accounts are required. This includes a thorough explanation of how a bank calculates its regulatory capital ratios.

8.6   International Cooperation

There is an element of discretion in the supervision of banks because banking activity is subject to different local regulations; there is no one global banking regulator. Bank supervisors work to ensure that their discretionary supervisory activities are carried out with transparency and accountability. Criteria for the review of capital adequacy for financial institutions should be publicly available.

International banks are active in a number of jurisdictions, and therefore are subject to supervision by their home authority (home supervisor) as well as each host authority in countries where they have banking operations (host supervisor). This situation is usually referred to in literature as home-host matters. The new Basel accords require closer practical cooperation between home and host supervisors to help reduce the supervisory burden on such international banking groups.

The home supervisor should lead the coordination effort between itself and the host supervisors (those supervisors who would oversee the bank's branch operations in another country) responsible for a banking group's operations. The aim should be to reduce the implementation burden on banks and conserve supervisory resources by avoiding redundant or uncoordinated validation work.

Following the global financial crisis of 2007–2009, many countries and economic zones implemented their own legislations to ensure the stability of their financial systems, this localized approach is at times referred to as "ring-fencing." This has greatly complicated the international banking environment, as there are both domestic regulations and a variety of international frameworks being implemented concurrently. Many countries are still implementing Basel II while others have already migrated to the Basel III enhancements. This inconsistency has increased the opportunity for regulatory arbitrage.

Banks, as would any other organization, will take advantage of the differences in both national and international regulatory systems. This concept, referred to as regulatory arbitrage, can include restructuring transactions, financial engineering, and geographic relocation. While taking advantage of regulatory distinctions is perfectly legal, the goal is to have international cooperation progress to the point that regulatory arbitrage opportunities have been minimized or, ideally, eliminated.

An example of a domestic development that shows how certain local regulations can cause complications although passed with the best intentions is the UK Banking Reform Act 2013 (largely based on the report known as the Vickers Report, after its chairman), outlined earlier in the book. Contrasting the UK Banking Reform Act to the Dodd-Frank act noted below, provides a good example of how jurisdictions, seeking to protect their industries and citizens, can cause issues in other parts of the world. Two national regulations, which have garnered much international attention, are discussed in the remainder of this section. These affect not only domestic banks but also international financial institutions that operate within the United States and the European Union.

8.6.1 The Dodd-Frank Act

In response to the global financial crisis of 2007–2009, the U.S. authorities passed the Dodd-Frank Wall Street Reform and Consumer Protection Act (Dodd-Frank) in 2010. The Act was aimed at strengthening the U.S. financial system and preventing a repeat of the collapse of major financial institutions. The Act covers both major financial institutions and the protection of consumers. It strengthens supervisory oversight and gives regulators additional powers to tackle financial fraud, conflicts of interest, corruption, and insider trading. The remainder of this subsection outlines the key areas covered by this Act.

Financial Stability Oversight Council

The Dodd-Frank Act created the Financial Stability Oversight Council (FSOC) to monitor and address risks that affect the financial industry. The FSOC makes recommendations to the United States' Federal Reserve for implementing strict rules for capital, leverage, liquidity, risk management, and other requirements as banks and nonbanks increase in size and complexity. In particular, it focuses on requirements for those areas that pose risks to the financial system.

The Council is chaired by the Treasury Secretary, and has nine members drawn from the following U.S. organizations: the Board of Governors of the Federal Reserve System, the Commodity Futures Trading Commission, Federal Housing Finance Agency, National Credit Union Administration, Office of the Comptroller of the Currency, Securities and Exchange Commission, and Consumer Financial Protection Bureau (see below). It covers both banks and nonbank financial institutions such as hedge funds, asset management firms, and insurance companies.

Too Big to Fail

Under the rules of the Dodd-Frank Act, the FSOC has the authority to break up any bank that is deemed "too big to fail." The FSOC can also require the bank to increase its reserve requirements, enforcing capital and leverage requirements to discourage it from becoming too big. Banks are also required to have plans for a structured and orderly shutdown in the event that they become insolvent. The overriding objective of the Act is to eliminate the use of taxpayer funds to rescue a future failing financial company.

The Volcker Rule

The Volcker Rule (named after the former U.S. Treasury secretary and Federal Reserve chair who proposed it) limits the ability of banks to engage in proprietary trading. Under the rule, a bank is permitted limited trading when necessary for it to operate—for example engaging in currency trading to offset the bank's own foreign currency positions. However, a bank directly owning, investing, or sponsoring hedge funds, private equity funds, or any proprietary trading operations for the purpose of making the bank a profit is deemed to be unacceptable under the Volcker Rule.

Derivative Trading

The Dodd-Frank Act strengthened the authority of the Securities and Exchange Commission (SEC) and of the Commodity Futures Trading Commission (CFTC), providing them with additional regulatory tools to better regulate over-the-counter (OTC) derivatives to limit excessive risk taking. The Act requires central clearing and exchange trading for most derivatives with a view to improving transparency, bringing OTC transactions into an exchange-type trading environment for the first time.

Regulation of Credit Agencies

One failing discovered during the financial crisis was the imprecise practices engaged in by credit rating agencies when rating derivatives and mortgage-backed securities. The Dodd-Frank Act addresses this by creating an Office of Credit Ratings at the Securities and Exchange Commission (SEC) to regulate credit rating agencies. Rating agencies are required to have their rating systems reviewed by the SEC and can be decertified if their activities are found to be deficient.

Consumer Protection

In addition to regulating banks that operate in the United States, the Dodd-Frank Act also addresses a perceived need for additional consumer protection by establishing and providing rule-making authority to a new agency, the Consumer Financial Protection Bureau (CFBP). The CFPB's authority extends to banks with more than USD 10 billion of assets and to all mortgage-related businesses, payday lenders, and other large nonbank financial institutions.

8.6.2 EU Capital Requirements Directive

The EU Capital Requirements Directive IV (CRD IV) goes beyond the simple adoption into the European Union of Basel III standards. In addition to strengthening a bank's ability to absorb losses, it also introduces new regulations that are aimed at reducing systemic effects, restoring trust, and improving the transparency of banks across the whole of the European Union. CRD IV comprises the Capital Requirements Regulation (CRR) and the Capital Requirements Directive (CRD). Under EU law, a directive gives each country a certain amount of discretion to implement EU requirements, whereas a regulation does not allow this discretion and is directly applicable to all banks across the European Union.

CRD IV also adds additional regulations on banks and supervisors to standardize the approach to risk regulation through the establishment of a

"Single Rulebook" that creates a single set of rules, which to a large extent removes national discretions. Local supervisors can change the regulations only when justified by national circumstances (e.g., specific issues with the real estate market in any one country), to ensure local financial stability, or to deal with specific issues related to a bank's risk profile. The aim is to ensure a uniform application of Basel III and limit the opportunity for regulatory arbitrage across the European Union.

The main additions to the Basel III framework are:

- *Remuneration.* In order to encourage banks to implement pay and bonus levels that do not encourage staff to take excessive risks, a remuneration framework was implemented. This framework limits an employee's bonus to a maximum of 100% of salary; however, shareholders retain the ability to increase this limit to 200%.
- *Corporate governance.* CRD IV includes rules aimed at improving risk oversight by boards of directors, enhancing the risk management function, and ensuring the effective monitoring of risk governance by supervisors.
- *Diversity.* Banks are required to improve the range of knowledge and experience at the board level with a view to improving risk oversight.
- *Enhanced transparency.* Banks have to disclose more information about their overseas activities and investments, including details on funds, profits, taxes, and subsidies in different jurisdictions. The intention of enhanced transparency is to restore the trust of EU citizens in banks and the financial sector.
- *Systemic risk buffer.* Under CRD IV, banks may need to hold an additional systemic risk buffer made up of Common Equity Tier 1 capital. The systemic risk buffer is not set on an individual bank basis, but is to be applied to the whole financial sector within each EU country. The decision to apply the buffer and the level at which it is set are at the discretion of each national supervisor. The aim of the buffer is to address long-term noncyclical systemic risks.
- *Other systemically important institutions buffer.* Basel III requires global systemically important financial institutions to hold additional capital. CRD IV goes further by allowing national supervisors to implement a buffer for other systemically important institutions (O-SIIs), which include domestically important institutions as well as those deemed important across the European Union. To limit the impact across the European Union, standardized criteria to identify O-SIIs are used by the national supervisor, and there is a 2% total of risk-weighted assets maximum limit on the size of the buffer.

8.7 Beyond Regulatory Capital

Meeting regulatory capital requirements does not relieve the board of directors and senior management of a bank of their responsibility to provide competent and prudent bank leadership and oversight. This includes the maintenance of adequate capital to support the bank's business activities beyond the scope of regulation. By design, regulatory capital defines the *minimum* capital requirement determined by the supervisor, whose primary concern is banking safety and stability for the general public.

EXAMPLE

In 2007, the global banking system started to experience capital adequacy issues related to the U.S. subprime mortgage market. In 2008, these issues became acute due to losses that were being incurred at unprecedented rates by banks as housing prices fell and borrowers defaulted on their loans. Banks were forced to raise capital from external sources. (Refer to the capital calculations in Figure 8.2.) For example, if UBS experienced losses related to the subprime market and credit bubble that resulted in a reduction of its Tier 1 capital by, for example, 35% or CHF 19,671 million, its capital ratio would have dropped to 9.6%. Although above the 8% minimum, it would be too close to provide confidence to the markets and its counterparties regarding its ability to withstand further losses in its portfolios. This example would also be the same for HSBC, Barclays, and BBVA.

In fact, real estate market values fell sharply in 2007 and 2008, affecting most of the banks around the globe. Ultimately, every bank became concerned about the balance sheet of its banking counterparties and questioned whether all possible losses were being disclosed and positions were being valued properly. Banks attempted to raise capital in any number of ways to shore up their balance sheets.

This resulted in a freezing of credit in the financial system as banks became unwilling to lend funds to each other and to their customers. This catastrophic situation forced governments to establish programs aimed at restoring confidence in the banking system and recapitalizing their banks so that the banks would resume lending money. As previously detailed in this chapter, much of the Basel III framework is aimed preventing a repeat of such a situation.

Regulatory capital mandates are designed to help ensure that in the event of distress or the failure of an individual bank, capital levels are adequate to prevent any individual bank's problem from becoming a systemwide problem. Consequently, under Basel II the time horizon relating to regulatory capital calculations tends to be short term—10 days for market risk capital, for example. Basel III takes a slightly different view of regulatory capital, as banks have to hold sufficient capital not just to survive the present short term, but also to be able to absorb losses from periods of significant stress.

Regulators want to ensure that the bank's capital would cover losses if its assets had to be liquidated quickly. Regulatory capital initiatives must be well defined, well tested, and broadly applicable. The methods for calculating regulatory capital are more rigid and focused on particular risks that all banks are likely to face, namely credit, market, and operational risk.

A key component of Pillar 2 is directed at supervisory evaluation of the quality of the bank's internal capital adequacy assessment process (ICAAP). Bank management must consider the long-term health and success of the bank, decide its risk tolerance, and set the capital level to be optimal with respect to its acceptable trade-off between risk and reward. Higher capital levels imply that fewer funds are available to lend out or invest, lowering profits. But higher capital levels also imply greater ability to absorb losses, which improves a bank's credit rating and lowers borrowing costs. Given the immense impact of this decision, bank managers must maintain a high-quality capital assessment process that addresses all the particular risks faced by that bank, not just those identified by regulators.

8.7.1 Defining Economic Capital

Economic capital is a related concept to regulatory capital. Whereas regulatory capital can be considered to be the capital a bank needs to meet the minimum requirements of the risk-based regulations, economic capital can be considered as the capital a bank needs to hold to run its business safely on a day-to-day basis. According to the Basel Committee on Banking Supervision (BCBS) of the Bank for International Settlements (BIS),

"Economic capital can be defined as the methods or practices that allow banks to consistently assess risk and attribute capital to cover the economic effects of risk-taking activities."

Economic capital reflects the capital level a bank must maintain to withstand large but unlikely losses so that it can survive over the long term. To survive in the long term, a bank needs to overcome periods during which extreme circumstances could cause it to sustain large losses. If the bank has capital levels to support it through such times, it will survive; if it does not have sufficient capital, it will fail. Economic capital measures potential, though unexpected, losses that would have to be covered by capital. Some banks define economic capital as the capital required to survive larger than expected losses; and some just consider losses beyond the unexpected level. However, all banks hold economic capital to survive very severe, extreme events.

Economic capital as a risk measure evolved from the value-at-risk (VaR) methodology (see Section 6.4.2). Both bank supervisors and bank management find VaR an important tool because it considers the vital question:

"For a particular confidence level (e.g., 95% of the time), what is an upper bound on how much the bank could lose in the next time period (e.g., next 24 hours, week, month, or year)?"

Recall from earlier discussions that VaR does not represent the absolute worst-case loss but the worst loss for some percentage of the time (e.g., 95%).

Importantly, VaR with a 95% confidence limit does not answer the question:

"How large can the losses be on the 5% of occasions when we exceed our VaR estimate?"

This is the question answered in our prior discussion about Expected Shortfall.

Economic capital considers the same question as VaR but is particularly concerned about the worst-case losses at a very high confidence level beyond what the bank considers normal losses of running a business. Economic capital modeling involves estimating a probability distribution for the bank's potential losses, deriving the likelihood of each possible loss value or ranges of loss values.

8.7.2 Calculating Economic Capital

Banks can calculate the economic capital needed for the whole bank, or they can calculate it separately for various risks or types of losses such as loan losses or trading losses. Banks have developed models that measure the potential extreme losses in scenarios that involve losses from a combination of their:

- Market risk (including that held in the banking book)
- Credit risk
- Operational risk
- Other risks

These models then estimate the capital necessary for the bank to survive worst-case losses from a combination of these risk areas. There are a number of measures used for economic capital. Typical methodologies used include:

- Standard deviation
- Value-at-risk (VaR)
- Expected shortfall (ES)
- Spectral and distorted risk measures

A detailed description of these methods is beyond the scope of the book, but any method used by banks must have the following characteristics:

- *Intuitive.* The method must make use of common risk terms, for example **unexpected loss.**
- *Stable.* It must not be subject to wide variations in results from small changes in the value of input parameters.
- *Easy to compute.* It should be as easy as possible to calculate, and any use of advanced modeling needs to be justified by the additional accuracy gained.
- *Easy to understand.* The bank's senior management must be able to understand the risk measure utilized.
- *Coherent.* The method should be equally applicable across risk types and portfolios, and the results should have the same meaning in all situations.
- *Simple and meaningful risk decomposition.* Any method must be capable of being applied equally to large or small businesses or individual exposures.

Clearly, there are similarities between the calculation of minimum regulatory capital discussed throughout Chapters 4 through 7 and the calculation of economic capital, and there are practical difficulties that both face. The data to create distributions of losses are difficult to assemble. Unlike regulatory capital, economic capital models can be internally developed models that try to capture specific characteristics of the individual bank and can be more flexible about capturing the effects of features such as diversification, liquidity risk, interest rate risk, and reputational risk. In addition, because economic capital is more concerned with the long-term survival of the bank, the typical time horizon is one year. Note that the time horizon defines the period over which losses are estimated, but does not imply how frequently a bank calculates economic or regulatory capital. That is, to calculate its economic capital, a bank may estimate its potential losses over the next year every day. Finally, note that economic capital is an internal bank metric; although bank supervisory agencies look at this and evaluate the bank's approach, economic capital is not the same as required regulatory capital.

Banks use economic capital models to decide on the level and structure of capital. The development and implementation of a well-designed economic capital model can help a bank identify, understand, mitigate, and manage its risks more effectively, leading ultimately to a more effective bank.

8.7.3   Risk-Adjusted Performance Measures

Since the formal development of economic capital as a bank management tool, banks have also used economic capital to support capital allocation and to evaluate profitability consistently across business lines. **Risk-adjusted return on capital (RAROC)** was developed by Bankers Trust in the late 1970s as a means of evaluating profitability from activities with very different risk profiles. Formally, RAROC is defined as follows:

$$\text{RAROC} = \frac{\text{Profit} - (\text{Economic Capital}) * r}{\text{Economic Capital}}$$

where r is the risk-free interest rate. Banks can use RAROC as a means of setting expected thresholds that must be met prior to initiating a new activity and as a means of evaluating the performance of different business units or activities.

EXAMPLE

Suppose that two business units (A and B) each return a profit of USD 5 million over the last year. However, suppose that business A is a much more risky business. In particular, for business A the economic capital required is USD 19 million and for business B it is USD 13 million. Suppose the risk-free interest rate is 5%.

RAROC shows business B to have a higher return on a risk-adjusted basis than business A. For business A, RAROC is 21.32%:
RAROC = [5 − (19.00) * 5%]/19.00 = 0.2132

For business B, RAROC is 33.46%:
RAROC = [5 − (13.00) * 5%]/13.00 = 0.3346

CHAPTER 9

Insurance Risk

T his chapter addresses the structure and risks of the insurance industry. Many banks offer insurance products alongside banking products, or own insurance companies as subsidiaries. As a result, the risks associated with the insurance industry can be a significant component of a bank's over-all risk profile. This chapter begins by describing the typical business model of insurance companies—which is quite different from the business model of a bank—and then examines the two principal types of insurance: property and casualty (P&C) and life insurance.

Chapter Outline

Key Learning Points
- Insurance is a contract between an insurer and a policyholder, whereby the insurer agrees to pay a sum of money to the policyholder if a specified event happens within a specified period of time.
- Insurance works on the principle of sharing the losses of a few people through small contributions made by a large number of people.
- There are two main types of insurance: property and casualty (P&C) and life insurance ("life and pensions").
- The main inherent risks of property and casualty insurance are underwriting risk, reserving risk, and claims management risk.
- The main inherent risks of life and pensions are longevity risk, mortality and morbidity risks, persistency risk, underwriting risk, and claims management risk.
- The required level of risk management and the controls adopted should reflect the materiality of the risks created by the products sold.
- Insurers usually reinsure some of their risks with reinsurance companies, who in turn, assume some of the risks that were previously held by the insurance company.
- There is no international accord for insurers that is equivalent to the Basel Accords for banks; however, there is a common regulatory approach related to insurance within Europe called Solvency 2. As with the Basel II Accord for banks, the Solvency 2 Directive provides for the use of advanced models for the key insurance risks and other risks (such as credit, market, and operational).
- The Financial Stability Board has identified large insurance companies that it considers to be global systemically important insurers (G-SIIs).
- Lloyd's of London is not an insurance company but a society of members, both corporate and individual, who underwrite in syndicates and on whose behalf professional underwriters accept risk.
- The growing use of sophisticated modeling techniques, external data and advanced analysis will increasingly influence the measurement of risk.

INSURANCE RISK

9.1   Introduction to the Insurance Industry

Insurance is a contract between an insurer and a policyholder, whereby the insurer agrees to pay to the policyholder a sum of money if a specified event happens within a specified period of time. For this service, the policyholder pays a relatively small sum of money, called a **premium**, to the insurer during the term of the contract.

The maximum amount that can be paid out to the policyholder is called the **sum assured**. If the actual loss suffered by the policyholder is less than the sum assured, then the policyholder will receive the actual loss, rather than the sum assured. Insurance works on the principle of sharing the losses of a few people among a large number of people who support the loss payout through their small contributions or premiums.

There are two main types of insurance: property and casualty (P&C) and life insurance. **Property and casualty** insurance covers losses arising from, for example, fires, car crashes, the sinking of a ship, and theft. Life insurance pays a sum of money on the death of the policyholder. **Life insurance** is often linked with **pensions**, with this aspect of insurance sometimes referred to as "life and pensions." Insurance use by a pension plan would work with the insurance company paying out a sum of money when the policyholder reaches a certain age or when other pre-agreed conditions are met.

9.1.1 The Business Model of Insurance Companies

The business model of insurance companies is very different from that of banks. Whereas banks tend to have short-term liabilities and long-term assets, insurance companies often have long-term liabilities but ample short-term assets (although these assets may be invested long-term).

Insurance companies make profits in two ways: from the difference between what they receive in premiums and pay out in claims, and from any profits that they receive by investing the premiums that they receive.

EXAMPLE

Insurance Company A receives and invests an annual premium of USD 500 for three years to insure a policyholder's car. At no point in those three years does the policyholder make a claim for an accident. The insurance company has made a profit of USD 1,500, before taking into account investment income and administrative expenses. In the fourth year, the policyholder crashes the car and makes a claim for USD 2,200. The insurance company is now facing a loss of USD 200 (four years of premiums at USD 500 per year minus a claim of USD 2,200).

However, the insurance company has made a profit of USD 300 from investing the premiums received from the policyholder. As a result, the insurance company has made an overall profit on the transaction of USD 100, before taking into account administrative expenses (total premiums of USD 2,000 plus investment income of USD 300 minus the claim of USD 2,200).

An important ratio that is used to assess the performance of insurance companies is the **combined ratio**. This can be expressed as:

$$\frac{Claims\ Paid + Operating\ Expenses}{Premiums\ Received}$$

If the insurance company is paying out more in claims and as operating expenses than it is receiving in premiums, this ratio will be more than 100%. If it is receiving more in premiums than it is paying out in claims and as operating expenses, the ratio will be less than 100%. Having a combined ratio that is less than 100% shows that a company does not have to rely on investment income in order to make an operating profit.

Another way that insurance companies differ from banks is that insurance companies generally have very long-term liabilities that are difficult to value. This is particularly true in the pensions business. For example, an insurance company may have entered into a policy to pay a policyholder USD 50,000 every year that the individual lives after the age of 60. If the policyholder is currently 40 years old, the insurance company needs to make sure that it will have funds available 20 years from now to start paying the benefits to the policyholder, and not knowing how long the policyholder will live, and for how many years it will have to continue paying out USD 50,000 per year.

One way that insurance companies try to ensure that they will have sufficient funds available to pay claims many years in the future is to invest the premiums that they receive in long-term assets—effectively matching the maturity of some of their assets and liabilities. However, their ability to do this is limited by the need to retain some liquid funds to pay out claims made by policyholders in the nearer term.

EXAMPLE

Equitable Life was a major British insurance company that specialized in providing pensions and life insurance. It was founded in 1762, but in 2000 it had to stop accepting new business and had to reduce payments to policyholders as a result of misjudging its ability to make long-term payouts to policyholders. During the 1970s and 1980s, when interest rates were high, Equitable Life made commitments to make large payments to policyholders when they retired. The company believed that it would be able to meet its obligations to make these large payments because it thought that, as a result of high interest rates, the investment income that it would receive on premiums would also be high. However, during the 1990s, interest rates declined to such low levels that it became clear to Equitable Life that it would not be able to earn enough on its investments to meet its obligations.

Even shorter-term liabilities can be difficult to estimate. For example, a company might insure an oil exploration company against the risk that the company will face damages claims for environmental pollution. The exploration company may face no damages for pollution in its normal operation, but it is also possible that if it has a major accident, the damages could be huge. In such cases, it is very difficult for an insurance company to decide how much to charge in premiums.

Many forms of insurance rely on the fact that a very large number of similar policies are written, and they assume that although some policies may cost the insurance company more than expected, taken as a whole, the vast majority of policies will behave in the way that the insurance company anticipates. In these cases, insurance companies use statistics to estimate the amount of claims that they will have to pay out. **Actuarial science** describes the statistical and mathematical tools used by insurance companies to assess the claims that they are likely to face.

EXAMPLE

Insurance Company B offers a life insurance product under which it agrees to pay USD 50,000 per year to policyholders every year they live after the age of 65. In order to price the product correctly, the company needs to estimate when policyholders are likely to die; it needs to estimate how many years it will be paying out USD 50,000 per year.

The company receives applications from two potential policyholders, both of whom are male and were born in 1975. On the application form, Applicant X states that he is a nonsmoker, while Applicant Y states that he does smoke cigarettes. From actuarial tables, the insurance company knows that the average life expectancy of males born in the applicants' country in 1975 is 78 years. However, the actuarial tables also state that the average life expectancy for male nonsmokers is 80 years while for smokers it is only 76 years. Assuming that there are no other factors that differentiate X and Y, the insurance company will charge a higher premium to X, the nonsmoker, because it expects to pay out USD 200,000 more to X than to Y (USD 50,000 per year for four years more than Y).

EXAMPLE

Insurance Company C provides automobile insurance to tens of thousands of policyholders. The company does not assess each policyholder on an individual basis in order to estimate whether they are likely to crash their car and make a claim. Instead, the company knows from statistical tables the percentage of all cars that are involved in accidents every year, and it also knows the average cost of repairing the cars after those accidents. Using those statistics, Company C can set its premiums at a level that will enable it to meet all claims (and have money left over as profit for itself) even though it does not know which cars will crash.

Now suppose that the government in Company C's country decides to raise the maximum speed limit on highways from 50 miles per hour to 60 miles per hour. If this change results in more cars being involved in crashes (and perhaps the crashes that occur being more serious than before, due to higher speeds), the insurance company's estimates may turn out to be wrong and the company might find itself paying out more money in claims than expected. Of course, the company would try to respond to this change by raising the premiums charged to motorists.

9.1.2   Differences between Property and Casualty Insurance and Life Insurance

Property and casualty (P&C) insurance is always a personal contract where the insurance company contracts with a customer directly for insurance protection. Life insurance is a nonpersonal insurance contract. This means that the policyholder and the person being insured do not necessarily have to be the same person (although in many cases they are).

P&C insurance insures homes, automobiles, and other personal property. This type of insurance is indemnity insurance. An indemnity is an amount paid by one party (the insurance company) to another (the policyholder) to compensate for a specific loss incurred by the policyholder. In the previous example, Company C's indemnity insurance pays enough money to repair or replace the insured cars of its policyholders in the event of accidents.

In contrast, life insurance insures a life or the life of someone with whom an association exists, such as a spouse, child, sibling, or business partner. When the insured individual dies, the life insurance policy pays a death benefit that is fixed. This is called a valued contract. A **valued contract** pays a fixed sum of money, regardless of the nature of the loss insured by the contract. The benefit of life insurance is that it can be structured to pay off some or all of the financial obligations that are left after a person dies. It can pay more than that, however, because life insurance pays a fixed amount. Death benefits can be used to pay some or all of the obligations that arise from the death, create wealth for the surviving beneficiaries, or replace income for survivors.

Both types of insurance are necessary to protect the financial value of both life and property. They serve different functions and fill specific diverse roles. P&C insurance is beneficial in that the insurance ensures that, almost regardless of the damage done, the property will be repaired or replaced. While P&C insurance generally has a maximum payout determined by the value of the property, it does not pay a fixed amount, so the insured is not required to estimate how much insurance must be purchased. When buying life insurance, the policyholder should generally buy only sufficient insurance to cover current and expected future financial liabilities. When purchasing P&C insurance, the maximum **coverage** should not extend beyond the total replacement value of the property.

9.1.3   Insurance Industry Participants

Insurance companies primarily distribute their products in one of three ways: through agents, through brokers, or through a bank insurance (or **"bancassurance"**) model. These distribution channels are described in Figure 9.1.

Role or Distribution Channel	Description
Corporate Insurance Agents	Many insurance corporate entities are allowed to operate as insurance agents. Historically, they have been quite successful due to huge databases, substantial resources and the ability to penetrate the market across various segments.
Insurance Brokers	Corporate insurance agents are only permitted to sell the products of only one company. Insurance Brokers, on the other hand, are allowed the sell the products of a wide variety of companies in the market. This allows them to offer a wide selection of choices to their customers.
Bank Insurance Model/ Bancassurance	The bank insurance model ('BIM'), also sometimes known as "bancassurance," is the term used to describe the partnership or relationship between a bank and an insurance company whereby the insurance company uses the bank sales channel in order to sell its insurance products. BIM allows the insurance company to maintain smaller direct sales teams as their products are sold through the bank to bank customers by bank staff and employees as well. This is considered cross-selling of insurance products and services by banking institutions. The etymology of bancassurance is from French "banc" (bank) + "assurance" (assurance).
Other Marketing Channels	This includes other types of marketing such as telemarketing, online selling, sales in shopping malls, and so on.

FIGURE 9.1 Typical Industry Structure and Key Participants

9.1.4   Significant Risks That Apply to the Insurance Business

Section 9.1.1 introduced some of the risks that insurance companies face in valuing long-term liabilities and ensuring that they will have sufficient assets when the time comes to cover those liabilities.

However, insurance companies face many other risks, some of which are similar to those faced by banks (for example, credit risk on the counterparties with whom they have invested their funds) and some of which are different.

Figure 9.2 shows how insurance-related risks (such as the ability to pay out claims) overlap with other risks. Experience shows that the biggest risks for insurance companies often lie in the area where different risks overlap. Major losses frequently occur when a number of controls, policies, and procedures fail to operate properly.

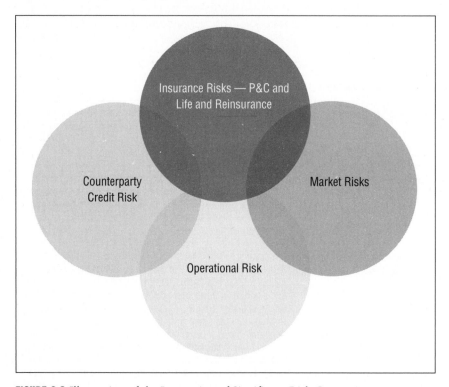

FIGURE 9.2 Illustration of the Interaction of Significant Risk Categories

9.2   Property and Casualty Insurance

Property and casualty (P&C) insurance is referred to differently in different parts of the world; property and casualty insurance in the United States and Canada, general insurance in the United Kingdom, and non-life insurance in Continental Europe.

There are various example types of property and casualty insurance, as identified in Figure 9.3.

Common Types of Insurance Contracts	Less Common Types of Insurance Contracts
Commercial P&C Liability (covering "Third Party": Bodily injury, property damage, limited contractual liability, etc.) Property Liability Automobile Liability Professional Liability Professional Indemnity	Crime Pollution Liability Various Inland Marine Policies Aircraft Terrorism Insurance

FIGURE 9.3 Example Types of Property and Casualty Insurance

EXAMPLE

RSA Insurance Group is a medium-size international P&C insurer. It describes itself as providing products that "protect people against the risks they face in their daily lives, both personal and commercial." The company provides personal and commercial insurance to more than 20 million customers globally. RSA offers a wide range of personal lines of insurance products, including automobile, home, travel, and pets. These products can be purchased directly, through a broker, or by an authorized partner. Commercial insurance caters to all sizes of businesses—from small and medium enterprises (SMEs) to large multinationals. Its products include marine, construction, power and renewable energy, automobile packages, liability, real estate, and property.

9.2.1   Inherent Risks of Property and Casualty Insurance

The main inherent risks, and their definitions, are:

- *Underwriting risk:* the risk that inappropriate business is contracted; this includes the:
  - Impact of underwriting cycle
  - Selection of undesirable risks
  - Fluctuations in the timing, frequency, and severity of insured events, relative to expectations at the time of underwriting
  - Inaccurate pricing of risk
  - Process that a financial services provider (e.g., insurer) uses to assess the eligibility of a customer to receive its products (e.g., insurance).
- *Reserving risk:* the risk that inappropriate reserves are held.
- *Claims management risk:* the risk that claims exceed expectations, or that inappropriate claims settlements are reached.
- *Claims reserving risk:* the risk of loss arising from an inadequate or inappropriate claims reserving policy or process.

9.2.2   Risk Appetite

It is essential for any company to formulate a risk appetite statement similar to that in banks, identifying the risks that the company faces, setting out a detailed appetite for such risks, and setting limits and metrics.

In the case of underwriting, the specific risk appetite may want to address, for example, that the company has no appetite for:

- Incurring censure, fines, or prosecution arising from underwriting activity.
- Failing to maintain a sound system of internal control around underwriting operations and practices.
- Damage to the company's own brands through undisciplined or inappropriate acceptance of risks.
- New classes of business not previously authorized, or developing an existing class of business outside of the company's current underwriting authority, without referring it to senior management responsible for that business.

9.2.3   Risk Identification, Mitigation, and Management

The insurer seeks to identify the fluctuations in the occurrence, amount, and timing of its insurance liabilities. It also seeks to identify aggregations of risk that may give rise to large single or multiple claims, including catastrophes. In addition, the insurance firm needs to identify changes to the external environment that may lead to an increase in P&C insurance risk.

Further, the firm needs to ensure at all times that it is not exposed to insurance risk in excess of its risk appetite. In doing so, the insurer should be both reactive, responding to actual increases in exposure, and proactive, responding to potential future increases. This involves close coordination among the processes of risk control, risk identification, risk mitigation, and risk measurement, as potential future exposures need to be identified and understood before effective action can be taken to control them. One example of how this can be implemented is for senior management to set individual underwriting limits for all employees and agents who have the authority to underwrite insurance risk. These include both monetary limits and limits on the types of product coverage that they can underwrite.

9.2.4 Minimum Standards of Risk Management and Controls

Minimum risk management standards include the following:

- Management information should be generated from P&C underwriting risk and used to provide insight, inform the operational planning process, and influence resource allocation, including capital planning.
- Risk appetite statements and tolerances should be clearly defined and refreshed on a regular basis (at least annually) and be regarded as an integral part of the planning process.
- Regular risk analysis reviews (at least on a quarterly basis) of P&C underwriting systems and processes should be actively performed to ensure that inherent underwriting risks are effectively managed.
- Adequate controls should be put in place by an independent validator, someone who is not directly involved with the process or activity being controlled.

Some key risk controls for different aspects of the insurance determination and claims process:

- *Reinsurance:*
  - Policies for determining and managing the inherent volatility associated with issuing any type of P&C insurance policy and the impact any losses would have on the company's P&C business.
- *Claims management risk:*
  - An implemented claims management process that guards against the inappropriate recording, estimating, handling, and settlement of P&C claims.

- Controls to address the following areas:
  - Claims verification
  - The claims estimating process
  - The claims handling process
  - Communications surrounding the claims experience
- *Underwriting risk:*
  - Processes and procedures that balance and manage the risks that are cycle smoothers (i.e., business that has limited price sensitivity) and cycle boosters (i.e., risks that are price sensitive within an account).
  - Products and policy wordings that are appropriate in relation to the type of risk being written, the market and country legal considerations, and discipline that is maintained through all stages of the underwriting cycle.
  - Compliance with the stated P&C reinsurance policy and the credit policy (i.e., risk of default of the reinsurer) for all purchases of reinsurance, both treaty and facultative (whereby the reinsurer gets to choose which policy it wants to reinsure from all those submitted to it at the same time by the P&C company).
  - Consistency with reinsurance treaties and with the philosophy statements provided to reinsurers.
- *Reserving risk:*
  - Assessment of whether reserves are sufficient to cover liabilities and whether excessive prudence exists. That is, do booked claims provisions contain margins beyond those required, taking into account regulation, professional actuarial guidance, and accounting standards?

The P&C firm must manage its insurance risks through avoidance, transfer, acceptance, or reduction of the likelihood of the occurrence or potential impact of a material operational risk exposure. This includes:

- Ensuring robust internal processes and systems are maintained.
- Accepting P&C insurance risks within the stated risk tolerance level.
- Embedding a risk culture throughout the financial institution via:
  - Aligning operational and individual goals with strategic goals
  - Including responsibility and accountability for risk management explicitly in job descriptions
  - Developing performance measures for effective risk management, ensuring that they are appropriate and sufficiently focused on future goals, and that they act as an early warning system
  - Developing a common language for risk management and ensuring that it is effectively communicated across the whole organization

9.3　Life Insurance

9.3.1　How Does Life Insurance Work?

Life insurance is designed to protect against the financial burdens that may accompany the death of the insured party. There are two options: term life and whole life. Both require the payment of, usually, a monthly premium by the insured, or someone representing the insured.

A term life policy will pay a death benefit in the event of death during the specific time, or term, covered by the policy. A term life policy has a start date and an end date. If death occurs the day after the policy ends, the insurance company does not pay a death benefit. The premiums that are paid for a term life policy cannot be recovered by the policyholder's estate after the term has ended.

A whole life policy provides **coverage** for the entire life of the insured. The insurance company invests the paid premiums, and some of the earnings are put into the insurance policy in the form of cash value.

EXAMPLE

Aviva Life is a major division of Aviva Insurance. It provides various types of life insurance coverage, depending on the needs of the customer. For example, offerings include standard life insurance, life insurance with critical illness coverage (insurance that pays out in the case of death or diagnosis with a critical illness), over 50s life insurance (guaranteed sum of money paid out at death), and income protection insurance (helps to pay the bills in the case of the earner's sickness or injury and inability to work).

9.3.2　Inherent Risks of Life Insurance

There are particular types of risks when a business offers life insurance products. These are the risks specific to protection and investment products, including those covering sickness and health. They include risks from longevity, mortality, morbidity, persistence, claims management, underwriting, product development, and expenses, among others.

Life insurance risks do not encompass risks associated with investments (covered under market risk) or risks directly associated with the selling process (distribution).

The key inherent risks and definitions for life insurance are:

- *Longevity risk*—The risk that customers now and in the future live longer than assumed in pricing the product, or longer than assumed in the current embedded value and reserving bases, or through changes in the base level of mortality and future improvements in life expectancy.
- *Mortality and morbidity risks*—The risks that the incidence of death (mortality) and sickness (morbidity) claims exceeds, in either number or amount, what has been assumed in the product pricing basis and current embedded value basis. Catastrophe risk also exists where multiple death claims exceed the reinsurance cover purchased.
- *Persistency risk*—The risk that policyholders terminate their policies in greater numbers or earlier than expected, or the policies are replaced by other insurers, resulting in losses from unrecouped expenses, lost future profits, and reputational risk from poor selling practices and customer servicing. Persistency is a complex area and an important risk from both a financial and a reputational perspective. Whether the percentage of policies lapsing or leaving is higher or lower than expected can have a material impact on reserving risk.
- *Claims management risk*—The risk that claims amounts are greater than expected, or greater than they should be, through poor claims handling processes, resulting in claims being paid when they should be rejected, or claims amounts being greater than acceptable.
- *Underwriting risk*—The risk that arises when poor underwriting practices allows risks to be accepted at inadequate premium levels, or allows proposals to be accepted that should actually be declined.
- *Product cycle risk*—The risk that an insurance company's management does not continually review the products in light of emerging experience, and as a result misses opportunities to review costs and/or remove poor products from sale.
- *Expense risk*—The risk that arises from inadequate management of acquisition and maintenance expenses, leading to losses where actual expenses cannot be met from premiums received.

It is the nature of these risks that some are more material than others, either at a business level by consequence of the products sold or at a total company (sometimes known as group) level when aggregated.

9.3.3 Risk Appetite

It is essential that companies formulate a risk appetite statement that their businesses are required to adhere to, covering each of the risks identified by the company and setting out detailed appetite limits and metrics.

The level of risk appetite for the institution is generally set in aggregate terms, which also include the level of risk associated with various individual risks. The risk appetite statement should be regularly reviewed in the light of the changing circumstances and business's risk profile.

The risk appetite statement for the risks noted below should contain at least the following:

- The longevity risk appetite should be framed in the context of the balance between (existing and new) annuity business plans and the firm's defined benefit pension schemes (retirement plans).
- The mortality and morbidity risk appetite should reference maximum sums assured for life coverage, critical illness, and disability income, combined with levels of reinsurance used and underwriting practice.
- The persistency risk appetite should initially cover maximum lapse rates for products sold.
- Underwriting and claims management appetite statements are difficult to frame quantitatively. However, it should be expected and expressly noted that businesses adopt high-quality processes that are assessed independently.
- The risk appetite statement should include the constraint that mortality and morbidity risk outside the company's risk appetite should be placed only with a financially strong reinsurer that has passed the company's risk assessment process and is on the company's approved reinsurance list.
- The risk appetite statement should espouse good product cycle management, that is, that it will not offer products that have become mispriced or outdated, and that products are managed and reviewed to ensure that adverse experience losses do not exceed agreed limits. Product reviews should also check that products continue to meet customer expectations.

9.3.4 Risk Identification, Mitigation, and Management

Life insurers' core measure of their exposure to insurance risk is **capital at risk**. The capital at risk is calculated in terms of the potential adverse deviation of actual experience from a best estimate of liabilities arising from each line of business. The best estimates of liabilities are informed by actuarial investigations into lapses (persistency), mortality, morbidity, and expenses, with analysis of deviation from assumptions underpinning products' pricing and existing reserves.

The controls described in the following sections provide methods and techniques for mitigating and managing each of these components of life insurance risk.

9.3.5 Minimum Standards of Risk Management and Controls

Minimum required risk management and controls are directly related to the materiality of the risks created by the products being sold.

- Management information for life insurance risk should be used to provide insight and inform the operational planning process, and to influence resource allocation, including capital.
- Risk appetite statements and tolerances should be clearly defined and refreshed on a regular basis (at least annually) and be an integral part of the planning process.
- Regular risk analysis reviews (at least on a quarterly basis) of life insurance systems and processes should be actively performed to ensure that inherent insurance risks are effectively managed.
- Appropriate internal controls should be put in place to ensure that the pre-defined requirements are met.

The key minimum standards of risk management and controls are:

- *Longevity, mortality, and morbidity risks:*
  - It is important that businesses analyze their own longevity mortality and morbidity experience, and benchmark against emerging industry experience where available, and remain abreast of the latest research on projected improvements

- *Persistency risk:*
  - Management must be aware of the persistency risks in the business that they write, and regularly monitor emerging experience as it becomes available, comparing that experience with original assumptions, and with market data wherever possible
  - Management must aim to manage persistency risk at all stages in the product cycle, both before the product is sold through careful product design, and throughout the life of the product

- *Claims management risk:*
  - A claims management process must be implemented that pays valid claims promptly and efficiently, and satisfies local statutes and regulations.
  - Sufficient detail on individual claims should be retained both to enable detailed analysis of historical experience and to enable investigation of individual claims in case of dispute.

- *Underwriting risk:*
  - A formally documented underwriting philosophy and supporting procedures must be put in place.
  - Appropriate underwriting skills and practices consistent with industry practice must be applied.
  - Independent reviews of underwriting, usually by reinsurers, should take place regularly. Underwriting practice should also be consistent with reinsurance arrangements and the experience assumed when pricing.
  - When writing unitized business, a clear unit pricing framework should be implemented, covering the calculation and checking of unit prices, the process to take when correcting errors, and addressing customer service, and regulatory requirements.

- *Reinsurance risk:*
  - Reinsurance is an important element of exposure management. A clear reinsurance strategy and associated procedures should be in place. The security of the reinsurer is of particular importance for long-term life business. The firm's policy on assessment and selection of reinsurers should be contained in the credit policy.

- *Product cycle risk:*
  - A clear process, including unambiguous accountability, for ongoing product management must be in place. All the insurance risk elements must be reviewed with appropriate regularity. This will include monitoring the experience of key parameters (such as lapses, mortality, and morbidity); management of reviewable rate contracts, accounting for portfolio claims trends and policy claims experience when relevant; and management of claims and claims handling (which can have a major impact on the results of health-related products such as critical illness and income replacement).

9.4   Reinsurance

Insurance companies usually reinsure some of their risks with reinsurance companies. The reinsurance company effectively assumes some of the risks that were previously held by the insurance company. There are two main reasons why insurance companies do this.

1. *Risk reduction.* An insurance company can pass on unwanted risks to a reinsurance company. It can transfer a specific group of risks to the reinsurance company (for example, the reinsurance company will make any payments arising from automobile insurance policies written by the insurance company between July 1, 2013, and September 30, 2014) or it may transfer part of the risks (for example, the insurance company will pay the first USD 5,000 on any automobile insurance claims on policies written between July 1, 2013, and September 30, 2014, but any amounts payable in excess of USD 5,000 will be paid by the reinsurance company).
2. *Ability to conduct more business.* By ceding risk in this way, the insurance company has reduced its liabilities and therefore is able to take on new business.

EXAMPLE

Insurance Company D is expanding rapidly as a result of attractive products that it has designed for the home insurance market. The company's marketing team believes that it will be able to increase sales of home insurance by 20% per year for the next three years. However, the company's chief financial officer warns that the company does not have sufficient capital to support such a large increase in business. The insurance company solves this problem by reinsuring part of its existing portfolio of home insurance policies, freeing its balance sheet to take on new business.

However, there are risks associated with reinsurance.

Reinsurance risk is the risk of loss arising from inadequate or inappropriate reinsurance cover.

Mortality and morbidity risks that exceed an insurance company's risk appetite must be placed only with a financially strong reinsurer that has passed the organization's risk assessment process and is on the insurance company's approved reinsurance counterparty list.

Reinsurance is used as a risk mitigation tool and support for product pricing. It is potentially exposed to loss arising from an arrangement being an inadequate or inappropriate method of risk transfer.

Risk management techniques associated with reinsurance include the following:

- Senior management should periodically review the company's reinsurance program. The review should consider the:
  - Purpose and strategy of the reinsurance program
  - Criteria for the placement of reinsurance
  - Retention policy
  - Exposure to and financial strength of reinsurers
  - Performance of in-force treaties and rejected claims
- Business should not be placed with a reinsurer without a signed agreement being in place. All agreements must be subject to review by the insurer's legal advisers prior to signature.
- To mitigate the risk that a reinsurer may refuse to meet a claim on the grounds that inappropriate underwriting procedures were in place, reinsurers should be provided with information on the procedures that are being adopted and operational controls. Reinsurers may also refuse to meet claims if they believe that the company has incorrectly paid out on a claim. This risk can be managed by having clear documentation with reinsurers on the agreement of claims and operational controls to ensure adherence to process. Relevant management committees and/or entity boards should review the outcome of audits by reinsurers.

EXAMPLE

AIG (American International Group) Re is an assumed treaty reinsurance division of AIG Property Casualty. **Assumed reinsurance** is the insurance risk that a reinsurer accepts (assumes) from a ceding company and is executed through a contract (treaty), rather than through separate negotiation for each policy that is reinsured. AIG Re offers both pro rata and excess loss treaty reinsurance cover. The business is predominantly written through brokers, but it also works directly with some customers to structure solutions designed to fit their needs. The company is required to be highly rated and well capitalized given the nature of its business. In addition to regular P&C areas of coverage, it also has specialized areas such as agriculture, marine, financial products (mortgages), and property catastrophe.

9.5   Other Types of Risk

9.5.1   Concentration Risk

Concentration risk in insurance, sometimes known as **accumulation risk,** is the risk arising from concentration of exposure in particular sectors of the market, as well as concentration of exposure to particular reinsurers or geographic accumulation. It is also the risk arising when similar risks across a wide range of products, although individually not material, aggregate to create a material risk for the business.

Concentrations of risk in specified reinsurers are regarded as a counter-party credit risk. Risk management techniques include applying a range of limits on the value of business that may be written on a single life or group of lives. The types of limits could include:

- *Group protection business*—Event limits restricting the total value of claims payable to a scheme from a single event at one location.
- *Individual life business*—Limits on the maximum insured value on a single life arising from one or more policies.
- *P&C insurance business*—Limits on the maximum loss that may arise on a single policy.

Although definitions are not consistent in the insurance industry, some key terms in this area are shown in Figure 9.4.

Type of Loss	Description
Maximum Probable Loss	The largest loss that the underwriter considers probable. Such an assessment would be made by the underwriter based upon his or her own experience and judgement
Maximum Possible Loss (MPL)	The worst loss that could possibly occur because of a single event, but assumes that protective controls will operate as they were intended
Maximum Foreseeable Loss (MFL)	The worst loss that can be foreseen due to a single event.

FIGURE 9.4 Types of Maximum Losses

9.5.2   Counterparty Credit Risk

Insurance companies and reinsurance companies incur credit risk for their counterparty exposures on investments and reinsurance transactions. As a result, they must understand and manage counterparty credit risk. This includes establishing principles and procedures for the selection of reinsurance or risk transfer counterparties, taking into account the creditworthiness and diversification of counterparties, as well as the legal jurisdictions in which they are situated.

9.5.3   Market Risk

Insurance entities incur market risk (such as asset risk, currency risk, etc.) on the investment of accumulated premiums and other funds. The company should have in place policies and procedures related to the following:

- Optimizing investment returns, setting asset allocation and diversification strategies and authorities for investment activities
- Approaching inherently risky financial instruments (e.g., derivatives, etc.)
- Understanding and managing counterparty credit risk, concentration risk, liquidity and other risks, and the impact of nonadmitted assets
- Matching policy benefits with the appropriate assets, where these are linked to the performance of particular investment instruments or groups of instruments

9.5.4   Pension Obligation Risk

Pension obligation risk is the risk of loss, or of adverse change in the value of insurance liabilities, resulting from events impacting the obligations of the internal pension scheme or retirement plan (e.g., increased longevity, increasing plan liabilities, and changes in accounting policy).

Where the insurance firm operates a defined benefit retirement plan—a type of pension plan promising a specific monthly benefit upon retirement based on various characteristics of the plan holder, such as age, earnings, years of service—pension obligation risk arises where the returns from investments held to meet the liabilities of plan members are less than expected, or as a result of greater than expected increases in the estimated value of the plan's liabilities.

Risk management techniques related to these types of plans include:

- At specified time intervals (e.g., every three years), the management of the defined benefit plan agrees on the appropriate assumption basis for calculating the funding valuation that is used to identify whether the pension funds are in surplus or deficit. The results of the funding valuation will be used to establish the level of contributions that are required to be paid into each plan to meet the current and future amounts expected to be paid to pensioners (retirees). Valuations of the plan liabilities and assets backing them should be reviewed at least twice a year as well.
- Due to the uncertainly of pension obligations, assumptions are necessary for estimating both the accumulated benefits to plan members (including current and future retirees) and the amount the company needs to invest to provide those benefits. The assumptions underpinning the calculation of pension liabilities are trends in mortality, plan membership changes, inflation, and interest rates. These assumptions should be subject to periodic stress testing to confirm that the funding liability is appropriate across a range of scenarios.

9.5.5 Catastrophe Risk

Catastrophe risk applies to both P&C and life insurance and reflects the risk of loss, or of adverse change in the value of insurance liabilities, resulting from the significant uncertainty of pricing and provisioning assumptions related to extreme or irregular events.

In the case of P&C business, for protection against business events such as natural disasters, epidemics, or terrorist attacks, there may be a significant increase in the number of incidences that may either exceed the level assumed/anticipated in the pricing basis or differ in terms of the timing and frequency of claims.

Exposure to catastrophe risk is managed by:

- Setting concentration limits by policy sizes, geographies, and product lines to limit the impact of a catastrophic event.
- Reinsurance to cover specific events or claims above a certain size. Reinsurance may also be used to mitigate catastrophe risks that may be outside the firm's tolerances or to enable the more effective pricing of insurance products.

Other risk management techniques related to catastrophe risk include:

- A full evaluation should be undertaken of the potential impact of catastrophic events on the profile and frequency of claims or other obligations that may arise under this policy, including stress and scenario testing to identify the full impact of extreme events.
- Regular reviews of concentration limits to ensure they remain appropriate, taking account of changes in the external environment, the profile of business written, and new business volumes. Actual exposures relative to limits should be subject to monitoring, with variances reported in management information.
- Annual reviews of catastrophe reinsurance arrangements to ensure that they continue to provide appropriate mitigation for exposure to catastrophic events.

9.6   Regulation and Supervision—Solvency 2 in the European Union

Globally, each political jurisdiction has its own risk and capital regulatory regime in place for insurance. There is no international accord for insurers that is equivalent to the Basel Accords for banks.

However, there is a common regulatory approach within Europe—called Solvency 2 that applies to the 28 member states of the European Union, plus three of the European Economic Area countries. The Solvency 2 Directive establishes a revised set of EU-wide capital requirements and as such represents a wholesale change in the risk assessment and capital adequacy regime for the European insurance industry. Other jurisdictions are considering similar implementations. Solvency 2 is still in the preparatory stage, with full implementation expected in 2016. While Solvency 2 is Europe-based, many believe that this regime will be implemented in other jurisdictions globally.

The insurance business in the EU is overseen by the European Insurance and Occupational Pensions Authority (EIOPA). EIOPA is comprised of high-level representatives from the insurance and occupational pensions' supervisory authorities of EU member states.

Some of the key risks identified by Solvency 2 that are unique to insurers, in comparison to banks, are underwriting risk, claims risk and actuarial risk (potential loss due to incorrect actuarial assumptions).

Similarly to the Basel II and III Accords for banks, in the Solvency 2 Directive advanced models are used for the key insurance risks as well as for other risks (such as credit risk, market risk, and operational risk). The Basel II/III Accords and the Solvency 2 Directive have similar aims: to create a prudential framework and standards of governance more appropriate to the true risks facing banks or insurance companies, and to establish incentives for banks or insurance companies to understand and manage their own risks better. They both have three pillars for risk and capital measurement.

The Solvency 2 legislation will replace the 13 existing EU insurance risk and capital systems. Solvency 2's three-pillar approach includes:

- **Pillar 1**—Quantitative requirements. Similarly to Basel II, Solvency 2 sets minimum capital levels, including all quantifiable risks within Pillar 1. This includes insurance risk (arising out of the volatility within the underwriting and reserves) and is intended to reflect the variety of risks and exposures that different insurers face in aggregate.
- **Pillar 2**—Requirements for the governance and risk management of insurers, as well as a capital add-on as required. In addition, there is a new **Own Risk and Solvency Assessment (ORSA)** reporting requirement.
- **Pillar 3**—Supervisory reporting and transparency requirements.

Figure 9.5 outlines the three-pillar approach under Solvency 2.

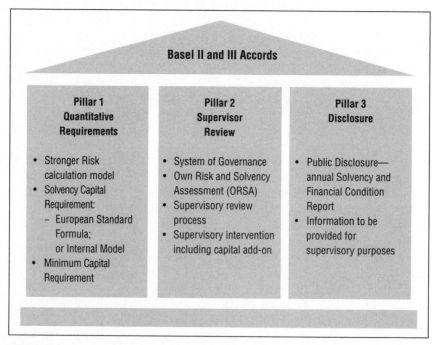

FIGURE 9.5 Solvency 2: Three-Pillar Approach

9.6.1   Internal Models Under Solvency 2

Solvency 2 aims to allow a full internal model approach. In fact, defining and developing internal models is an explicit Solvency 2 Directive requirement. The use of mathematical models to assess risk recognizes the broad range and scale of risks faced by insurers and provides them with the opportunity to build models that better reflect the interaction between risks in their own firms. Model use also allows firms to include in their risk assessment the mitigation effects of their risk mitigation techniques (e.g., diversification). Internal models are developed by the financial institution to determine capital requirements on the basis of the company's specific risk profile.

The most significant difference between Basel II/III and Solvency 2 is the treatment of full internal models.

Pillar 1 of Basel II/III allows a full internal portfolio model approach only for market risk and operational risk. For credit risk, which is the largest component of a bank's capital requirement, companies are only allowed to use internal models to determine parameters (probability of default, loss given default, and exposure at default) to feed into a supervisory-prescribed model. In the field of operational risk for Basel II/III, firms can choose the Advanced Measurement Approach (AMA) backed up by a sophisticated internal model (including scenario and loss distribution approaches).

Solvency 2 permits firms to apply for approval to use full or partial internal models for the calculation of their regulatory capital requirements, as an alternative to applying the results of the standard formula. The internal modeling activity is required to be integrated into the risk management activity of the firm.

Figure 9.6 is a schematic of an internal model. It is the key mechanism for the identification, assessment, measurement, monitoring, and reporting of risk profiles, across the firm, in order to enhance risk management capabilities and assist in the determination of Solvency 2–based and economic capital requirements (both at consolidated/group and for material specified solo levels).

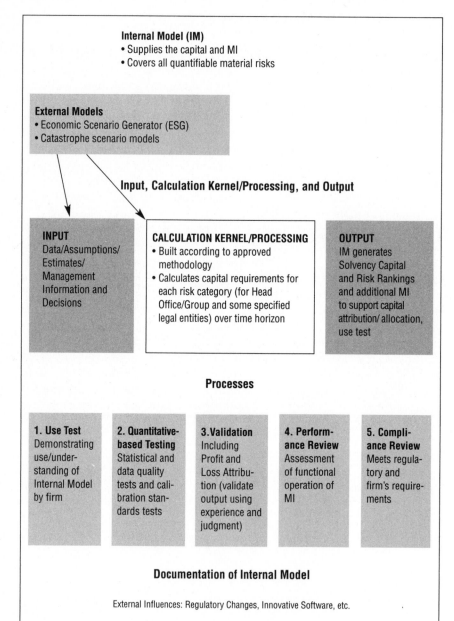

FIGURE 9.6 Example Schematic of an Internal Model Under Solvency 2

9.6.2   Solvency 2 and Basel II/III—Similarities and Differences

Solvency 2 and Basel II/III have a number of similarities and differences, as described in Figure 9.7.

Similarities	Differences
Similar aims, which are: - To create a prudential framework more appropriate to the true risks facing the respective organizations (credit institutions for Basel II and insurance companies for Solvency 2) - To create incentives for companies to understand and manage their own risks better.	Basel II/III is international, while Solvency 2 is generally European Union (EU) specific
Three Pillar approach	Insurers have market, credit, liquidity and operational risks like banks but also actuarial and other insurer-specific risks
- Move away from one-size-fits-all capital approach (e.g. flat % for capital allocation) to a more risk sensitive approach. - Different methods of calculating capital (TSA, AMA, etc.)	Risk is the business of Insurers
Increased focus on operational risk calculation vs. prior regulatory regimes	Insurers in some jurisdictions (e.g., UK) already have an internal capital process (ICA) and thus this is a less radical change from Solvency I to Solvency 2 than from Basel I to Basel II

FIGURE 9.7 Solvency 2 and Basel II/III—Similarities and Differences

9.6.3   Global Systemically Important Insurers (G-SIIs)

The Financial Stability Board has identified large insurance companies that it considers to be global systemically important insurers (G-SIIs). These G-SIIs have been identified based on criteria such as size, global activity, and the amount of noninsurance businesses they have. Size continues to play a significant role in the designation methodology.

One material obligation of an insurer designated a G-SII is the need to draw up recovery and resolution plans to limit the economic fallout if they were to go out of business.

EXAMPLE

The nine G-SIIs initially named by the Financial Stability Board in July 2013 are:

- Allianz SE
- American International Group, Inc.
- Assicurazioni Generali S.p.A.
- Aviva plc
- Axa S.A.
- MetLife, Inc.
- Ping An Insurance (Group) Company of China, Ltd.
- Prudential Financial, Inc.
- Prudential plc

Because there are no global solvency standards, it is difficult to assess what the implications will be for the companies on this list; however, the overall European Solvency 2 standards of this designation will apply to some of them.

9.6.4   Proportionality

The principle of proportionality requires that the governance and control system (including regulations) be proportionate to the nature, scale, and complexity of the risks inherent in the business of an insurance undertaking. This applies to both the low end and the high end of the risk spectrum. Proportionality justifies simpler and less burdensome ways of meeting requirements for low-risk-profile areas. Proportionality says that for more complex risk areas there is an increased likelihood that undertakings will need to apply to more sophisticated methods and techniques.

9.7   The Role of Lloyd's of London

Lloyd's of London, while not an insurance company, or a company at all, is one of the more important insurance industry players in the world. Lloyd's is a market that provides specialist, or tailored, insurance coverage by forming syndicates of investors to invest in providing coverage for specifically defined needs. Lloyd's currently has 57 managing agents who are responsible for managing the activities of 93 different syndicates.

The capital required to support the underwriting and insurance coverage of each syndicate comes from corporate investors, insurance companies and individuals, although the majority of the capital for Lloyd's market comes from corporations. Syndicate investors are technically obligated to be a part of a syndicate for a year, but many will stay beyond that time frame.

Each syndicate is operated independent of the other, with no overlapping insurance coverage or legal obligations.

Lloyd's brokers, who are specialists in various types of risks, bring business to the market, the investors, and their syndicates. The risks placed by the brokers with the underwriters originate from clients and other brokers and intermediaries from all over the world. Together, the syndicates underwriting at Lloyd's form one of the world's largest commercial insurers and a leading reinsurer.

Figure 9.8 identifies the structure and participants in Lloyd's of London.

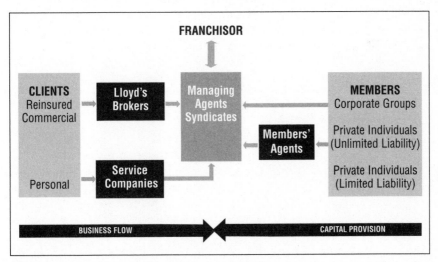

FIGURE 9.8 Lloyd's of London—Overview and Participants

9.8   Summary

The insurance and banking industries play vitally important and complementary roles in our global risk-based capital system. While operating as separate fields of specialty, the issues they face, and the manner in which they are required to operate are very similar. Both are being challenged by the need to ensure they are identifying and assessing risks properly. The requirement for a robust and dynamic control system within each company, between industry players, and across borders, as well as their relationships and interactions with regulators are virtually identical. As seen in this chapter on insurance, and throughout the book when discussing the intricacies of the banking industry, there are many ways things can go wrong, with very material and negative resulting consequences. Working in either industry requires a basic understanding of how each operates, why controls are so important, and how to recognize when things may be moving along the wrong path so that issues can be raised within the company at the earliest possible opportunity, to be analyzed and dealt with before they become so large they materially impact the company's operations.

Foundations of Financial Risk is designed to provide that base level of awareness and understanding, bringing into focus in a high level and comprehensive way the issues faced each and every day by those engaged in the banking and insurance industry. Having this broad-based knowledge not only helps create a culture of risk awareness within a company, but also lends mightily to the ongoing objective of guarding against and mitigating the impact of errors and omissions that affect systemic risk in a world that is ever and increasingly interconnected and multinational.

Glossary

Advanced Measurement Approach   The Advanced Measurement Approach is a sophisticated approach to calculate operational risk capital, allowing the bank to use internally generated models to calculate their operational risk capital requirements.

Asset and liability management (ALM)   Asset and liability management (ALM) in a bank manages the risks that arise due to the mismatches between assets and liabilities in terms of maturity, liquidity, interest rates, etc., and typically focuses on the banking book's interest rate risk and the bank's liquidity risk.

Asset-backed security (ABS)   Asset-backed securities, backed by pools of mortgage loans or other types of securitizable cash flow generating assets, are sold to investors who then receive payments based on the cash flows generated by the assets in the underlying pool.

Asset-based loan   Asset-based loans allow the borrower to pledge a specific asset or a combination of assets, such as inventory, machinery, or equipment, as collateral to cover a loan.

Asset conversion loan   Asset conversion loans (self-liquidating loans) are loans that are repaid by converting the asset that is used to collateralize the loan into cash.

Asset transformation   Asset transformation is the process of creating new assets (loan) from liabilities (deposits) with different characteristics by converting small denomination, immediately available, and relatively risk-free bank deposits into loans—new relatively risky, large denomination assets—that are repaid following a set schedule.

Assets   Assets are the various loans, investments, and anything of value that the bank owns.

Balance sheet   The balance sheet shows all the assets, liabilities, and equity the bank has at one particular point in time.

Balloon payments   Balloon payment is a large payment at maturity that includes the repayment of the principal and in certain cases all the accumulated interest.

Bank   A bank takes deposits, makes loans, arranges payments, holds a banking license, and is subject to regulatory supervision by a banking regulator.

Bank for International Settlements   The Bank for International Settlements, BIS, established in Basel, Switzerland, in 1930, is the principal center of international central bank cooperation.

Bank panic   A bank panic occurs when a large number of depositors at multiple different banks simultaneously demand the return of their deposits.

Bank regulation   The process of writing the rules that govern how banks operate (for example, setting minimum capital requirements).

Bank run   A bank run occurs when a large number of depositors at one bank simultaneously demand the return of their deposits.

Banking book   The banking book of a bank is the portfolio of assets, primarily loans, a bank expects to hold until maturity when the loan is repaid fully; typically refers to the loans the bank underwrites.

Banking license   A banking license, issued by a banking regulator or supervisor, allows a bank to engage in banking activities under the condition that the bank agrees to be supervised by regulatory or supervisory authorities.

Bank supervision   The process of enforcing the rules that govern how banks operate. Usually, supervision is divided into "off-site supervision" whereby supervisors review written information and statistics submitted by the bank and "on-site supervision" whereby inspectors from the supervisory agency make visits to a bank to meet managers and directors and see for themselves how a bank is operating.

Basel Accords   The Basel Accords (Basel I Accord, the Market Risk Amendment, and Basel II Accord) are the cornerstones of international risk-based banking regulation, the results of a collaborative attempt by banking regulators from major developed countries to create a globally valid and widely applicable framework for banks and bank risk management.

Basel Committee on Banking Supervision   The Basel Committee on Banking Supervision, a forum for regulatory cooperation between its member countries on banking supervision-related matters, was established by the central bank governors and consists of senior representatives of bank supervisory authorities and central banks from major economies.

Basic Indicator Approach (BIA)   The Basic Indicator Approach uses the bank's total gross income as a risk indicator for the bank's operational risk exposure and sets the required level of operational risk capital at 15% of the bank's annual positive gross income averaged over the previous three years.

Basis point   A basis point is one-hundredth of one percent, or 0.0001.

Beta factor (operational risk)   The beta factor is the fixed percentage of average positive annual gross income (over three years) of the eight different business lines a bank may have and is used to calculate its operational risk capital.

Bid-ask spread   The bid-ask spread is the difference between the buy price or rate (bid) and sell price or rate (ask) of a financial instrument.

Board of directors   The board of directors has the ultimate responsibility for the management and performance of a company, is responsible for the bank's governance, and is elected by the shareholders.

Bond   A bond is a legally binding contract through which the borrower (also referred to as the issuer of the bond) borrows the principal, an amount specified in the bond, from an investor and in exchange pays a specified amount of interest, usually at regular intervals, and repays the principal either at maturity or during the life of the bond.

Borrower   A borrower receives money from a lender in exchange for a promise to repay the full amount borrowed (the principal) plus an additional amount (interest) at a future date(s).

Bottom-up approach   The bottom-up approach analyzes all processes within each business unit separately and benchmarks each unit's risk profile; it then aggregates identified risks first at the business line and eventually at a corporate level to generate a company-wide risk profile.

Business risk   Business risk is the potential loss due to a weakening in the competitive position.

Call option   A call option is a right to buy, while a put option is a right to sell, another financial or real asset. These rights are similar to insurance policies and their price is termed the "premium."

Capital adequacy   Capital adequacy is achieved when a bank's capital ratio meets or exceeds the minimum capital ratio, which under the Basel Accords is 8% of risk-weighted assets and can be satisfied with Tier 1, Tier 2, and Tier 3 capital. Tier 1 capital has to account for at least 4% of risk-weighted assets; the remainder can be satisfied through Tier 2 and, in the case of market risk capital, Tier 3 capital. National banking regulators can deviate from these minimum capital adequacy ratios.

Capital ratio   Capital ratio is the relationship between risk-weighted assets and regulatory capital.

Cash flow-based loan   A cash flow-based loan provides funds that are repaid from the cash flow generated from the borrower's operations.

Central bank   A central bank is the principal monetary authority of a country, or a group of countries, and may also exercise regulatory and supervisory responsibilities over other banks, arrange payment between banks, and when needed, provide stability to the financial and banking system.

Charged-off loan   A charged-off loan is a loan that has been removed from the bank's financial statements because the bank believes that it will collect nothing of the loan from the borrower.

Circulating Assets   Highly liquid, current assets also known as floating or working assets. Examples include cash, work-in-progress, and inventory that are expected to be consumed or sold within the course of an operating cycle and replaced by similar assets.

Clearinghouse   A clearinghouse guarantees the financial performance of a trade on an exchange by becoming the buyer to each seller and the seller to each buyer and clears the trade between the parties by processing payments and the exchange of instruments.

Collateral   Collateral is an asset pledged by a borrower to secure a loan or other credit and is forfeited to the lender in the event of the borrower's default.

Commercial bank   A commercial bank offers a wide range of highly specialized loans to large businesses, acts as an intermediary in raising funds, and provides specialized financial services including payment, investment, and risk management services.

Commercial paper Commercial paper is an unsecured, short-term debt security with a maturity range of 30 to 50 days or less issued by a typically large, financially strong, organization that uses the proceeds to finance its operations.

Committed facility A committed facility is a loan whose terms and conditions—such as margins, fees, and duration—are clearly defined in a formal agreement by the bank and are imposed on the borrower, and the facility is funded.

Commodity Commodities are generally physical items such as food, oil, metal, or other fixed substances that are relatively homogenous in nature.

Commodity risk Commodity risk is the potential loss from an adverse change in commodity prices. This applies to all commodity positions and any derivative commodity positions such as futures contracts.

Compensating balances Compensating balances are deposits the bank requires the borrower to deposit for the duration of the commitment in exchange for extending a committed or an uncommitted facility.

Compliance risk Compliance risk is the risk that a bank suffers losses as a result of its failure to comply with laws and regulations or with internal policies and procedures that govern the way it operates.

Confidence level Confidence level expresses the degree of statistical confidence in an estimate.

Consortium A consortium denotes a cooperative underwriting of loans by a select group of banks.

Contagion The risk that one bank or financial system may start to experience problems as a result of problems at another bank or financial system. Sometimes contagion can spread as a result of loss of confidence or fear, rather than as a result of clear financial relationships.

Cooperative banks Financial institutions that are owned by their customers. Cooperative banks usually focus on retail business and have strong ties to local communities, although some cooperative banks have become very large and have international networks.

Core banking services The core banking services are deposit collection, loan underwriting, and payment services.

Corporate borrower Corporate borrowers range from small local companies to large global conglomerates.

Corporate governance Corporate governance is a set of relationships framed by corporate bylaws, articles of association, charters, and applicable statutory or other legal rules and principles, between the board of directors, shareholders, and other stakeholders of a organization that outlines the relationship among these groups, sets rules how the organization should be managed, and sets its operational framework.

Cost of funds The cost of funds is the interest rate, required return, or other compensation associated with securing and using capital.

Counterparty credit risk Counterparty credit risk is the risk that the other party to a contract or agreement will fail to perform under the terms of an agreement.

Coupon rate   The coupon rate is a percentage of the principal borrowed, and determines the coupon payment, the promised and regularly paid interest payment to the buyer of a bond or other debt security.

Covenant   A covenant is an agreement that requires one party to refrain from or engage in specified actions and is imposed on the borrower by a lender to prevent a potential deterioration in the borrower's financial and business condition.

Coverage   The financial protection that is provided by an insurance policy

Credit analysis   Credit analysis or credit assessment is the process of assessing risk as measured by a borrower's ability to repay the loan.

Credit concentration risk   Credit concentration risk is the risk stemming from a single large exposure or group of smaller exposures that are adversely impacted by similar variations in conditions, events, or circumstances.

Credit derivative   A derivative instrument, such as an option, swap, or forward, that enables a firm to manage their exposure to credit risk. For example, a credit default swap (in one of its forms) transfers to another counterparty the risk that a lender will not be repaid. The lender pays a fee for this protection to the other counterparty.

Credit position   Although banks classically are "long" the credit market (net lenders, loan assets in the balance sheet), it is also possible to be short credit. This is achieved in the credit derivatives or bond repo markets and can be profitable when a borrower's credit deteriorates. Irrespective of whether the bank is long or short credit, it will always have a position in credit risky assets. In the extreme event, where the bank is neither long nor short credit risk, it is said to have a neutral, or zero credit position. This is rare across an entire bank, but can occur in sub-portfolios or on individual trading desks.

Credit rating agency (CRA)   A credit rating agency evaluates the creditworthiness of various borrowers, issuers, or credits.

Credit risk   Credit risk is the risk of loss due to non-payment of a loan, bond, or other credit.

Credit risk capital   Credit risk capital is capital allocated against possible credit losses.

Credit risk mitigation technique   A credit mitigation technique reduces credit risk through the use of such things as collateral, loan guarantees, securitization, or insurance.

Credit score   A credit score is a number that relates the relative strength of each borrower to a larger group of borrowers and indicates the relative chance of default.

Credit unions   Financial institutions that are owned by their customers and focus on serving low-income customers. They offer a limited range of deposit and loan products and usually operate within a single local community.

Currency   A currency is a generally accepted form of money—coins and bills—used in a country or a group of countries and issued by a government, central bank, or monetary authority.

Cyclical financing   Cyclical financing funds temporary and recurring increases in inventory, production, and sales due to changes in the business cycle.

Default   Default, the failure to pay interest or principal according to contractual terms, occurs when a debtor is unable to make a timely payment.

Default risk   Default risk is the potential loss due to default.

Deposit   A deposit is money entrusted to a bank for safekeeping in a bank account that allows the depositor to withdraw these funds and any interest paid by the bank on the deposit.

Deposit insurance   Deposit insurance is a promise by a government or an insurance system that, in the event of a bank failure, bank depositors will receive their deposits with that bank either partly or fully.

Derivative   A (financial) derivative is an instrument whose value "derives" from the value of a related underlying financial asset or commodity, and includes swaps, options, forwards, and futures.

Disclosure   Disclosure is the dissemination of material information about the conditions of a business that allows for a proper and transparent evaluation of that business.

Dividend   A dividend is that part of the earnings of a corporation that is distributed to its owners. A dividend is a distribution to shareholders and typically entails the payment of cash or additional shares.

Economic capital   Economic capital is the amount of capital the bank needs in the case of loss events, covers all risks across a bank, and is essential for the bank to survive in the long term.

Effective duration   Effective duration goes further than other duration measures and tries to find the same price sensitivity per yield change while additionally taking embedded options into account. Bonds with call and put features, such as callable bonds, putable bonds and U.S. Mortgage Backed Securities, with their implied early redemption option, do not respond well to traditional duration estimates, because these do not take any value change due to the embedded option into account. So, effective duration not only takes into account that the bond's cash flows can change when interest rates change, but also that the cash flows from the embedded options can change independently thereof.

Equity   Equity is the capital raised from shareholders plus retained earnings and reflects the ownership interest in a corporation.

Equity risk   Equity risk is the potential loss due to an adverse change in the price of stock.

Eurozone   The group of countries that have adopted the Euro as their common currency. Following the accession of Latvia on January 1 2014, the Eurozone had 18 members.

Exchange   A (financial) exchange is a formal, organized physical or electronic marketplace where trades between investors follow standardized procedures.

Exchange rate   Exchange rates reflect the relative value of one currency in relation to another currency.

Expected loss (EL) An expected loss describes the mean annual aggregate of losses or, more practically, the size of losses that can be expected to occur.

Exposure at default (EAD) Exposure at default is the maximum loss the lender may suffer in case of a default.

External risk External risk is associated with a potential loss caused by external parties, is beyond the direct control of the corporation, and includes natural disasters, power shortage, or terrorism.

Fair market value Fair market value is the price the asset would fetch if sold immediately on the market to a willing buyer.

File for administration (Chapter 11) Chapter 11 refers to a section in the U.S. bankruptcy code that provides for a company to seek protection from its creditors. A company that is "in Chapter 11" is able to reorganize its affairs, subject to court approval, and continue operating (again, in a manner approved by the court). After the conditions of the court-approved reorganization are fulfilled, the company emerges from Chapter 11 and can operate again in a normal manner. Chapter 11 bankruptcy differs from some other forms of bankruptcy that entail the disposal of assets by an administrator and the end of the company itself.

Financial asset A financial asset derives its value from a specific contractual claim and includes bonds, loans, stocks, money, currency, derivatives, deposits, etc.

Financial instrument A financial instrument is a representation of an ownership interest claim or the contractual or contingent claim to receive or deliver cash, or another financial instrument or asset, and can either be a cash instrument (e.g., cash, securities, loans, bonds, notes, equity) or a derivative instrument (e.g., forward, future, option, swap).

Financial intermediation Financial intermediation is the process bringing together those who need financing, such as businesses and governments, with those who provide financing, such as lenders, banks, and private investors, and facilitating the flow of capital between them.

Financial stability Financial stability indicates that shocks and disturbances impacting the financial markets and financial institutions do not restrict their ability to continue intermediating financing, carrying out payments, and redistributing risk satisfactorily.

Financial Stability Board The Financial Stability Board is an international body that co-ordinates the work of national financial authorities and international standard setters. Its members are ministries and finance and financial regulators.

Five Cs of Credit The Five Cs of Credit is an abbreviation of a widely used credit analysis framework that focuses on the character of borrower, the capital provided by the borrower, the business, economic and other conditions faced by the borrower, the financial and legal capacity of the borrower, and the various types of collateral and other types of credit support mechanisms offered by the borrower.

Fixed rate loan A fixed rate loan is a loan whose interest rate does not change during the life of the loan.

Floating rate loan   A floating rate loan is a loan whose interest rate is tied to an underlying index or base rate and, as a result, may change during the life of the loan.

Foreign currency cross rate   A foreign currency cross rate is the exchange rate between two currencies against a third.

Foreign exchange rate   A foreign exchange rate specifies the price one currency in terms of another currency.

Foreign exchange risk   Foreign exchange risk is the potential loss due to an adverse change in foreign exchange rates.

Forward   A forward (contract), a derivative, is a nontransferable contract that defines the delivery of specified asset (e.g., commodities, currencies, bonds or stocks), at a specified price, of a specified quantity, on a specified future date.

Fractional reserve banking   Fractional reserve banking is a banking system where only a small fraction of the total deposits must be held in reserve, with the balance available to be invested in loans and other securities.

Funding liquidity   Funding liquidity refers to a bank's ability to have funds available to repay depositors on demand and to fund loans.

Funding liquidity risk   Funding liquidity risk refers to a bank's potential inability to have funds available to repay depositors on demand and to fund loans when needed.

Futures   A futures (contract), a derivative, is a standardized and transferable contract traded on an exchange that defines the delivery of specified asset (e.g., commodities, currencies, bonds, or stocks), at a specified price, of a specified quantity, on a specified future date.

G20 (AC)   The G20 comprises 19 countries and the European Union and it acts to co-ordinate economic co-operation and decision making among its members. Decisions taken by the G20 have a wide impact throughout the global economy.

General or systematic market risk   Systematic risk represents the effect of unexpected changes in macroeconomic and financial market conditions on the performance of a wide range of assets, and represents the risk of an adverse movement in market prices that are applied across a range of financial assets, including fixed income, loans, equity, and commodities.

Headline risk   Headline, or reputation, risk is the potential loss due to a decrease in a bank's standing in public opinion.

Hedging   Hedging attempts to reduce risk by matching a position with an opposite and offsetting position in a financial instrument that tracks or mirrors the value changes in the position.

High frequency/low impact, HFLI events   HFLI events occur frequently, but each event has a low impact on the operations of the bank.

Hybrid security   A hybrid security is a financial instrument that has both equity and debt features.

Idiosyncratic risk   Idiosyncratic risk represents risks that are particular to the conditions and circumstances of one or a defined group of individual borrowers, assets or securities.

Illiquidity   Illiquidity is the inability to make payments when they are due.

Income statement   The income statement records all the revenues (income) and costs (expenses) that the bank has encountered over a specific time period, such as one month, one quarter, or one year.

Inflation rate   Inflation rate, the price of money, is the change in the purchasing power of money expressed as an annual percentage change.

Innovative capital   Innovative capital includes complex financial instruments that have both equity and debt features.

Insolvency   Insolvency occurs when liabilities exceed assets; while not synonymous with bankruptcy or illiquidity, it typically leads to either or both.

Institutional borrower   An institutional borrower is a financially sophisticated organization such as a large publicly traded company, a hedge fund, a large bank, or a large insurer, who borrows substantial amounts of capital using debt securities or direct borrowing.

Insurance   Insurance provides financial compensation for loss; in exchange for periodic payments the insurer guarantees the insured a sum of money upon the occurrence of an adverse specific event.

Interbank loan   An interbank loan is a loan between banks.

Interconnectivity (AC)   A set of relationships that link financial institutions and financial systems so that a problem in one may lead to a problem in another.

Interest rate   Interest rate, the price of credit, is the rate charged for accessing and using borrowed funds.

Interest rate margin   The interest rate margin is the difference between the interest income the bank earns on its assets and the interest expense it pays on its liabilities.

Interest rate risk   Interest rate risk is the potential loss of value due to the variability of interest rates.

Interest rate risk in the banking book   The interest rate risk in the banking book reflects the fact that bank assets and liabilities have different maturities, are priced off different interest rates, and are repriced at different points in time.

Internal Models Approach   The Internal Models Approach relies on the bank's own internal risk management models and determines the regulatory minimum capital requirement for market risk based on the bank's VaR calculations.

Internal process risk   Internal process risk is the potential loss resulting from improper execution of processes and procedures in conducting a bank's day-to-day operations and internal processes.

Internal Ratings-Based (IRB) Approach   The Internal Ratings-Based Approach to determine the regulatory minimum capital requirement for credit risk uses the bank's own information. IRB includes two different procedures that have methodological differences to forecast the different risk factors.

International bank   An international bank is a large commercial, investment, or merchant bank with operations in different countries.

International Organization of Securities Commissions (IOSCO) (AC)   IOSCO develops standards and proposes regulations to govern the activities of non-bank financial markets such as share trading and bond markets. Its members are national regulatory bodies responsible for the oversight of securities markets.

Investment bank   An investment bank predominantly deals with corporate and institutional customers, issues financial securities in the financial and capital markets, provides advice on transactions such as mergers and acquisitions, manages investments, and trades on its own account.

Investment grade credit rating   An investment grade credit rating is one at the high end of the credit rating scale and is typically considered to imply a low probability of default.

Investment portfolio   An investment portfolio held by a bank or an individual contains various investments that typically include stocks (equity), bonds, loans, financial derivatives (options, futures, etc.), investible commodities such as gold or platinum, real estate, or similar assets of value.

Junior debt   Junior debt is subordinated to more senior debt but has priority over equity.

Legal risk   Legal risk includes, but is not limited to, the risk associated with the uncertainty of legal actions or the application or interpretation of contracts, laws, or regulations and can include potential exposure to fines, penalties, or punitive damages resulting from supervisory actions, as well as private settlements.

Lender of last resort   The lender of last resort, typically a central bank, assists banks facing unusually large and unexpected funding and other liquidity problems, or a systemic crisis by providing financing to the banks.

Lessee/lessor   A lessee contracts with a lessor to use an asset that lessor owns, and in exchange for the lessee's right to use the asset, it will make regular contractual payment(s) to the lessor.

Letter of credit   A letter of credit guarantees payment by a bank on behalf of its customer who pays a fee to the bank for providing the guarantee.

Level amortization   Level amortization repays the principal and interest on the loan with equal payments that include both interest and principal payments.

Leverage   Leverage, reflects the amount or proportion of debt used in the financing structure of an organization; the higher the leverage the greater the proportion of debt the company uses.

Leverage buy-out (LBO) transaction   The purchase of a company that is funded with significant amounts of debt.

Liabilities   Liabilities consist of a bank's deposits and its borrowings.

LIBOR   LIBOR, London Interbank Offered Rate, is a daily reference rate based on the average interest rate banks in London charge other banks, on the offer side of the transaction, when borrowing and lending.

Licensing   Licensing provides license holders the right to operate a bank and the licensing process involves an evaluation of an entity's intent and ability to observe the regulatory guidelines that will govern the bank's operations, financial soundness, and managerial actions.

Lien   The legal claim on the ownership of an asset that is given by a borrower to a lender as a way of offering security for the loan.

Line of credit   Line of credit is a typically short-term, uncommitted credit facility.

Liquidity   Liquidity refers to either market (transactional) or funding (payment) liquidity.

Liquidity coverage ratio One of the two liquidity standards introduced in the Basel III Accord. The standard is that banks should hold sufficient high quality liquidity assets (HQLA) to be able to withstand (by selling or pledging those assets) the net outflow of liquidity arising from financial stress lasting 30 days. (See also "Net Stable Funding Ratio.")

Liquidity crisis Liquidity crisis is a situation when the bank is not able to make payments when they are due, secure needed funds, or trade in the markets.

Liquidity risk Liquidity risk can be market (transactional) liquidity risk and funding (payment) liquidity risk.

Loan agreement The loan agreement is a legal contract between the bank and the borrower and includes a description of undertakings and understandings, such as the principal, the stated interest rate and its calculation, the schedule of payments and repayments, the use of collateral, covenants, etc.

Loan loss reserve A loan loss reserve, or "allowance for loan losses" or a "credit loss reserve," is the portion of loans set aside to absorb anticipated loan losses.

Loan-to-value, LTV, ratio Loan-to-value ratio is the ratio of the loan and the collateral supporting the loan.

Long position A long position, the opposite of short position, represents the ownership position of an asset; when the asset's value increases, the position increases in value and when the asset's value declines, the position decreases in value.

Long-term lending Long-term lending has a maturity exceeding 15 years and finances major capital projects or expenditures.

Loss given default (LGD) The actual loss the lender suffers in the wake of a default: a function of the RR and the EAD. LGD is influenced by debt type, asset type, recourse, assignment terms, and payment delays.

Low frequency/high impact, LFHI events LFHI events occur infrequently, but each event has a significant impact on the operations of the bank.

Macro-prudential supervision (GS) Supervision that focuses on the stability of a financial system as a whole, rather than on its components. Individual banks may be working within the regulations but collectively their actions could lead to instability in a financial system.

Margin Margin (requirement) is the amount investors must post to their brokers and the brokers are obligated to post with the clearinghouse, and is determined by various considerations, including the different types of instruments the broker trades on the exchange, the risk of the instrument, and the overall trading volume.

Margin call Margin call is the additional amount that needs to be deposited to fulfill the margin requirement imposed by the clearinghouse or the broker.

Marked-to-market Marked-to-market (accounting) assigns a value to an asset that reflects the value it would fetch on the market.

Market discipline Market discipline is the external monitoring and influencing of another bank's risk-taking activities based on the disclosure of relevant financial, risk or other information that allows external assessment of risk-taking.

Market liquidity risk Market liquidity risk refers to the ability to trade assets with negligible price concessions.

Market or trading liquidity   Market or trading liquidity refers to the ability to trade in and out of a position without significant price concessions.

Market risk   Market risk is defined as the risk of losses in on- and off-balance-sheet positions arising from movements in market prices and under the Basel II Accord encompasses the risks pertaining to interest rate related instruments and equities in the trading book, and foreign exchange risk and commodities risk throughout the bank.

Market Risk Amendment   The Market Risk Amendment of 1996 required banks to maintain regulatory minimum capital against the bank's positions in various market-traded financial assets such as foreign exchange, fixed income, equity, commodities, and derivatives. It is now superseded by the Basel II Accord which incorporated significant proportions of the amendment.

Market risk capital   Market risk capital is capital allocated against possible market losses.

Maturity   Maturity is the time period until a loan, bond, or other credit is repaid fully.

Median   To find the median, list the values of the data set in numerical order and identify which value appears in the middle of the list.

Mean   To find the mean add up the values in the data set and then divide by the number of values.

Medium-term lending   Medium-term lending has a maturity not exceeding three or five years and finances on-going investments in machinery, equipment or facilities, or cyclical needs.

Micro-prudential supervision   The supervision of individual banks to ensure that on an individual basis they remain strong.

Mode   To find the mode, identify which value in the data set occurs most frequently.

Monetary stability   Monetary stability reflects the extent that the value of money can be maintained and, as a synonym for price stability, implies low and stable inflation.

Money   Money serves as a medium of exchange, legal tender, and basis for trade, and acts as a unit of account and store of value.

Money creation   Money creation is the creation of additional money, within a fractional reserve banking system, by bank lending.

Money multiplier   The money multiplier, the inverse of the reserve requirement, indicates how much additional money each unit of money, deposited with a bank, creates.

Mortgage   A mortgage finances the purchase of real estate that serves as collateral.

Net income   Net income is the difference between total revenue and expenses.

Net interest income   Net interest income equals the difference between the interest income the bank earns on its loans and other financial assets, and the interest expense it pays to its depositors and other lenders.

Net stable funding ratio   One of the two liquidity standards introduced in the Basel III Accord. The standard is that banks should have sufficient Available Secure Funding to cover Required Secure Funding over a period of one year.

Non-investment grade credit rating   Noninvestment grade credit rating is a low credit rating and implies a relatively high probability of default.

Nonperforming loan   Nonperforming loan is a loan whose borrower fails to make, or makes delayed, payment.

Non-systemic risk   Non-systemic risk is risk that is restricted to a limited number of entities, typically one company, and does not affect others.

Notional principal amount (NPA)   The name for the nominal value of a derivatives contract. Real principal amounts are rarely exchanged under derivative contracts, so the NPA is not a measure of the value of the contract. Rather, the NPA serves as a basis upon which the cash flows (payments and receipts) in the contract are to be calculated.

Off-balance-sheet activity   Off-balance-sheet activities are not recorded on the balance sheet, and include asset, debt, or financing-related activities such as derivatives or loan commitments and other contingent exposures that could pose a risk to the bank.

Operational loss event   Operational loss event is a loss that is the result of operational failure.

Operational risk   Operational risk is the risk of loss resulting from inadequate or failed internal processes, people, and systems, or from external events. This definition includes legal risk but excludes strategic and reputational risk.

Operational risk capital   Operational risk capital is capital allocated against possible operational losses.

Option   An option conveys the right but not the obligation to buy or sell an underlying asset; the two main types of options are a call option and a put option.

Over-the-counter (OTC) market   The over-the-counter market is a decentralized market without a physical marketplace, where both standardized and nonstandardized securities and other financial instruments are traded.

Own Risk & Solvency Assessment (ORSA) requirement   Under Solvency 2's Pillar II the Own Risk & Solvency Assessment (ORSA) is a new specialized reporting requirement on risk and capital matters.

Paid-in-capital   Paid-in-capital is the (equity) capital that the owners have invested in the corporation.

Past-due loan   A past due loan is a loan whose repayment of principal and interest are in doubt because the borrower has missed several payments to the bank or the bank has a clear indication that the borrower may not repay the loan.

Payment system   A payment system is the infrastructure that settles financial and other transactions or transfers funds between financial institutions using established procedures and protocols.

People risk   People risk is associated with a potential loss resulting from intentional or unintentional employee actions, such as improper recordkeeping, misuse of information, or fraud.

Performing loan   A performing loan is a loan whose borrower is making payments as agreed.

Permanent financing   Permanent financing provides capital either through equity or long-term debt to purchase, develop, and operate long-term fixed assets, such as factories, equipment, and machinery.

Pillars 1, 2, and 3 of the Basel II Accord   The Basel II Accord consists of three pillars. Pillar 1 focuses on minimum capital requirements for the three major risks bank face: credit risk, operational risk, and market risk. Pillar 2 focuses on supervisory review and processes for capital adequacy. Pillar 3 focuses on market discipline and transparency.

Portfolio   A portfolio is a collection of investments, such as stocks, bonds, and cash equivalents, held by an institution or a private individual.

Portfolio management   Portfolio management involves determining the contents and the structure of the portfolio, monitoring its performance, making any changes, and deciding which assets to acquire and which assets to divest.

Project finance   Project finance provides funds for the completion of large scale industrial or infrastructure projects where the assets of the project are pledged as collateral for the loan and the realized income or cash flow from the completed project is expected to repay the loan.

Prime lending rate   The prime lending rate is the rate the banks typically charge their best customers.

Principal   The principal is the amount borrowed on a credit and excludes interest or other charges.

Private offering   A private offering raises capital by selling new securities to a selected group of individuals that typically meet certain criteria, but not to the public.

Probability of default (PD)   The probability of default is the probability that a borrower defaults.

Provision for loan loss   Provision for loan loss is a cost recorded on the income statement that represents funds set aside to absorb anticipated loan losses.

Public borrower   A public borrower is typically a sovereign state, provincial, or a local government including their sub-entities or agencies.

Public offering   A public offering raises capital by selling new securities to the public.

Put option   A put option gives its holder the right, but not the obligation, to sell a specified asset for a specified price at some future date.

Recovery rate (RR)   The recovery rate is that fraction of a defaulted obligation that can be recovered.

Regulatory capital requirement   Regulatory capital requirement specifies how much minimum capital a bank must hold to guard against the various—market, credit, and operational—risks it takes.

Repurchase agreement or repo   A repurchase agreement, repo, is a contract between two parties in which one party sells the other a security at a specified price with the obligation to buy the security back at a later date for another specified price; they are widely used by central banks to provide support to meet a bank's short-term liquidity.

Reputational or headline risk   Reputational, or headline, risk is the potential loss resulting from a decrease in a bank's standing in public opinion.

Reserve requirement   The reserve requirement, in the fractional reserve banking system, is the proportion of funds a bank must keep in reserve to meet regulatory requirements and limits how much money an initial deposit could potentially create.

Retail bank   Retail banks primarily service individuals, or consumers, and small and medium enterprises (SMEs).

Retail borrower   A retail borrower is an individual ("consumer") who borrows money to purchase homes, cars, and other goods or services.

Retained earnings   Retained earnings is that part of corporate earnings not returned to the owners as dividends.

Risk appetite   Risk appetite is the level of risk exposure an investor is willing to assume in exchange for the potential for a profit.

Risk management   Risk management is a structured approach to monitoring, measuring, and managing exposures to reduce the potential impact of an uncertain happening.

Risk-adjusted return on capital (RAROC)   RAROC, a risk-based profitability measurement, calculates the risk-adjusted financial performance of an operation or business unit.

Risk-weighted assets   Risk-weighted assets equal the sum of various financial assets multiplied by their respective risk-weights and off-balance-sheet items weighted for their credit risk according to the regulatory requirements outlined by banking regulators and supervisors.

Savings accounts   Savings accounts typically limit the number of withdrawals a depositor can make over a specified period of time.

Savings and loans (S&Ls)   S&Ls, or thrifts, primarily offer loans to individuals to finance residential housing, car, and other retail or consumer purchases.

Scenario analysis   Scenario analysis, or what-if analysis, assesses the potential outcome of various scenarios by setting up several possible situations and analyzing the potential outcomes of each situation.

Seasonal financing   A seasonal loan finances a temporary and predictable short-term demand, such as seasonal increases in inventory or farm-related financing.

Securitization   Securitization is a process where relatively illiquid cash flow producing assets (e.g., mortgages, credit cards, and loans) are pooled into a portfolio, and the purchase of these assets in the portfolio is financed by securities issued to investors, who then share the cash flows generated by the portfolio.

Securitizing assets   Securitization is a process where relatively illiquid assets—mortgages, credit cards, and loans—are pooled into a portfolio and the portfolio is then transformed into a security; as a result the credit risk of the individual assets is transferred to the investors who buy the securitized product.

Security   A (financial) security is a fungible financial instrument that may be required to be registered with a regulatory authority.

Senior debt   Senior debt has priority in default over all other more junior and subordinated debt.

Settlement risk   Settlement, or Herstatt, risk is the risk that a counterparty fails to perform as agreed and does not deliver a security, or its value after the other counterparty has already delivered on the same transaction.

Shadow banking   The provision of credit, depository and other financial services by institutions and vehicles other than banks.

Shareholder   A shareholder, stockholder, or equity holder, is one of the owners of a corporation; a shareholder typically has the right to elect the board of directors, vote on corporate matters, and may receive dividends.

Shareholders' equity   Shareholders' equity, the difference between assets and liabilities, is the shareholders' investment in the company, which typically equals the amount the shareholders have invested in the company and retained earnings.

Short position   A short position, the opposite of long position, represents either of an option, or selling a futures position; when the asset's value increases, the position declines in value and when the asset's value declines, the position increases in value.

Short-term lending   Short-term lending has a maturity less than one year and finances temporary requirements or seasonal needs.

Sinking-fund amortization   Sinking fund amortization repays the principal and interest on the loan with payments, where the principal repayment is a constant, but the interest payments change as the outstanding balance is reduced.

Small and medium enterprise (SME)   A small and medium enterprise is usually a partnership, proprietorship, owner-operator, or other types of small business and corporation whose sales, assets, and headcount falls below a certain limit.

Solvency   Solvency is when assets exceed liabilities, and typically implies the ability to repay debts and other obligations when they come due.

Sovereign borrower   A sovereign borrower is a government of an independent state or a country that issues bonds or borrows to finance large capital or infrastructure investments, such as roads or railways, or to fund government spending.

Specific, non systematic, unique risk   Specific, non systematic, unique risk is the risk of an adverse movement in the price of one individual security or financial asset due to factors specific to that particular security or issuer.

Speculation   Speculation involves the buying (long position), holding, selling, and short selling (short position) of financial assets, commodities, foreign exchange, or derivatives, with the expectation that price fluctuations will generate a profit; a position that is not hedged; buying or selling an asset with the hope of earning a gain.

Spillover effect   Spillover effect is a spreading of concern.

Spread duration   Floating rate assets have an effective duration close to zero, but spread duration comparable to normal fixed rate assets. This makes it easier to compare the two types of investments.

Stakeholder   A stakeholder is someone with an interest in the future of a business, enterprise, or organization, and usually includes individual customers, borrowers, depositors, investors, employees, shareholders, regulators, and the public.

Standardized approach   The Standardized Approach to calculate the bank's credit and market risk capital is the simplest approach outlined in the Basel II Accord for these risks. For operational risk, this is an intermediate level approach.

Strategic risk   Strategic risk is the potential loss due to poor business decisions or their incorrect execution.

Stress testing   Stress testing assesses the potential outcome of specific changes that are fundamental, material, and adverse.

Supervisory review   Supervisory review is a process that national bank regulatory or supervisory authorities use to evaluate a bank's capital adequacy in relation to the risks and capital the bank has.

Swap   A swap, a derivative, allows two counterparties to exchange streams of future cash flows with each other.

Systemic risk   Systemic risk is the risk of a system-wide breakdown in the banking or financial system.

Systems risk   Systems risk is the loss resulting from the insufficient protection of information technology against disruption, damage, or hazards such as systems failure, security breaches, or data theft.

Temporary financing   Temporary financing provides capital through short- or medium-term debt; includes seasonal and cyclical loans.

Tier 1 capital   Tier 1 capital in the Basel Accords is the core capital of the bank and refers to equity capital and to certain types of disclosed reserves, as well as particular debt/ equity hybrid securities.

Tier 2 capital   Tier 2 capital in the Basel Accords is supplementary capital and refers to undisclosed and certain disclosed reserves, general provisions, general loan loss reserves, hybrid capital instruments, and subordinated debt.

Tier 3 capital   Tier 3 capital in the Basel Accords is a specific type of supplementary capital and refers to certain types of short-term debt that can partially satisfy regulatory minimum capital requirements for market risk only.

'Too big to fail' firms   Financial institutions that are considered so important to their domestic financial system, or to the global financial system, that governments and regulators would not allow them to fail.

Top-down approach   The top-down approach initially provides an overview of the bank's overall risk exposure and then analyzes identifiable risks first at the business line and then at the business unit level; as the analysis moves to business line and business unit level, the analysis is conducted in increasingly greater detail.

Trade receivables   Trade receivables result from credit sales, where the company extends credit to its customers to purchase its products or services in anticipation of payment.

Trading   Trading is the exchange between traders.

Trading book   The trading book of a bank is the portfolio of various positions in financial assets, instruments, and commodities that a bank holds with the intention to invest, to trade, or to hedge other positions in the trading book.

Transaction accounts   Transaction accounts are accounts where the depositor can withdraw the deposits on demand using checks, debit cards, or similar payment instructions.

Uncommitted facility   An uncommitted facility is a loan with loosely specified terms and conditions but with an understanding that the funds will be made available by the lender when the borrower demands.

Underwriting   Underwriting assesses the borrower's eligibility to receive a credit, a loan or a bond, by analyzing financial and other information furnished by the potential borrower or obtained elsewhere.

Unexpected loss   An unexpected loss describes the loss in excess of the expected loss and is expressed with a certain confidence level.

Universal bank   Universal banks complement their offering of core banking services with a wide range of other financial services, particularly insurance.

Value-at-risk (VaR)   Value-at-risk measures risk by calculating the potential loss exceeding a specified confidence level using statistical analysis.

Wholesale bank   A wholesale bank is an investment or merchant bank that serves, corporations with banking and advisory services that are specific to the need of large businesses.

Written-down loan   A loan that has been revalued at a lower value based on the bank's determination that it will not be able to recover fully the amount it has lent to the borrower.

Yield curve   A yield curve illustrates the relationship between bond yields and their maturity.

Index